COOKING
GLUTEN-FREE!

A Food Lover's Collection of Chef and Family Recipes
Without Gluten or Wheat

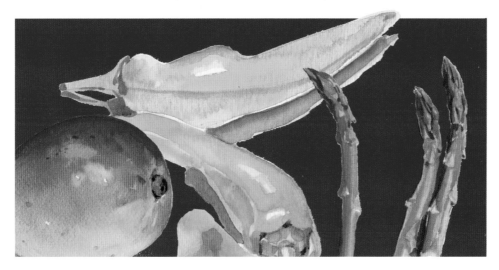

Karen Robertson
Illustrated by J. Diane Robertson

Celiac Publishing, Seattle, Washington

Second Edition, revised 2003

Published by Celiac Publishing, Seattle, Washington

Design by DD Dowden
Printed in South Korea

10   9   8   7   6   5   4   3   2

Library of Congress Control Number: 2002092249

    Robertson, Karen

        Cooking Gluten-Free!

        A Food Lover's Collection of Chef and Family Recipes Without Gluten or Wheat / Karen
           Robertson; watercolors by J. Diane Robertson

        1. Gluten-free diet—Recipes.

        ISBN   0-9708660-1-1

Celiac Publishing
P.O. Box 99603
Seattle, WA 98139
celiacpublishing@earthlink.net
www.cookingglutenfree.com

CELIAC
PUBLISHING

With Love to Carmen and Sam

CONTENTS

Acknowledgments 2

Foreword 4

Preface 6

Introduction 8

How to Get Started 10

The Recipes

Breakfast 15

Appetizers 23

Entrées by Season

    Spring 33

    Summer 53

    Fall 75

    Winter 95

Accompaniments 119

Long Simmering Soup, Chili, & Stock 155

Breads 161

Sweets 179

Appendix 213

    The Gluten-Free Diet, Patient Support Organizations, Dairy-Free Substitutions,
    Recipe Conversion Ideas, Gluten Intolerant Children, Lunch and Snack Ideas,
    Outdoor Cooking, Pantry Basics, Utensils & Cookware,
    Chef Contributors, Sources, Measurement Conversion Chart,
    Gluten-Free Flour, Glossary of Cooking Terms

Index 236

ACKNOWLEDGMENTS

SO MANY PEOPLE HAVE PLAYED A PART in making this book possible. My sincere thanks go to everyone who took the time to make a contribution.

I owe a great deal to my husband, Alan, who endured many years of cookbook writing and happily took on the role of supreme taste tester (along with our gluten intolerant children, Carmen and Sam). He also deserves credit for both teaching me how to cook and contributing many of the grill recipes. The book was brought to life with the gorgeous watercolors generously donated by Alan's mother, Diane Robertson. Without her efforts, this book would be missing a very important element. Thank you, Diane!

I also owe many thanks to both my editors and my designer. Barbara Figueroa, a former chef and restaurant owner, has brought her talents to this book through editing, rewriting, recipe contribution, and consulting. Her tireless efforts significantly improved the manuscript! And a special thank you to Kathy Winkenwerder for providing a "fresh set of eyes" and great insight during the important final edit. DD Dowden designed a beautiful, functional book, and cheerfully kept me on track every step of the way. I was very lucky to find these talented people. Many thanks also go to Chris Cauble for overseeing the printing and design work. It would have been impossible to achieve my goal without him.

The gathering of recipes from renowned chefs across the country was greatly facilitated through the efforts of many people. Josh Raynolds (Rosenthal Wine Merchants), Larry Stone (Master Sommelier at Rubicon), and Dan Phillips (The Grateful Palate) all connected me to some of the best chefs in America. I am especially honored to know Dan McCarthy of McCarthy & Schiering Wine Merchants, who aided tremendously in this effort, and who also selected the wine pairings for many of the recipes throughout the book.

A special note of gratitude goes to Christopher Kimball and Ludger Szmania, two chefs who believed in this book from the beginning and made it possible for me to get my project off the ground. Thanks also go to the many contributing chefs who took the time to create recipes for the home cook: Gerry Hayden, Hans Bergmann, Christian Svalesen, Tom Douglas, Lynne Vea, Ludger Szmania, Todd Gray, Suzanne Goin, Kathy Casey, Erol Tugrul, Barbara Figueroa, Charlie Trotter, Dennis Leary, Bob Kinkead, Linda Yamada, Michael Kornick, Christopher Kimball, Thoa Nguyen, and Marcella Rosene.

Goldie Caughlan and Marilyn McCormick are credited with inspiring me to learn more about the food we consume. I thank them both for having faith in my ability to teach gluten-free cooking classes. I also give special thanks to Cynthia Lair, Karol Redfern Hamper, and Linda Carlson as my mentors throughout the book publishing process.

I have been very fortunate to know and work with Bette Hagman, the pioneer of gluten-free cooking. She has graciously answered my many questions, and has supported my efforts in writing this book.

Joanne VanRoden, Amy Bogino Eernissee, Debra Daniels-Zeller, Edel Amundson, Jerry and Julie Hawkins, Heather Shaw, Diane Robertson, Marian Robertson, Bill Bassett, Lorna Sass, Wendy Wark, Cynthia Lair, Judy Bullock, and Bill Fredericks have all earned kudos for the recipes they contributed.

The top-quality baked goods in this book would not be possible without Wendy Wark's superior flour mix. I owe her much gratitude for allowing me to use this formula as the basis of all of my baked goods. And thanks to Rebecca Reilly for developing some excellent gluten-free recipes in her book. Once I tasted a few recipes from these two women, I knew there was hope for delicious gluten-free treats!

Cynthia S. Rudert, M.D., F.A.C.P., is to be credited with penning the book's foreword. She is one of the foremost authorities on celiac disease in the United States today. I am indeed blessed to have met her, and appreciate her eagerness to take part in the writing of this book.

My gratitude goes out to Shelley Case, R.D., who specializes in celiac disease, for helping me understand the finer points of the gluten-free diet. I am also fortunate to know Cynthia Kupper, C.R.D., Executive Director of the Gluten Intolerance Group. She has been a tremendous resource for me over the years in putting this book together with the most accurate information available. Her unrelenting work for GIG and her efforts to join the various celiac groups in North America together with one voice are to be commended.

A final thank-you goes to all the Gluten Intolerance Group members, especially Michele Benson and Jennifer Smith, for their encouraging feedback on my gluten-free recipes and their insightful recommendations for this book.

FOREWORD

CELIAC DISEASE IS THE MOST COMMON INHERITED GENETIC ILLNESS IN AMERICA. Fortunately, it is a condition that will generally show marked improvement through strict adherence to a lifelong gluten-free diet. Upon eliminating wheat, oats, rye, and barley, the microscopic damage to the small intestine will immediately begin to improve. There are ongoing studies evaluating the safety of oats in the diet of celiac patients. At the present time, oats are not recommended for patients in the United States, where cultivation in fields cross-rotated with wheat is permitted. Dermatitis herpetiformis patients must observe the same dietary guidelines. Individuals with DH almost always have underlying celiac disease, though they might exhibit few, if any, gastrointestinal problems.

In our country, we are just beginning to realize how common celiac disease is. The University of Maryland's Center for Celiac Research is conducting an ongoing multi-center serologic study, and has tested over 10,000 individuals in order to better understand its prevalence in the United States. Preliminary data indicates that it may affect one out of every 170 Americans in the general population. In fact, if you have a relative with the disorder, the chance that you also have it may be as high as one in twelve.

It has recently come to light that if you adhere strictly to a gluten-free diet, you will decrease the likelihood of developing another associated autoimmune disease, such as Addison's disease, B-12 deficiency, myasthenia gravis, Raynaud's disease, scleroderma, Sjogren's syndrome, lupus erythematosus, thyroid disease, or autoimmune chronic active hepatitis. (For example, the incidence of Type I Diabetes, or insulin dependent diabetes mellitus, in people with CD/DH is believed to be twice that of the general population.) Anyone with ongoing gastrointestinal

4

symptoms should be evaluated for celiac disease, now thought to occur in one out of every thirty individuals referred to a gastroenterologist for any reason.

In my experience, the most common symptom associated with the disorder is fatigue. In fact, many of my patients have been misdiagnosed with chronic fatigue syndrome before celiac disease was discovered to be the actual cause. Interestingly, symptoms may vary depending on the individual. Some patients suffer from unexplained abdominal pain, gas, or bloating; others may have constipation or diarrhea. By the time extensive damage has been done to the small intestine, malnutrition, weakness, and weight loss is inevitable. Certain individuals may actually have difficulty losing weight. A gluten-free diet is a healthy diet, and it is wonderful to be able to treat celiac patients without submitting them to a life-long medication regimen. Of course, it is important to address other coexisting problems, such as vitamin and mineral deficiencies. Chronic malabsorption of calcium can lead to osteopenia or osteoporosis, even in adolescence.

The vast majority of patients note substantial improvement and even total resolution of their symptoms on a gluten-free diet. If their symptoms continue, or recur, I would be concerned about inadvertent gluten ingestion.

Please turn to your physician for testing if you are the relative of a celiac patient. It is not unusual for the condition to be misdiagnosed as "irritable bowel syndrome" or "spastic colon." The initial phase involves screening for antigliadin IgG and IgA antibodies, antiendomysial antibodies, tissue transglutaminase, and serum IgA level. It is also necessary to have a biopsy obtained from several portions of the small intestine during a procedure called endoscopy (esophagogastroduodenoscopy), as blood tests may be normal in up to twenty percent of individuals with celiac disease, and therefore cannot be relied upon for conclusive results.

If you are diagnosed with celiac disease, you should be under the care of a physician with related experience, in order to manage continued or recurrent symptoms and other coexisting medical disorders. I urge you to join support groups and play an active role in your recovery. Finally, read this book; a gluten-free diet for life can be both therapeutic and absolutely delicious!

Cynthia S. Rudert, M.D., F.A.C.P.
Medical Advisor, Celiac Disease Foundation
Medical Advisor, Gluten Intolerance Group
Medical Director, Gluten Sensitive Support Group of Atlanta
Founding Member, Celiac Standardization Group

The Medical Quarters, Suite 312
5555 Peachtree Dunwoody Road, NE
Atlanta, Georgia 30342
(404) 943-9820

PREFACE

COOKING GLUTEN-FREE! was written for people with a gluten or wheat intolerance and for those who dine with them daily. Gluten intolerance is known as celiac disease and/or dermatitis herpetiformis. A person with gluten intolerance must avoid wheat, oats, rye, barley, spelt, triticale, and kamut or risk intestinal damage. The standard American diet is dominated by these forbidden grains, which makes a gluten-free diet a tremendous challenge. Gluten is also "hidden" in many foods that contain malt or malt flavoring, modified food starch, hydrolyzed vegetable protein, etc.

A special diet causes great frustration and a huge life change, so it is helpful to know that gluten-free food can be absolutely delicious; it is simply a matter of using quality recipes and ingredients. This book was designed to help you wade through the jungle of gluten-free recipes so you won't have to waste your time and money on the bad ones. Included are proven recipes for such essentials as desserts, flour tortillas, breads, hamburger buns, breadsticks, pancakes, waffles, and sweet breads; there are also recipes with which to compose wonderful menus for your weekly repertoire. Recommended mail order pastas, crackers, and snacks are also listed. There is hope!

The great chefs rely heavily on fresh ingredients, so that much of what they cook is gluten-free (excluding bread and pasta); they also possess the know-how to make gluten-free substitutions when necessary. In developing this book I asked some of the finest chefs in America to contribute gluten-free meals that would be easy for you to prepare at home.

When our children were diagnosed with celiac disease, I decided it was easier to cook one gluten-free meal for the whole family rather than feed our children differently. The key was getting organized with gluten-free ingredients and finding recipes combining ease of preparation with taste appeal. Our entire family now has a healthier diet and we have amassed a collection of recipes with which to make delectable meals and treats. Cooking gluten-free involves some initial "start up" time while you learn what to buy and how to cook without gluten.

Positive thinking is quite powerful. Once you understand the basics and have some experience, you will be pleased with what you can create. Cooking is a great way for families to reconnect at the end of the day; it brings people together and makes a house a home. There is no doubt that other activities will need to be rearranged or put on hold awhile. Your top priority must be support of the gluten intolerant person, especially in the first year following diagnosis.

A chapter is included to help parents of gluten-intolerant children cope with the many challenges they face. An optimistic outlook and a commitment to your role as a personal chef/dietician are very important.

Trying to figure out what to have for dinner requires creativity. This book does the creative thinking for you and quickly solves the "what's for dinner?" dilemma. A variety of quick meals (☺) are included, though most entrées with side dishes can be prepared within 30-45 minutes from start to finish.

Since a gluten-free diet is stricter than a wheat-free diet, the book's content is tailored to the former. Anyone on a wheat-free diet will find the book very beneficial as well.

You will notice recipes including healthy flours such as brown rice, amaranth, and quinoa. Other recommended ingredients include organic shortening, tofu, fruit puree sweeteners, etc. Try to incorporate these ingredients for a healthier overall diet. Some recipes include alternative flours. Amaranth, quinoa, buckwheat, teff, and millet are gluten-free providing you can find a pure source (grown in dedicated fields and processed on dedicated equipment). You can research this issue further by contacting the Gluten Intolerance Group, Celiac Sprue Association/USA, Canadian Celiac Association, and Celiac Disease Foundation.

Everyone wants to experience a good meal that is satisfying to both eyes and tummy and is easy to prepare. This book provides recipes and guidance to achieve this goal.

INTRODUCTION

THE ENTRÉE RECIPES in this volume are arranged by season so you can take advantage of fresh produce at its peak, and because seasons tend to dictate our "food moods." However, you will find some items such as tomatillos, which are plentiful in summer, used in a winter recipe. Many foods are available year round, thanks to our global economy, and it is refreshing to have a taste of summer even in wintertime.

Some meals are labeled "quick" for those nights when time is at a premium. You will find ways to shorten your time in the kitchen as cooking becomes a part of your life. Rest assured that you won't have to spend each day cooking from scratch! Your homemade gluten-free food can be stored in the freezer for those "no time to cook" nights of the week, while on other nights you can create a simple dinner such as gluten-free pasta with fresh vegetables. Most recipes for each meal can be prepared in 30-45 minutes, and you will learn how to prepare certain parts in advance to ease the stress of getting dinner on the table when everyone is hungry.

Since the book is written with the novice cook in mind, directions are provided for very simple recipes, and cooking terms are defined in the glossary.

Accompaniments

Salads, vegetables, and other side dishes are covered here. Most entrées include a suggested accompaniment from this section.

Breads

Essentials such as sandwich breads, tortillas, pizza crusts, sweet breads, muffins, etc. fill this chapter.

Sweets

Recipes include scrumptious cakes, cookies, pies, elegant fruit desserts, and chocolate confections.

Chef Recipes

Throughout the book, you will find recipes contributed by celebrated chefs and well-known cookbook authors throughout the country.

The appendix is a wealth of information for anyone who must remove gluten or wheat from his or her diet.

Warning

Since a gluten-free diet is the "prescription" for those with celiac disease, a strict caveat is in order. Given the numerous recommendations by allergists and naturopaths to eliminate wheat from the diet, it is important that the patient know the pitfalls of eliminating wheat before ruling out celiac disease. A traditional wheat-free diet does not address foods containing hidden gluten. Any gluten consumption will depress the immune system of a celiac patient.

As many allergists and naturopaths are unfamiliar with the condition, you must enlist the help of a knowledgeable gastroenterologist, who will run a simple diagnostic blood screening test. In order for test results to be accurate, only a qualified lab should run the test, and the patient should still be consuming wheat at a normal level. Many people have undermined their chances for a proper diagnosis by embarking on a wheat-free or gluten-free diet prior to testing. (Call any of the celiac organizations for lab names and recommended physicians.)

Patients with untreated celiac disease have an increased risk for developing: lupus, thyroid disease, Addison's disease, scleroderma, Grave's disease, Sjogren's syndrome, and diabetes. This is not a complete list. Please contact the Gluten Intolerance Group, Celiac Sprue Association, Canadian Celiac Association, or Celiac Disease Foundation to learn more about celiac disease, and to get all the facts from a qualified source.

HOW TO GET STARTED

YOU WILL FIND IT EASIER TO BEGIN by relying heavily on prepackaged gluten-free food, and by devoting your energies to researching brand names and availability. The multiple tasks of cooking and baking throughout the week may become overwhelming unless you plan with expediency in mind. As most people get tired of "fast food" after awhile, there is much incentive to acquire an ever-broadening repertoire of cooking skills. (Before meeting my husband, I was not much of a cook, testament that anyone can become quite proficient with the right instruction!) A big challenge with gluten-free cooking is weeding through the many recipes available and determining which are worthwhile. Recording a list of favorites will assist you in your efforts.

The right tools in the kitchen can make cooking easy and successful. Good quality cookware, knives, and a few gadgets can really save time. Many American kitchens are outfitted with thin cookware that burns food easily and knives that are dull, lightweight, and uncomfortable. In *The Cook's Bible*, Christopher Kimball gives his recommendations for basic cookware and utensils. Buy his book, or check it out from the library; it will help you buy the right equipment and teach you so much about cooking! My list of preferred kitchenware is shown in the Appendix of this book.

If fat is a concern, be aware that packaged gluten-free foods have many of the same unhealthy characteristics as the regular grocery store fare. A case in point is the addition of refined sugar as a flavor enhancer. Simple carbohydrates, unless utilized for energy, quickly turn to glucose in the bloodstream and are stored as fat. When you cook your own food, you know the exact ingredients, and can save the sugar (in small amounts) for dessert. If you balance your daily intake from the basic food groups and exercise daily, you can still eat great gluten-free sweets in moderation while maintaining your desired weight. The key word is balance. Many of the healthier flours, such as quinoa, amaranth, and brown rice flour are used in this book, and make for healthier treats than those based on white flour.

The key to cooking gluten-free is setting oneself up with all the necessary resources. This may seem like a daunting task at first, but once you are set up it is simple to maintain and you will feel like a pro! Take it slow at first so that you don't exhaust yourself—it is difficult enough to adapt to this huge change in your life, but with time and practice you will be an excellent cook!

Pantry Basics

It is time to reorganize your pantry. This will be an ongoing process as you try the various recipes in this book. You may not have a bottle of Madeira in your cabinet right now, but the bottle you buy for a particular recipe will serve you well for a number of other dishes. Don't avoid a recipe because of a bare-bones cupboard. Buy the ingredients and expand your horizons! Review pantry basics in the Appendix, but don't rush out to buy everything right away. Take your time and add to your pantry week by week.

It is helpful to have a cabinet near your stove top to hold the variety of cooking wines, oils, vinegars, and spices you will need while cooking. A separate shelf for all the special gluten-free flours and baking ingredients is also good to have. It is, of course, advantageous to have your foodstuffs grouped together logically so that you can see when you need to restock. Keep a shopping list, categorized by source (store or mail order house), and reorder promptly, allowing for delivery time, when any given item runs low.

Cookware and Utensils

Try to buy the best utensils and cookware you can afford. You are making an investment in your future, since celiac disease is a lifelong condition. It will represent a sizeable initial expense, but you will save money in the long run as you enjoy your own fine cooking rather than eating out or buying convenience foods. One item, the Kitchenaid mixer, stands out above all others as a recommended purchase. Gluten-free baked goods are a different beast altogether, and proper mixing of the batter or dough depends on a heavy-duty standing mixer for success.

Where to Shop?

Produce

If the chain groceries in your neighborhood don't have good produce, try to find a specialty grocer or farmer's market. Since the gluten-free diet is so restrictive, it pays to find a place with fresh, appetizing fruits and vegetables (frozen is a good alternative for some items). Make a point of befriending the produce person at your store, who can direct you to ingredients that you might otherwise have trouble finding. It is terribly time-consuming to shop by reading all the produce signs in search of an unfamiliar item; however, once you learn to recognize it by sight, the process will go much faster. If you have access to them, use organic fruits and vegetables; it is the way to go for long-term health.

Mail Order

There are many good mail order sources for gluten-free food. Contact them all to discover which products you like best (some are listed in the Appendix). Since beans are a great source of nutrients for people on a gluten-free diet, and the standard grocery store line is pretty humdrum, check out specialty catalogs (or organic markets) for interesting fresh varieties.

Specialty Food Stores = Quality and Freshness

If you are fortunate enough to have a fish market, butcher, gourmet market, or farmers market nearby, take advantage of what they have to offer. You can more readily get answers to your questions about freshness, organic growing methods, or freedom from hormones. The knowledgeable staff at these stores can also tell you whether shrimp or scallops are packed in a wheat slurry, or whether sausages and lunch meat contain gluten. Frequenting these shops also helps you avoid the additives found in lower-grade products. In order to make all the "store hopping" a bearable task, keep in mind that this is how the Europeans shop, and that you are getting the freshest, highest quality gluten-free food possible.

Outdoor Grilling In All Seasons

It may sound crazy (and if you live somewhere with snow on the ground throughout the winter, it is crazy), but many people grill outdoors 12 months a year. In Seattle, the climate is fairly temperate, so we have an outdoor grill set up under cover and use it all year long. Many stores do not stock charcoal throughout the winter, so you may need to stock up in the fall or find a wood stove store that carries charcoal all year round. Charcoal grilling is the best by far, but there are some good gas grills to which you can add wood chips for better flavor. Try apple wood, cherry wood, alder wood, etc. for a variety of aromas.

Plan Your Time

This is easier said than done; however, make this your number one goal and you'll be glad you did. Before you begin to cook, read each recipe you will be preparing. In this way, you can make your grocery list, determine how much time you will need, know what you can chop up in advance, and prioritize the steps involved. Try to sit down and plan three meals at a time so you don't end up at the grocery store every day. Finding the time to do this is difficult, but it makes life much easier knowing what is on the menu and having all your ducks in line. If your upcoming week is a busy one, consider spending time on the weekend making pizza crusts, soups, or sauces, and freeze them for use during the week.

Designate a day to bake bread, and make a special treat every other week for the cookie jar or the lunch box. (I find it helpful to have extra brownies frozen individually, so that if our children are invited to a birthday party, they can each take a brownie to eat while the other kids are having wheat flour cake.) Stock your kitchen with five pounds each of the types of flour you use most often, as well as an ample supply of xanthan gum.

Mise en Place

This is a French term for having everything ready up to the point of cooking. The most time-consuming part of cooking is the chopping, grating, and other prep work that must be done prior to combining the ingredients (which is why you rarely see it demonstrated start to finish on a cooking show). Buy a variety of glass bowls, chop up everything needed for the recipe ahead of time, and place the ingredients in the bowls. By doing this you insure against last minute mistakes. If you freeze your meat, take defrosting time into consideration too. Be sure any marinade you use is made early enough so the meat has time to marinate. If you use a charcoal grill, light it in advance so that the coals are ready when you need them. These steps seem obvious, but they are easily overlooked when one is pressed for time.

Think about each recipe in the meal, and take the cooking time of each element into account so that everything is ready at the same time and nothing is overcooked. (For example, start the chicken entrée, and begin steaming the broccoli during the last ten minutes of cooking time.) It takes a bit of practice, but after cooking a meal once or twice you will begin to get the hang of it and learn to anticipate potential problems. After doing this for a while, you will be a pro at pulling together a meal quickly, and your hard work will have paid off.

Ingredient and Resource Notes

Fresh ground pepper and sea salt are my choices, as are the fresh herbs now available in most grocery stores. It is best to choose unprocessed vegetable oils such as corn, olive, canola, walnut, sesame, sunflower, and safflower. Butter is a better choice than margarine, which is rarely used in gourmet kitchens. Organic shortening is a healthy new product that you might try instead of regular shortening, which contains artery-clogging hydrogenated oils (as does margarine). Products that may be difficult to find in the average grocery store are listed in the Appendix, along with mail order sources.

Cookbooks and Classes

Expand your knowledge base by taking some cooking classes. Many talented chefs offer cooking classes in their restaurants. Many natural food stores offer some of the best classes around. I have even taken an excellent chocolate truffle-making class through a university extension program.

One cookbook I recommend for people with multiple sensitivities is Carol Fenster's *Special Diet Solutions*, which offers good substitution ideas for those who must avoid gluten, dairy, eggs, yeast, or refined sugar. Bette Hagman covers the subject of gluten-free bread in great detail in her book, *The Gluten-Free Gourmet Bakes Bread*. Wendy Wark has developed my favorite flour mix of all in her book, *Living Healthy with Celiac Disease*. Wendy has graciously permitted me to use several of her recipes, including her All Purpose Gluten-Free Flour Mix (found on page 181). Another indispensable resource for the novice cook is *The New Food Lover's Companion* by Sharon Tyler Herbst. The book is a comprehensive guide of over 4000 food, wine and culinary terms published by Barron's. I have found this volume to be as fascinating as it is informative.

Cook's Illustrated magazine is a great monthly resource. There are no advertisements, just page after page of great cooking ideas and "how to" tips.

Eating Out

If you enjoy fine dining, you will likely find a chef willing to cook gluten-free once you explain the diet to him or her during an off-peak period. However, be aware that most short order restaurant cooks cannot avoid hidden gluten, since much of the food they use is prepackaged and frozen. Even a simple hamburger may have been bought as a frozen patty with fillers (a common purchasing specification in many such restaurants). Also, short order cooks are usually in a hurry, and may overlook cross-contamination potential on preparation and cooking surfaces. As a family, we find it easier, less expensive, and safer to cook gluten-free at home most of the time. Since both of our children are still young, and it is imperative to keep their gluten intake as close to zero as possible, I am able to ensure their health through knowledge of every ingredient used in making their dinner.

Over the years, I have made note of the problems most people have with gluten-free cooking, and have attempted to resolve them in this book. Here's hoping it addresses your own challenges, either potential or actual, and that you find it both helpful and easy to use.

Granola Cereal 16

Granola Bars 17

Fruit Smoothies 18

Smoked Salmon Potato Pancakes with
Dill Yogurt Cheese 19

Pancakes and Waffles 20

French Toast 21

Cinnamon Rolls 21

Old-Fashioned Cake Donuts 22

BREAKFAST

Granola Cereal

This granola is lighter and fresher than others we have tried. It is a good cereal or yogurt topping. A small food processor makes grinding the nuts and seeds effortless.

ingredients:

2 cups unsweetened coconut

1 cup chopped or coarsely ground walnuts
  or almonds

⅔ cup chopped or coarsely ground
  pumpkin seeds or sunflower kernels

2 cups coarsely ground soy nuts

2 tablespoons flax seed,
  finely ground (optional)

2 cups gluten-free brown rice crisp cereal
  (see Sources)

½ cup honey

2 teaspoons vanilla

½ cup vegetable oil

comment:

Nuts contain high-quality fats that are especially beneficial for active children and adults. 90 percent of the fat in nuts is unsaturated fat, which is heart-healthy and can lower LDL (bad) cholesterol. Nuts and seeds are rich sources of protein, fiber, B vitamins, calcium, minerals, and Vitamin E.

makes 8 cups

Preheat oven to 225°F. Lightly oil two large jelly roll pans (12½ x 17½-inch) with a bit of vegetable oil.

Combine coconut, walnuts, pumpkin seeds, soy nuts, flax seed, and cereal in a medium bowl. In a small saucepan mix honey, vanilla, and oil. Bring to a boil, stirring constantly. Quickly remove from heat when mixture begins to bubble. Pour honey mixture over granola and stir until thoroughly moistened. Spread mixture in an even layer on prepared pans. Bake for 1½ hours, stirring every 30 minutes.

Granola Bars

Make the granola one day and granola bars the next day for a freezer full of quick snacks.

ingredients:

8 cups granola (page 16)

¾ cup semi-sweet chocolate chips

1 cup chopped dried dates, figs, raisins,
  or cranberries

1½ cups peanut butter or almond butter

1¼ cups dark corn syrup

comment:

Soy nuts are a great way to add the benefits of soy into your diet. Flax seed provides calcium, iron, niacin, phosphorous, and vitamin E, as well as omega-3 fatty acids. Both soy and flax seed are rich in phytoestrogens (plant hormones) that appear to decrease menopausal symptoms, lower cholesterol, increase bone density, and protect against cancer. Be sure to refrigerate or freeze flax seed, and only grind enough for what you plan to use each day.

makes 45-50 granola bars

In a large bowl, mix granola with chocolate chips and dried fruit. Heat peanut butter and corn syrup over low heat in a medium saucepan, stirring occasionally, until texture is smooth and consistency becomes thinner. Equally divide granola mix into two large bowls. Pour ½ peanut butter syrup over one bowl of granola, stirring well. Repeat this step with second bowl of granola mix and remaining peanut butter syrup. With your hand in a plastic bag, spread mixture evenly ¾-inch thick into a lightly oiled 12 ½ x 17 ½-inch jelly roll pan. Refrigerate for an hour, then cut into bars. Wrap and freeze individual bars for quick on-the-go snacks. If you include flax seed, granola bars should be refrigerated or frozen.

variations:

If you decide to omit the chocolate chips, add ¼ cup each of peanut butter and corn syrup to the mixture.

Gluten-free brown rice syrup is a good substitution for corn syrup; you may also try a concentrated fruit juice sweetener.

Fruit Smoothies

For breakfast on the run, get the day started with a quick, healthy smoothie.

ingredients:

1 banana, peeled

½ cup berries, frozen or fresh

½ cup orange juice or other juice

⅓ cup plain yogurt or silken tofu

1 tablespoon maple syrup or honey

1 teaspoon flax seed, freshly ground
  (optional)

Protein powder to taste (optional)

makes 12 ounces

Place all ingredients in a blender. Blend on high speed until smooth.

Smoked Salmon Potato Pancakes with Dill Yogurt Cheese

A nice addition to a Sunday brunch, this recipe also makes a great appetizer.

ingredients:

One recipe of Dill Yogurt Cheese (page 27)

One recipe of Potato Pancakes (page 144)

4 ounces thinly sliced smoked salmon
   (such as lox)

2 tablespoons capers in distilled vinegar,
   drained

4 servings

To serve, spread 1-2 tablespoons cheese mixture on each potato pancake. Top with a slice of smoked salmon and a few capers.

Pancakes and Waffles

Pure maple syrup, warmed and poured over a stack of pancakes, is a weekend indulgence!
Try sprinkling raisins, dried cherries, cranberries, fresh blueberries, or thin slices of a tart, juicy apple onto pancake batter while it cooks to add variety.
This recipe is adapted from Wendy Wark's *Living Healthy with Celiac Disease* (AnAffect 1998). Use the same recipe for waffles.

ingredients:

1 cup buckwheat flour

1 cup Wendy Wark's gluten-free flour
   mix (page 181)

½ teaspoon salt

1 teaspoon cream of tartar

½ teaspoon baking soda

2 teaspoons baking powder

¼ cup sugar

½ cup melted butter or vegetable oil

3 eggs

1½ cups milk

4 servings

Heat a non-stick griddle or a heavy-bottomed frying pan to 350°-375°F.

Whisk together flours, salt, cream of tartar, baking soda, baking powder, sugar, butter, and eggs in a medium bowl. Stir just enough to dampen the batter, do not overbeat. Cautiously add milk until you reach desired consistency. (You may not need all the milk.) Pour ¼ cup of batter onto the cooking surface. Cook until the pancake is full of bubbles on top and the underside is lightly browned, then flip with a spatula and cook the other side until it is lightly browned. Remove from griddle or pan and set aside on a warm plate while cooking the remaining pancakes. Serve with warm maple syrup.

Note: The amount of milk determines the thickness of these pancakes.

French Toast

ingredients:

3 eggs

½ cup milk

¼ teaspoon each of cinnamon and nutmeg

8 slices day old gluten-free bread

½ cup pure maple syrup, warmed

4 servings (two slices per serving)

Heat a non-stick griddle to 350°-375°F.

Whisk together eggs, milk, and cinnamon in a bowl large enough to lay a slice of bread flat. Dip both sides of bread into egg mixture, coating completely. Place on griddle and cook until browned on both sides. Repeat with each slice of bread, keeping cooked slices warm in a 200°F. oven. Serve with warm maple syrup.

variation: Top each slice with a ½ tablespoon of roasted tahini. Tahini is a creamy paste made from hulled sesame seeds, and it adds a nice dimension to French toast.

Cinnamon Rolls

Every now and then you must treat yourself to a cinnamon roll! Packing them tightly into a baking dish helps to keep them moist throughout.
Adapted from Wendy Wark's *Living Healthy with Celiac Disease* (AnAffect, 1998).

ingredients:

1 recipe Workable Wonder Dough (page 169)

3 tablespoons butter, melted

⅔ cup brown sugar

3 tablespoons ground cinnamon

½ cup raisins

1 ⅓ cups confectioners' sugar

3-4 tablespoons milk

makes nine 2-inch rolls

Butter an 8-inch round cake pan.

Roll out dough to a 9 x 18-inch rectangle, approximately ½-inch in thickness. Brush dough with 3 tablespoons melted butter. Sprinkle sugar, cinnamon, and raisins evenly over the dough. Beginning at one of the 9-inch sides, roll dough into a log shape. Using a sharp, clean knife, cut log into 9 equal pieces. Arrange rolls in prepared pan, packing tightly together and keeping the swirl side up. Cover with a warm, wet towel and let rise one hour. Bake at 400°F. for 15-20 minutes. While cinnamon rolls are baking, whisk together confectioners' sugar and milk in a small bowl. Drizzle mixture over hot, baked cinnamon rolls.

Old Fashioned Cake Donuts

A special treat! Serve donuts with a dusting of powdered sugar or a Chocolate Glaze (page 198).

ingredients:

1 egg, lightly beaten

½ cup milk

½ cup sugar

2 teaspoons baking powder

¼ teaspoon nutmeg

½ teaspoon salt

1 tablespoon butter, melted

1¾-2 cups Wendy Wark's gluten-free
    flour mix* (page 181)

¾ teaspoon xanthan gum

Vegetable oil for frying

Confectioners' sugar or Chocolate Glaze

*Amount of flour needed depends on humidity

makes twelve 3-inch donuts

Mix egg, milk, sugar, baking powder, nutmeg, salt, and butter in a medium bowl. Combine flour and xanthan gum in a small bowl. Add flour mix until just incorporated. The dough will be very soft. Cover and refrigerate for one hour.

On a lightly floured surface, gradually work additional flour into the dough until it is no longer sticky. Roll out to ½-inch thickness and cut out 3-inch rounds with a well-floured cookie cutter or a knife. Cut out a 1-inch hole from the middle of each and save to make donut holes. Place donuts and donut holes on a sheet of wax paper on a baking sheet. Allow to air-dry for 10 minutes to help reduce oil absorption while frying. In a heavy-bottomed pan or a deep fryer, heat 3-4 inches of vegetable oil to 360°F. Fry 2-3 donuts at a time, turning once to brown on both sides, for about 6 minutes. Drain on paper toweling. Dust with confectioners' sugar or glaze with chocolate before serving.

Notes: You may substitute cocoa for ½ cup of the flour mix to make chocolate donuts. Feel free to experiment with other flavors by adding spices or by mixing in lemon or orange zest.
All ingredients should be room temperature.

Hummus 24

Mexican Salsa 25

Cheese Board 26

Artichoke Pesto 27

Dill Yogurt Cheese 27

Baked Cheese Wafers 28
 Marcella Rosene, Pasta & Co.

Roasted Pumpkin Seeds 28

Tapenade 29

Channa Dal Spread 30

Spicy Shrimp Skewers 31

Peach Salsa 31

Tomatillo Salsa 32

APPETIZERS

Hummus

This recipe is from Cynthia Lair's *Feeding the Whole Family* (Moon Smile Press, 1997), which offers wonderful whole foods recipes for babies, young children, and their parents. Cynthia's book is a great way to start cooking with healthy, tasty ingredients that you may not have tried before, such as sea vegetables, various beans, and soy products. This recipe is very quick if you have a pressure cooker. I have recently purchased one of the new, safer pressure cookers from Kuhn Rikon, and it is wonderful. Canned beans can replace chickpeas as a variation on the theme.

ingredients:

2 cups cooked chickpeas (garbanzo beans)

5 tablespoons tahini

½ tablespoon sea salt

⅓ cup freshly squeezed lemon juice
   (juice of 1½-2 lemons)

2-3 cloves garlic

3 tablespoons extra virgin olive oil

¼ cup (approximately) cooking liquid from
   beans (or water)

Chopped parsley (optional)

Paprika (optional)

makes 2¾-3 cups

Place cooked chickpeas in food processor or blender with tahini, salt, lemon juice, garlic, and olive oil. Blend until smooth. Add cooking liquid from beans or water to desired consistency. Garnish with chopped parsley or paprika if desired. Stores well, refrigerated, for at least a week.

For babies 10 months and older

Reserve some plain cooked chickpeas and mash. Some may enjoy picking up and eating plain cooked chickpeas; be sure they are well cooked.

variation for children

Hummus may be too spicy; try reducing lemon juice and garlic by half.

Comment: Hummus is a traditional Middle Eastern dish that is great as either a dip or a sandwich spread. The combination of chickpeas and tahini adds up to a high-protein formula. (Tahini is a creamy paste made from hulled sesame seeds.)

Mexican Salsa

This salsa is among the most popular in Mexico, and it combines cooked and uncooked ingredients, resulting in a more complex flavor.

ingredients:

2 cups water

3 jalapeños, stemmed

2 plum tomatoes

2 medium tomatillos, husks removed and
    sticky exterior washed

2 small onions, peeled and quartered

6 cloves garlic

½ teaspoon salt

15 sprigs fresh cilantro, chopped

makes 2 cups

Bring water to a boil in a medium saucepan. Add 2 whole jalapeños, tomatoes, tomatillos, 1 onion, and 4 cloves garlic. Boil for 15 minutes, remove from heat, and let cool a bit.

In the bowl of a food processor, place 1 halved jalapeño, 2 quartered garlic cloves, 1 onion, and salt. Chop coarsely. Add chopped cilantro and gradually add cooked vegetables to the fresh mixture in the food processor and blend. Add a little cooking water if necessary to thin the sauce.

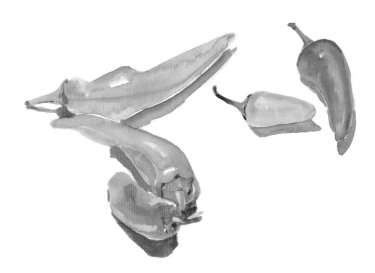

Cheese Board

An array of cheese, pears, apples, figs, and dates can serve as either an appetizer or as a course to precede dessert. It is both fun and easy to put together. When tasting, try different combinations (such as blue cheese with pears and dates, a wonderful harmonization of flavors).

ingredients:

1 pound of assorted cheeses, such as pecorino
(an Italian sheep's milk cheese),
Camembert, Brie, and blue cheese
6-7 dried figs or dates, quartered
3-4 fresh pears, cored and sliced
(choose from D'Anjou, Bartlett, or Bosc)
10 ounces rice crackers

6 servings

Arrange cheese, dried figs or dates, and pears on a wooden cutting board and serve.

variation:
Tart apples make a nice substitution for the pears.

wine suggestion: Italian Pinot Grigio

Artichoke Pesto

A tasty dip with crackers.

ingredients:

1 can (13 ounces) whole artichoke hearts
    (drained, with 3 tablespoons liquid reserved)
½ cup grated Parmesan cheese
Juice from 1 lemon
1 small garlic clove, passed through a
    garlic press or minced
2 tablespoons olive oil

makes 1 ¼ cups

Combine artichoke hearts, reserved liquid from artichokes, Parmesan, lemon juice, and garlic in the bowl of a small food processor. Pulse on high for a minute, then slowly drizzle in olive oil while machine is running until well incorporated.

Dill Yogurt Cheese

A good low-fat substitute for sour cream or cream cheese. This recipe combines it with sour cream for a tangier flavor.

ingredients:

8 ounces non-fat plain, gluten-free yogurt,
    drained of liquid (see Note)
½ cup gluten-free sour cream
¼ cup chopped fresh dill

makes 1 ½ cups

Combine drained yogurt with sour cream and dill. Mix well.

Note: Once the liquid is drained from yogurt it becomes yogurt cheese. Donvier makes a yogurt strainer that is easy to use. Simply place the yogurt in the mesh basket, cover, and refrigerate. The liquid will drain out in about 2 hours. You can fashion your own strainer by suspending a mesh sieve over a bowl.

Baked Cheese Wafers

This recipe is adapted from the *Pasta & Co. By Request* cookbook by Marcella Rosene (Pasta & Co., 1991). Pasta & Co. is Seattle's premier, upscale take-out food shop with five locations.

ingredients:

6 ounces Monterey jack cheese,
    cut into sixteen ¼-inch slices
1 heaping teaspoon Pasta & Co. House
    Herbs or herbes de Provence

makes 16 wafers

Preheat oven to 400°F.

Arrange 8 cheese slices with plenty of space in between on a non-stick baking sheet. Sprinkle with herbs. Bake exactly 10 minutes. Lift each cheese wafer onto a cooling rack covered with paper towels. Repeat process with remaining 8 slices.

Note: Herbes de Provence is found in the spice section in large grocery stores. It includes basil, fennel, lavender, marjoram, rosemary, sage, summer savory, and thyme, all of which are commonly used in southern France.

Roasted Pumpkin Seeds

Pumpkin seeds, also known as pepitas, are popular in Mexican cooking. Sprinkle roasted pumpkin seeds over salads, use as a garnish, or eat as a healthy snack. Stores that offer organic produce often sell pumpkin seeds in bulk.

ingredients:

Olive oil
1-2 cups pumpkin seeds, raw and unsalted

makes 1-2 cups

Preheat oven to 250°F.

Lightly coat or spray a large jelly roll pan or baking sheet with oil. Scatter pumpkin seeds evenly over the pan and season with salt. Bake for 1-2 hours (the latter makes for a crunchier result). Cool and store in an airtight container.

Tapenade

Marian Robertson introduced this tapenade to our family, and we are grateful! All ingredients can be kept on hand for last minute preparation.

ingredients:

1 jar (7 ounces) roasted red peppers,
     drained
1 can (6 ounces) whole artichokes,
     drained and quartered
½ cup fresh parsley, large stem removed
½ cup grated Parmesan

¼ cup olive oil
3 cloves garlic, finely chopped or
     passed through a garlic press
1 tablespoon lemon juice
¼ cup gluten-free capers, drained

makes 2 cups

Place all ingredients in a food processor. Mix until well blended.
Serve on gluten-free crackers or bread.

wine suggestion: Italian Dolcetto d'Alba

Channa Dal Spread

Debra Daniels-Zeller teaches a Bean Cuisine cooking class at our local natural foods market, PCC Natural Markets.
Her class is a wealth of information on beans and cooking how-to. Beans provide many of the nutrients that people on a gluten-free diet may lack.
They are high in protein, low in fat, and are good sources of calcium, iron, B vitamins, niacin, and zinc. They are also rich in soluble fiber.
A special benefit for diabetics is the gradual release of the glucose in beans into the bloodstream, which helps stabilize sugar levels.

ingredients:

1 cup channa dal, soaked overnight

1 strip kombu, cut into small pieces

4 cups water

3 tablespoons chopped sun-dried tomatoes

½ cup hot water or water used for
　cooking beans

½ tablespoon olive oil

1 medium onion, chopped

2 jalapeños, seeded and minced

2 cloves garlic, minced

2 teaspoons chili powder

½ teaspoon cumin

Generous dash of cayenne (optional)

Salt to taste

⅓ cup chopped cilantro

makes 3 cups

Place soaked beans, kombu, and water in a soup pot. Bring to a boil, then reduce heat. Cover and simmer for 45 minutes, or until beans are very tender.

While beans are cooking, soak sun-dried tomatoes in hot water until softened.

Heat a heavy skillet over medium heat. Add olive oil, onion, and jalapeños. Stir briefly, then reduce heat, cover, and cook until onions are soft. Add garlic, chili powder, cumin, and cayenne if desired. Continue to cook until vegetables are very soft.

When beans have finished cooking, drain, reserving liquid. Puree beans and jalapeño mixture in a food processor or blender with the sun-dried tomatoes (using more of the bean cooking liquid if needed) until it forms a smooth paste. Season to taste with salt and pepper. Pulse in chopped cilantro at the end.

Spoon into a serving bowl. It can be used as a spread, or you can add a bit more water and make a dip.

wine suggestion:　California Sauvignon Blanc

Comment: You will find this nutty spread to be downright delicious. Channa dal beans are hulled and split baby garbanzo beans. They can be found in natural food markets, specialty food stores, and through mail order houses (see Sources). Garbanzo, red, or pinto beans are possible substitutes, but the flavor will not be the same.

Spicy Shrimp Skewers

Our neighbor, Bill Bassett, likes to cook, and comes up with interesting creations all the time.
He made this one night as an appetizer to accompany my Lopez Taquitos (page 50). They were great together!

ingredients:

1 pound medium shrimp, shelled, rinsed,
   and deveined

1½ tablespoons cumin (or less to taste)

1 medium jalapeño, stemmed and
   finely chopped

2-3 tablespoons olive oil

1 lime, cut in half

6 servings

Prepare an outdoor grill. Thread shrimp onto bamboo skewers. In a small bowl, combine cumin, jalapeño, and olive oil. Brush shrimp skewers with seasoning mixture. When coals are hot, sprinkle skewers with salt and pepper and arrange in an even layer on the grill. Cook shrimp until just opaque in the center, squeezing the juice of half a lime over each side while grilling. Serve immediately.

wine suggestion:　French Chablis

Peach Salsa

This is an unusual yet tasty salsa for chips. It would be fun and interesting over halibut as well.

ingredients:

4 Italian plum tomatoes, cut into ¼-inch dice

1 cup (¼-inch dice) fresh, peeled peaches

½ cup finely diced red onion

16 large basil leaves, finely chopped

4 teaspoons balsamic vinegar

¼ cup extra-virgin olive oil

makes 2 cups

Combine tomatoes, peaches, onion, basil, balsamic vinegar, and olive oil in a large bowl. Season with salt and pepper. Serve.

wine suggestion:　French Sancerre

Tomatillo Salsa

A salsa to serve as an appetizer or as an accompaniment to an omelet. When buying tomatillos, look for firm fruit with tight fitting husks. If the fruit has started to shrink in the husk, it is aging. Tomatillos are available year round; however, the smaller fruit found during the winter months will necessitate buying ten or eleven for this recipe.

ingredients:

7 medium tomatillos, husks removed and
    sticky exterior washed
Salt and freshly ground pepper
½ cup chopped parsley or cilantro
¼ cup olive oil
1 tablespoon lime juice
2-3 tablespoons diced sweet onion
Half of a medium cucumber, diced
1 medium avocado, diced

makes 2 cups

In the bowl of a small food processor, puree 3 tomatillos with salt, pepper, and parsley. Slowly add olive oil. Chop the remaining tomatillos and toss with the lime juice, onion, cucumber, and tomatillo puree. Add the avocado and gently mix. The salsa can be used right away, or covered and refrigerated for about one hour.

Chiles Rellenos with Mango Salsa 34

🕐 Fried Rice with Cashews and Snow Peas 36

🕐 Spinach Chèvre Pasta with Marinara Sauce 37

🕐 Pan-Fried Chicken with Leeks 38

Savory Crustless Tart with Artichokes and Bacon 39

Northwest Paella 40
  Chef Barbara Figueroa

🕐 Dungeness Crab Caesar Salad 41

Pacific Rim Flank Steak 42

Chicken Fajitas with Sweet Peppers 43

🕐 Braised Tuna with Ginger and Soy 44
  Chef Christopher Kimball

🕐 Pork Tenderloin Medallions 45

Pan-Fried Crab Cakes with Tomato Coulis and Cilantro Oil 46
  Chef Christian Svalesen

Butterflied Leg of Lamb 47

🕐 Roasted Asparagus Quesadillas with Cactus Salsa 48

Roast Chicken 49

Lopez Taquitos 50

Vegetarian Lasagna 51

SPRING

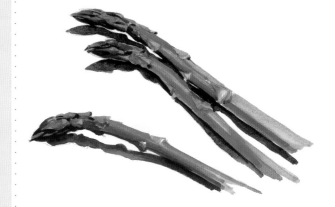

🕐 – indicates a quick meal

Chiles Rellenos with Mango Salsa

This is a great meatless meal, with flavors that go wonderfully together. Make a large batch to guarantee leftovers for lunch the next day. Serve with black beans for a nice color contrast, or with refried beans.

ingredients:

mango salsa

2 cups peeled, chopped mango
   (about 2 whole mangoes)
½ cup chopped red onion
1 cup chopped red bell pepper
3-4 tablespoons finely chopped fresh cilantro
3 tablespoons lime juice

chiles

9 ounces Monterey Jack cheese, grated
12 ounces mozzarella cheese, grated
7 ounces feta cheese, crumbled
8 poblano or Anaheim chiles, or
   4 cans (7 ounces each) whole green chiles

4 servings (two per person)

For Mango Salsa: Mix all ingredients in a nonreactive bowl. Cover and refrigerate.

Preheat oven to 400°F.

Combine cheeses in a medium bowl and mix well.

Roasting Fresh Chiles: To prepare, char peppers under the broiler, turning periodically to blacken on all sides. Transfer peppers to a paper bag and seal. When peppers are cool, remove the blackened skins, which will come off easily.

Cut a slit in each chile and remove seeds and membranes. Fill each chile with a handful of cheese mixture. Place chiles on a baking sheet and top with remaining cheese mixture. Bake until cheese melts and chiles are heated through (about 5 minutes). Transfer chiles to plates and spoon salsa over each.

wine suggestion: California Sauvignon Blanc

Note: The poblano chile is a dark green to black variety; its flavor is somewhat earthy rather than spicy. Peak season is summer to early fall, although many markets sell them year round. Anaheims are lighter green and milder in flavor.

Variation for Children: Quesadillas

4 servings

Substitute 8 corn tortillas for the chiles in the recipe on the preceding page.

Place four corn tortillas on a non-stick baking sheet, cover with cheese mixture, and place another tortilla on top of each. Sprinkle with more of the cheese mixture and cook as directed for chiles rellenos. Cut each tortilla into six equal wedge-shaped pieces.

If you are not familiar with mangoes, they can be quite difficult to work with, thanks to the large, flat seed inside. Sunfresh brand mangoes are a good alternative to fresh mangoes; they are sliced and vacuum packed in jars, and are usually found in the refrigerated section of grocery stores near the produce. Fresh mangoes in season (around midsummer) are wonderful. Look for skin that is either orange or red with a little green. Fruit should be soft and unblemished. Large mangoes are better, since they yield a greater proportion of fruit. To prepare, first peel the fruit, then score the outside all the way around. With the knife tip, slice off the mango squares, cutting through until you feel resistance from the seed.

Fried Rice with Cashews and Snow Peas

A quick meal that is satisfying. Serve with Miso Soup (page 89) or as a one-dish meal.

ingredients:

¾ cup cashews

4 servings of cooked rice

2 eggs

¼ teaspoon salt

2 tablespoons peanut oil

3 scallions, chopped

1 pound chicken or pork tenderloin, sliced
 ¼-inch thick in 1-inch pieces

½ teaspoon minced fresh ginger or
 ginger juice (see Sources)

1 teaspoon toasted sesame oil

1 cup snow peas, stringed, or
 frozen green peas

2 tablespoons gluten-free tamari or gluten-
 free soy sauce

4 servings

Preheat oven to 325°F.

Spread cashews out on a baking sheet. Bake for 5-10 minutes until light golden in color. Watch carefully to avoid burning.

Have cooked rice ready before starting. Beat eggs with salt in a small bowl. Heat 1 tablespoon of peanut oil in a large skillet or wok. Add scallions and eggs and stir-fry until set. Remove from pan and set aside. Heat another tablespoon of oil. Add meat and briefly cook over high heat. Add ginger, sesame oil, peas, and cashews. Stir-fry for 2 minutes. Stir in tamari, eggs, and rice, mixing together gently to combine ingredients. Heat through and serve.

variations:

Carrots, asparagus, or green beans can be added or used in place of the peas.

Tofu is a good substitution for chicken or pork. Frozen tofu provides the best texture for this dish. Be sure to thaw tofu completely. Drain tofu by placing it on a plate, resting another plate on top, and setting a 1-pound weight atop the second plate. After 10 minutes or so discard excess water. Chop tofu into ½-inch cubes, substitute for the meat in the recipe.

Spinach Chèvre Pasta with Marinara Sauce

This comforting entrée features a wonderfully light, low-fat creamy marinara sauce with spinach. The sauce is adapted from a recipe in Marcella Rosene's *Pasta & Co. By Request* cookbook (Pasta & Co., 1991). Pasta & Co. is Seattle's premier upscale take-out food shop with five locations. They have also begun to stock gluten-free pasta.

ingredients:

Marinara Sauce

3 tablespoons olive oil

1 teaspoon red pepper flakes or dash of chili oil

3 cloves of garlic, finely chopped or passed
   through a garlic press

2 cups dry white wine

2 cans (28 ounces each) high quality
   crushed tomatoes

2 ounces tomato paste

½ teaspoon salt

Black pepper to taste

2-3 tablespoons fresh basil

2-3 tablespoons fresh oregano

1 pound gluten-free penne pasta
   (Tinkyada or Bi-Aglut is best)

2 ounces fresh spinach, washed and dried

5 ounces soft creamy goat cheese (chèvre)

4 servings

Heat olive oil in a medium saucepan over moderate heat. Add red pepper flakes and garlic. Cook for one minute, stirring frequently and being careful not to brown the garlic. Add wine and simmer for 10 minutes until reduced by half. Add tomatoes and tomato paste, cover, and simmer on low heat for 20 minutes, stirring occasionally. Taste sauce for seasoning, adding salt, pepper, and sugar as needed. Add fresh herbs. Simmer a few minutes longer.

Prepare pasta according to package directions. Place cooked pasta on a dinner plate, top with a handful of fresh spinach, ladle marinara sauce on top of spinach (the heat from the sauce and pasta will lightly wilt the spinach), and top with goat cheese. Serve immediately.

wine suggestion: Italian Pinot Bianco

Marinara Sauce: This flavorful sauce can be easily made with 10 minutes of preparation time and 30 minutes of cooking time. If you like a lighter sauce, omit the tomato paste. The sauce will keep frozen for several months; you can make several double batches and freeze for future use.

Pan-Fried Chicken with Leeks

A very quick meal with a nice twist to the typical chicken dinner. Serve with Master Recipe for Long Grain White Rice (page 151), it is the best method I've discovered for cooking rice perfectly every time. To keep things simple, the vegetable accompaniment consists of thick slices of ripe, juicy tomato.

ingredients:

3 large leeks

1 tablespoon olive oil

2 cloves garlic, finely minced or
*   passed through a garlic press*

1 whole boneless, skinless chicken breast,
*   cut into 2-inch strips*

3-4 boneless, skinless chicken thighs,
*   cut into 2-inch strips*

½-¾ cup gluten-free chicken stock

¼ cup cream

4 servings

Rinse leeks well and cut off the root ends. Slice white part diagonally into ¾-inch pieces.

Heat oil in a large skillet over low heat. Add garlic and leeks. Cook, stirring occasionally, until leeks are softened. Remove from skillet and set aside. Increase heat to high. Add chicken to skillet and cook, stirring, until lightly browned. Add chicken stock and reduce by half. Add cream. Season with salt and pepper. Scrape the browned bits from the bottom of the skillet, using a wooden spoon, and stir until cream is well incorporated. Serve over rice.

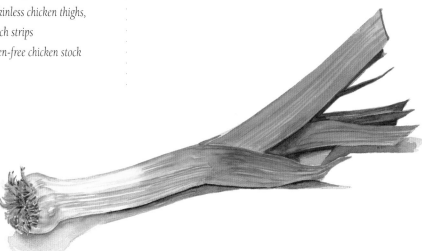

Savory Crustless Tart with Artichokes and Bacon

Be sure to save stale gluten-free bread to make bread crumbs for this recipe. Serve with either Basil Spinach Salad (page 121) or Apple Sauté (page 135). Recipe adapted from *Breakfast in Bed*, Carol Frieberg (Sasquatch Books, 1990).

ingredients:

8 slices bacon

½ medium onion, chopped

1 can (13 ounces) of whole artichoke hearts, chopped (plus ¼ can reserved liquid)

6 eggs, slightly beaten

⅓ cup grated Parmesan cheese

⅓ cup gluten-free bread crumbs

Grated Monterey Jack cheese

Chopped chives or parsley for garnish

4 servings

Preheat oven to 325°F.

Butter a 9-inch quiche or pie plate.

Cook bacon over low heat until crisp in a medium skillet. Remove from pan and drain on paper toweling. Remove all but 2 tablespoons of bacon fat from skillet. When bacon cools, crumble into small pieces.

Cook onion in bacon fat over low heat, stirring occasionally, until translucent. Add artichokes and reserved artichoke liquid. Heat for 2 minutes, stirring and scraping skillet with a wooden spoon to deglaze. In a large bowl, lightly beat eggs; add Parmesan cheese, bread crumbs, artichoke mixture, and bacon. Mix well and place in prepared dish. Bake for 25 minutes, or until just set. Sprinkle top with grated cheese and bake for 5 minutes more. Garnish with chopped chives or parsley.

Northwest Paella

Chef Barbara Figueroa – Seattle, Washington

Barbara Figueroa is a former executive chef and restaurateur who has spent her career in such kitchens as Spago, Le Cirque, and the Sorrento Hotel.
She is currently the director of food and beverage at the Warwick Hotel, and has been a contributor to various publications as well as the editor of this book.

ingredients:

3 tablespoons olive oil

2 medium onions, diced

2 large red bell peppers, diced

3 pounds chicken thighs

3 cloves garlic, minced

1½ pounds rice, preferably basmati or Texmati

1 quart (generous) rich gluten-free chicken stock
(about 20 ounces)

2 cups canned plum tomatoes
(seeded and coarsely chopped),
plus 1½ cups of their juice, strained

1 pound gluten-free chorizo, cut in ½-inch rounds
(may substitute with gluten-free spicy sausage)

½ teaspoon saffron

2-3 bay leaves

4 pounds assorted seafood (prawns, mussels,
clams, squid, cubes of salmon or halibut fillet,
crab or whatever is seasonally available), cleaned

1½ pounds snow peas or sugar snaps, stringed
(snow peas may be cut in half diagonally)

¼ cup (rounded) chopped Italian parsley

Additional sprigs of Italian parsley for garnish

chef's comments:

A one-dish perennial favorite of both young and old. The flavors marry well over a few days' time, lending the recipe to "big batch" production.

12 servings

Heat olive oil in a large heavy pot over moderate flame. Add onions and peppers. Sauté until onions barely begin to soften. Add chicken thighs and garlic. Cook until chicken is seared on all sides. Add rice. Lower heat. Cook, stirring, over moderate low heat, until grains take on a translucent appearance. Add 1 quart of the stock, tomatoes, and tomato juice. Bring to a boil. Add chorizo, saffron, and bay leaves. Reduce heat to low. Cover and simmer, stirring occasionally, until rice is barely cooked. Season with salt and pepper. Immediately turn out onto a flat pan to cool.

Cook peas until crisp-tender in boiling salted water. Drain and shock in ice water. Drain again thoroughly.

To serve, reheat rice mixture in a moderate (about 350°F.) oven, covered with foil. When rice is reheated, bring remaining stock to a simmer. Add seafood, cover, and steam until done, removing pieces as they finish cooking. Toss seafood (and its steaming liquid, which should be minimal), peas, and parsley with rice mixture. Garnish with parsley sprigs.

wine suggestion:

A white Rioja is a classic with this dish, but you might want to try a French Sauvignon Blanc from the Loire Valley, or a northern Italian Pinot Grigio.

Dungeness Crab Caesar Salad

This is one of the few recipes that include a store-bought salad dressing. I prefer to make my own dressings, however, the best Caesar dressings made at home include a raw or briefly cooked egg. With young children in the house, I am hesitant to serve egg in this manner. One of the chef contributors to this book is Ludger Szmania. His bottled Caesar Salad Dressing is superior to any others we have tried. Distribution in stores is limited to the Northwest (see Sources). Annie's Caesar Dressing is a good alternative and is available through Mrs. Roben's catalog (see Sources) and in many natural food stores.

ingredients:

4 large slices gluten-free bread, cubed

1 head romaine lettuce, washed and dried

Szmania's Caesar Salad Dressing

Parmesan cheese, grated

½ pound fresh Dungeness crab meat,
    picked over to remove bits of shell

4 servings

Preheat oven to 400°F.

Spread cubed bread in an even layer on a large baking sheet. Bake for 10 minutes until croutons are crispy.

Tear romaine into bite-sized pieces and transfer to a large salad bowl. Toss dressing with romaine until well coated. Add croutons and Parmesan and toss again. Serve salad on individual plates and top with fresh crab. Season with salt and pepper to taste.

wine suggestion: Alsatian Pinot Blanc

Note: An alternative to baking the bread cubes is to sauté them in butter in a skillet. I have tried both methods, and baking the croutons produces a crispier crouton that also takes the flavor of the Caesar dressing better.

Pacific Rim Flank Steak

An easy marinade to tenderize and flavor a tougher cut of meat. If you plan to serve this on a weeknight be sure to marinate the meat early in the day. (It takes only about five minutes to put the marinade together.) When serving, cut thin slices across the grain of the meat for a more tender result. Serve with Fresh Artichokes (page 138) and Tinkyada fettuccine. Toss each pound of pasta with 4-5 tablespoons of Homemade Pesto (page 69), or with butter and Parmesan cheese.

ingredients:

1½–2 pounds flank steak

Marinade:

¾ cup vegetable oil
¼ cup gluten-free tamari or
    gluten-free soy sauce
3 tablespoons honey
2 tablespoons red wine vinegar
1 clove garlic, finely minced or
    passed through a garlic press
One 1-inch piece of ginger, minced

4 servings

Place flank steak in a nonreactive dish. Combine all marinade ingredients and pour marinade over the meat. Cover and refrigerate for at least 5 hours, turning meat several times.

Preheat grill.

Cook flank steak two inches above hot coals, 4-5 minutes on each side. (You may also broil it for about the same amount of time.)

wine suggestion: Washington Merlot

Note: Hot coal test: you will be able to hold your hand above the grate for only 2 seconds.

Chicken Fajitas with Sweet Peppers

A fairly quick meal; once you make the tortillas a few times the process will be faster. While the chicken is marinating, you can slice the onions and peppers and make the tortillas in about 15 minutes. Serve fajitas with Homemade Refried Beans (page 153) for a more complete meal.

ingredients:

1½ pounds boneless, skinless chicken breast,
   cut into thin 2-inch strips
⅓ cup olive oil or cilantro oil
   (found in gourmet markets)
⅓ cup chopped fresh cilantro
Juice of one lime
1½ tablespoons ground cumin
4 cloves garlic, finely chopped or
   passed through a garlic press
1 recipe of Homemade Tortillas (page 167)
⅓ cup sliced onions
1½ cups sliced assorted sweet peppers

4 servings

In a nonreactive medium bowl, combine chicken, oil, cilantro, lime juice, cumin, and garlic. Refrigerate.

Prepare flour tortillas (see recipe).

While tortillas are being held in the oven, heat a large skillet. Remove chicken from marinade and stir-fry until cooked through. Add sweet peppers and onions, seasoning with salt and pepper. Serve in warm tortillas with your favorite salsa and sour cream. (NOTE: If you prefer to grill the chicken, simply sauté the peppers and onions in a small amount of olive oil. When chicken is cooked through, slice into 2-inch strips and serve.)

wine suggestion: French Côtes du Rhône

Braised Tuna with Ginger and Soy

Chef Christopher Kimball

Founder, editor, and publisher of *Cook's Illustrated* magazine.* Author of *The Cook's Bible* and *The Yellow Farmhouse Cookbook*
Recipe adapted from *The Cook's Bible* (Little Brown, 1996)

ingredients:

5 tablespoons rice wine vinegar

⅓ cup tamari (gluten-free soy sauce)

⅓ cup white wine

⅛ teaspoon ground cardamom

½ teaspoon sugar

3 tablespoons peanut oil

4 fresh tuna steaks

1 small onion, diced

1 tablespoon peeled and minced gingerroot

3 cloves garlic, minced

2 teaspoons toasted sesame oil (see Sources)

2 scallions, diced

chef's comments:

Roasted (or toasted) sesame oil is available in health food stores. It has a great deal more flavor than regular sesame oil, which should not be substituted in this recipe. If you cannot find it, simply omit it from the recipe. Serve with Master Recipe for Long Grain White Rice (page 151).

4 servings

Preheat oven to 375°F.

Combine vinegar, tamari, wine, cardamom, and sugar in a small bowl. Put 2 tablespoons peanut oil into a Dutch oven or flameproof casserole dish over medium-high heat. When oil is hot, add tuna steaks (in batches if pan is crowded) and sear for about 2 minutes. Turn tuna over and cook for 1 minute more. Remove steaks from pan and keep warm.

Add remaining tablespoon of peanut oil to pan. Cook onion and ginger over medium heat, stirring frequently, for 4 minutes. Add garlic and cook, stirring frequently, for another 3 minutes. Add the reserved vinegar mixture and bring to a boil. Add the tuna steaks, cover, and bake in preheated oven until done (about 7 minutes, depending on the thickness of the steaks). Check after 4-5 minutes to avoid overcooking. Remove steaks from pan and keep warm.

Place pan on top of stove and reduce liquid over medium-high heat for 1 to 2 minutes. Add sesame oil and scallions. Season with salt and pepper. Continue cooking for another minute, or until reduced and flavorful. Pour liquid over tuna steaks and serve.

wine suggestion:

Pinot Blanc. Try two winners from the *Cook's Illustrated* May/June 1999 issue taste test: the 1997 Steele Bien Nacindo Vineyard or the 1997 Lockwood.

*__Cook's Illustrated__ is a wonderful magazine for seasoned cooks as well as those just learning. Each month well-researched and tested recipes are featured to provide you the best way to prepare the dish. Another good source from Christopher Kimball is __The Cook's Bible__, a fabulous book with over 400 recipes for just about anything you want to cook. It is like having a cooking instructor constantly at your side.

Pork Tenderloin Medallions

An easy, flavorful dinner you will enjoy time and again. Serve with Oven Roasted Red Potatoes (page 139) and
Fried Sage Green Beans (page 139); it is also nice served over Tinkyada gluten-free fettuccine.

ingredients:

2 pounds pork tenderloin

4 heaping tablespoons gluten-free
    Dijon mustard

3 teaspoons green peppercorns

1 tablespoon olive oil

2 cloves garlic, finely minced or passed
    through a garlic press

2 tablespoons butter

6 tablespoons white wine

4 tablespoons whipping cream

4 servings

Slice the pork tenderloin into round slices ¼-inch thick. Arrange slices side by side and sprinkle with salt and pepper. Spread mustard on one side of each slice. Using either a mortar and pestle or the back of a spoon in a small bowl, thoroughly crush the green peppercorns and set aside.

Heat the oil in a large, heavy-bottomed skillet on high heat. Add the garlic and heat for a moment without allowing garlic to brown. Add the meat and cook for a few minutes on each side until golden brown. (The bottom of the pan will develop a crust as the meat and mustard brown.) Add the crushed peppercorns and butter, stirring well to incorporate. Once meat is cooked, remove to a plate and keep covered to retain heat.

Over high heat, deglaze pan by adding the wine and reducing by half, scraping the bottom of the pan to loosen browned meat and mustard bits stuck to the pan. Add the cream and incorporate well. Return meat to the pan, coating thoroughly with the sauce. Serve immediately.

wine suggestion: Oregon Pinot Noir

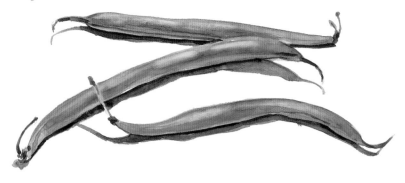

Pan-Fried Crab Cakes with Tomato Coulis and Cilantro Oil

Chef Christian Svalesen, 36° – Dallas, Texas

Chef Svalesen was featured in the 1998 *Wine Spectator* as a hot young chef. When Chris heard of this book, he enthusiastically put together some easy and scrumptious recipes. These crab cakes are fabulous! Chris uses Jonah crab from Maine. Dungeness crab from Alaska is an excellent substitution. Find a good source for seafood and enjoy! Serve with salad of daikon and radish sprouts.

ingredients:

Cilantro Oil

1 cup cilantro oil (if not available at your
   market, use olive oil)

1 bunch cilantro, washed with stems removed

2 cloves of garlic, finely minced or passed
   through a garlic press

Tomato Coulis

6 Roma tomatoes, chopped

2 cloves garlic, finely minced or passed
   through a garlic press

Crab Cakes

1 pound crab meat, picked over for shells

1 egg, slightly beaten

½ cup gluten-free mayonnaise

½ cup gluten-free bread crumbs

¼ cup finely chopped red and
   green bell peppers

¼ cup finely chopped onion

1 tablespoon Worcestershire sauce

8 shots of Tabasco

⅛ cup finely chopped cilantro

1 tablespoon olive oil

1 tablespoon butter

4 servings (two crab cakes per person)

For Cilantro Oil: Puree olive oil, cilantro, and garlic together in a small food processor or in a blender. Season with salt and pepper.

For Tomato Coulis: Puree tomatoes and garlic in a food processor. Place in a medium saucepan and simmer until thickened (about 30-40 minutes). Strain out excess liquid in a fine mesh strainer. Season with salt and pepper.

For Crab Cakes: In a medium bowl, mix together crab, egg, mayonnaise, bread crumbs, peppers, onion, Worcestershire sauce, Tabasco, and cilantro. Season with salt and pepper. Form eight patties weighing two ounces each. (Extra crab cakes can be frozen.)

In a medium broiler-safe skillet, pan-fry crab cakes over medium heat in olive oil and butter. Brown one side, then place under broiler to brown the other side for 2 minutes. Place a portion of tomato coulis on a dinner plate next to two crab cakes and drizzle with cilantro oil.

wine suggestion: Shiraz (the name given the Syrah grape in Australia, where it is a popular varietal)

Note: Save extra cilantro oil to toss with pasta or a salad for another meal.

Butterflied Leg of Lamb

So easy and delicious, and not as challenging as it sounds. Ask your butcher to butterfly the lamb for you. This recipe comes from Joanne VanRoden, owner of Wellspring Cookbooks. Her daughter is a friend of mine, and dinner at Anne's house is always an occasion to remember! Serve as a spring holiday meal with Roasted Vegetables (page 149), Garlic Mashed Potatoes (page 140), and Gorgonzola–Pear Salad (page 121). Conclude with the Cheese Board (page 26).

ingredients:

4-5 pounds butterflied leg of lamb

¼ cup gluten-free tamari or gluten-free
   soy sauce

¾ cup red wine
   (a Burgundy or a full-bodied Syrah)

3 tablespoons honey

1 tablespoon gluten-free Dijon mustard

3 cloves garlic, passed through a
   garlic press or minced

3 tablespoons fresh rosemary
   (or 2 teaspoons dried rosemary)

¼ teaspoon freshly ground pepper

Juice and zest of 1 orange and 1 lemon

1 cup gluten-free beef broth

8 servings

Place meat in a large nonreactive baking dish. In a small bowl, whisk together tamari, red wine, honey, mustard, garlic, rosemary, pepper, juice, and zest. Pour marinade over the meat and refrigerate overnight, or for at least 12 hours.

Prepare an outdoor grill by mounding the charcoal about 6 inches below grating at its highest point. Preheat the grill. Reserve the marinade and pat the meat dry. Cook meat over hot coals (about 12 minutes per side for meat that is 1½ -2 inches thick, or until internal temperature is 130º-135ºF. for medium rare). Cover with foil and let rest for 5-8 minutes on cutting board.

Make a sauce for the meat by reducing reserved marinade and beef broth by half in a small pot. Taste, seasoning with salt and pepper as necessary.

To serve, cut lamb diagonally across the grain in ½-inch thick slices. Place several slices in the center of a warm plate and spoon sauce over and around the lamb.

wine suggestion: French Red Rhône

Notes: Zesting an orange or lemon can be done with a zester or with a very fine grater. The grater is a quicker method. Grate over a large bowl to capture the flavorful orange and lemon oils that are released as you grate.
By removing the shank bone and ball joint from the leg of lamb,
the butcher can create a flat piece of meat that is easy to grill.

Roasted Asparagus Quesadillas with Cactus Salsa

My friend Edel has a son with multiple allergies. She faces many of the same challenges as gluten intolerant people but in different food categories.
She must check ingredients with manufacturers and watch everything that her son eats or contacts. Through it all she has developed interesting recipes, including this one.
Serve as a good weekend lunch or a quick on-the-go dinner. Cactus salsa is sold in specialty grocery stores.

ingredients:

1 bunch of asparagus (thin stalks)
Olive oil
1 cup white sharp cheddar cheese, grated
½ cup cactus salsa or green salsa
8 corn tortillas

4 servings

Preheat oven to 400°F.

Wash and dry asparagus. Holding a stalk of asparagus, bend until it snaps in two, discarding the lower portion. Repeat with remaining stalks. Place asparagus in one layer on a baking sheet, spray (or brush) lightly with olive oil, and season with salt and pepper. Roll stalks to coat with oil and seasoning on all sides. Bake for 10 minutes (or 20 minutes for thick asparagus).

Heat a skillet or griddle and warm a tortilla on each side. Place 4 asparagus stalks, 2 tablespoons cheese, and 2 tablespoons salsa on one half of tortilla. Fold tortilla over to cover ingredients. Repeat steps to fill other tortillas. You might also like to top with additional cheese, melting cheese briefly under the broiler.

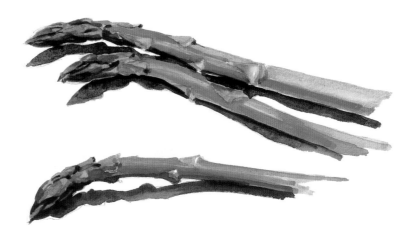

Roast Chicken

I consider this the best way to cook a whole chicken, as it is very easy and the chicken will be quite succulent.

There will also be plenty of leftovers to use in a chicken salad later in the week.

You will need an upright poultry roasting column; this item is made of stainless steel, clay, or other material, and can be purchased in gourmet cookware shops.

ingredients:

1 whole chicken
   (weighing between 3½ and 5 pounds)
2-3 tablespoons of lemon juice
2-3 fresh sprigs each of rosemary, thyme,
   and sage (or 2-3 tablespoons each of
   dried rosemary, thyme, and sage,
   tied in a cheesecloth bag)
1 tablespoon butter, melted

Recipe requires an hour or more preparation/cooking time.

4 servings

Preheat oven to 400°F. Be sure you have pulled any extra racks out of the oven before they get hot. (The lowest rack is probably the only one you will need.) Use a shallow baking pan with an easy to clean surface, and have a roasting column ready.

Remove the giblets and neck of the chicken. Rinse the chicken inside and out, and pat dry with a paper towel. Place chicken in baking pan, pour the lemon juice inside the cavity, and season both cavity and exterior of chicken with salt and pepper. Place herbs on top of the roasting column and insert the column into the bird (neck up and legs down). Tie the legs together with cooking twine. Baste chicken with melted butter (use lemon juice for low-fat basting).

Pour 1½ cups water into the baking pan. Roast chicken for one hour, or until a meat thermometer inserted into the thickest part of the thigh reads 170°–175°F. Let rest 20 minutes before carving.

wine suggestion: Spanish Rioja

Note: Save carcass for homemade chicken stock, freezing in a freezer bag for future use.

Lopez Taquitos

"Taquito" actually means little taco, but you often find them in Mexican restaurants in the form of a corn tortilla wrapped tightly around a meat filling and deep-fried until crisp. We pan-fry our taquitos in a small amount of oil, and the end result is quite similar with less mess and fewer calories. This recipe was created by Diane Robertson, who painted the watercolors for this book.

Make-ahead steps include cooking and shredding the chicken, assembling the taquitos, preparing the salsa, and cooking the beans before refrying them.
Serve with Mexican Salsa (page 25), Homemade Refried Beans (page 153), and rice.

ingredients:

1½ quarts of water, lightly salted

4 chicken breasts, boneless and skinless

6 garlic cloves

1 cup red bell pepper, finely chopped

1 cup green bell pepper, finely chopped

1 medium onion, sliced

3-4 garlic cloves, finely chopped or
    passed through a garlic press

1 cup mushrooms, finely chopped

2 tablespoons olive oil

20 corn tortillas

¾ cup Parmesan cheese

Vegetable oil

Recipe requires an hour or more preparation/cooking time.

6 servings

Place water, chicken, and garlic cloves in a large saucepan. Bring water to a boil, then remove pan from heat and let chicken and garlic sit in the water, covered, for 20 minutes. Remove chicken from water. Let cool, then shred into bite size pieces.

In a large saucepan or skillet, sauté chicken with red and green peppers, onion, garlic, and mushrooms in the olive oil. Season with salt and pepper.

Heat a large skillet over medium low heat, and add enough oil to cover the bottom of the pan. Dip a corn tortilla into oil and coat completely. (This softens the tortilla for filling and rolling.) Place on a paper towel to drain. Spread a few tablespoons of chicken mixture down the middle of the open tortilla, sprinkle with some Parmesan, and roll up tightly. (This step can be done a day ahead.)

When ready to serve, heat ¾-inch of oil in a large skillet. Over medium-high heat, fry the taquitos until crisp and heated through, about 3 minutes per side. Drain well on paper toweling. Keep taquitos warm in a 250°F. oven until ready to serve.

wine suggestion: Dry French Rosé

Vegetarian Lasagna

My sister-in-law Heather Shaw, an excellent cook, gave me this recipe. Her lasagna, made with a vegetarian sauce, tastes fresh and, we think, much better than lasagna made with meat. Gluten-free pasta does not lend itself to freezing, so plan to eat this the day you make it.

ingredients:

Sauce

1 medium onion, chopped

2 cloves garlic, finely chopped or passed through a garlic press

¼ cup olive oil

3 zucchini, sliced ⅛ inch thick

1 can (28 ounces) whole tomatoes, chopped (including the juice, seeds strained out)

1 can (6 ounces) tomato paste

¼ cup each of Italian flat leaf parsley and basil, finely chopped (or 1 tablespoon each dried parsley and basil)

1 package (5 ounces) gluten-free lasagna noodles (Ener-G Foods brand is recommended, see Sources)

8 ounces gluten-free ricotta cheese

8 ounces mozzarella cheese, grated

4 ounces Parmesan cheese, grated

> **Recipe requires an hour or more preparation/cooking time.**

4 servings

Butter a 12-cup baking dish.

Lightly sauté onions and garlic in olive oil. Add zucchini and cook for 10 minutes, or until zucchini softens a bit. Add tomatoes (with juice) and tomato paste. Add parsley and basil. Season with salt and pepper. Mix well and simmer for 30 minutes.

Preheat oven to 350°F.

Cook lasagna noodles very al dente. (They will cook further in the oven.) Arrange a layer of cooked noodles in the buttered baking dish. Spread half the sauce over the noodles. Sprinkle half the mozzarella and a third of the Parmesan cheese over the sauce. Drop half the ricotta cheese by tablespoons over the mozzarella and Parmesan. Add another layer of cooked noodles, remaining sauce, remaining mozzarella, another third of the Parmesan, and remaining ricotta. Arrange final layer of cooked noodles and top with remaining Parmesan cheese. Bake for 30 minutes.

Note: Freezing gluten-free pasta dishes will cause the pasta texture to change. However, you can make extra sauce and freeze it for a future quick meal.

variation for meat sauce: Substitute ½ pound of ground meat and ½ pound sweet Italian sausage for the zucchini.

wine suggestion: Italian Valpolicella

🕐 Chicken Salad 55

Grilled Mahi Mahi with Tomatillo Sauce 56
Chef Bob Kinkead

Barbecued Tri Tip 57

🕐 Halibut and Chips 58

Jerk Chicken with Cilantro Mango Salsa 59

Grilled Swordfish Steak over Grilled Eggplant Tapenade with Basil Oil 60
Chef Christian Svalesen

🕐 Beef Kebabs 61

🕐 Red Sauce with Sweet Butter Clams and Pasta 62
Marcella Rosene, Pasta & Co.

Yellow Tomato Soup with Avocado, Red Onion, and Mint 63
Chef Todd Gray

🕐 Apple Cider-Dijon Salmon 64

Thyme-Marinated Flank Steaks 65

Seared Sea Scallop-Green Papaya Salad with Cranberry Essence 66
Chef Linda Yamada

Pan-Fried Chicken and Black Bean Salad 67

(continued on next page)

SUMMER

🕐 – *indicates a quick meal*

Mexican Green Soup 68
  Chef Christian Svalesen

Pizza 69

Sautéed Salmon with Caramelized Onion-Strewn Grits and Portobello Mushroom-Red Wine Sauce 70
  Chef Charlie Trotter

Mustard Crusted Black Cod with White Asparagus, Black Trumpet Mushrooms, Leek-Potato Puree, and Seville Orange Vinaigrette 72
  Chef Dennis Leary

Slow Barbecue Baby Back Ribs 74

Chicken Salad

Chicken salad is an easy, satisfying summer meal; it is easier yet when using leftover chicken. Try the variation with apples, or create your own interesting combination. Wrap in Homemade Tortillas (page 167) and serve with fresh sliced peaches.

ingredients

2 cups cooked chicken, chopped

½ cup red cabbage, chopped

½ cup red pepper, chopped

3 scallions, chopped

3-4 tablespoons gluten-free mayonnaise

4 servings

Combine chicken, cabbage, red pepper, scallions, and mayonnaise in a medium bowl. Season with salt and pepper and serve.

wine suggestion: Chianti Classico

variation:
Granny Smith Chicken Salad

Substitute one large organic Granny Smith apple, cored and cubed, for cabbage and pepper. Substitute one finely chopped shallot for scallions. Instead of fresh peaches, serve with watermelon slices.

Grilled Mahi-Mahi with Tomatillo Sauce

Chef Bob Kinkead, Kinkead's — Washington D.C.

In 1983, *Food & Wine* magazine named Bob Kinkead one of the nations' most promising culinary talents. He has lived up to that title over the years with multiple nominations and awards from the James Beard Foundation. Countless magazines, from *Esquire* to *Gourmet*, have featured Chef Kinkead. He has served as executive chef and partner at 21 Federal in Nantucket and Twenty-One Federal in Washington D.C. He now owns Kinkead's, where he continues to work his magic.

Serve with Jicama Slaw (page 134) and black beans.

ingredients:

Tomatillo Sauce

6 scallions
6 tomatillos, husked
1 poblano chile
2 Anaheim chiles
1 small onion, quartered
Olive oil
5 cloves garlic, peeled and minced
1 tablespoon whole cumin seed, toasted
Juice of 4 limes
1 jalapeño, finely minced
1 bunch cilantro leaves, stems removed

Six 5-ounce mahi-mahi fillets,
   skinned and boned
Cilantro sprigs and lime wedges for garnish

6 servings

Preheat an outdoor grill.

Chop scallion greens, leaving the white part whole for grilling. Toss white scallion bottoms, tomatillos, poblanos, Anaheims, and onion in a bit of olive oil and season with salt and pepper. Grill vegetables on a hot grill and remove when cooked on all sides. Place the chiles in a plastic bag and seal. When chiles are cool enough to touch, peel and dice.

In a blender, place white scallion bottoms, tomatillos, Anaheim chiles, garlic, cumin, and lime juice. Puree until smooth. Season with salt and pepper. Empty mixture into a nonreactive (glass or plastic) container. Without cleaning out the blender, add the scallion greens, poblanos, grilled onion, jalapeño, and cilantro leaves. Puree until smooth. Season with salt and pepper. Empty mixture into a separate container. (The sauces are pureed separately to keep a nice bright green color.)

Lightly oil the mahi-mahi fillets and season with salt and pepper. Cook on a hot grill for 4 minutes on the first side, then turn and cook for 2-3 minutes on the other side, or until just done in the middle.

To finish the sauce, bring the tomatillo puree to a boil. Add the cilantro puree. Remove from heat when heated through. Adjust seasoning and pour sauce onto 6 warm plates. Top with a mahi-mahi fillet. Garnish with a cilantro sprig and lime wedge.

wine suggestion: California Chardonnay

Barbecued Tri Tip

This triangle cut of meat is from the sirloin tip. Slow grilling is the trick. Wood chips and charcoal make this a wonderfully flavorful meal.
Serve with Pasta Salad (page 126) and Green Beans (page 139).

ingredients:

1-2 pound tri tip steak

Seasoned salt (Lawry's is recommended)

2 cups large wood chips (cherry wood,
    apple wood, or hickory wood chips)

4 servings

Sprinkle meat lightly on both sides with seasoned salt. Refrigerate.

Prepare an outdoor grill by mounding the charcoal about nine inches below the grating at its highest point. Preheat the grill. While grill is preheating, soak wood chips in water. Once coals are hot (you should be able to hold your hand above the grating for only 2 seconds), spread them out in an even layer. Drain wood chips and place a handful on the hot coals. Put grating in place, heat for a few minutes, then clean with a wire brush. Place meat on grill and cook, turning once, for about 45 minutes (or until internal temperature is 120°F-130°F. for rare beef, 130°F-135°F. for medium-rare beef).

wine suggestion: Washington Merlot

Halibut and Chips

Though not deep-fried, here's a quick homemade version of fish and chips that will satisfy your craving and is actually much better than any fish and chips you could buy. A tartar sauce recipe is included if you want to use it though halibut and ling cod are delicate fish. Serve with "chips" (Homemade Fries page 148) and Cole Slaw (page 128).

ingredients:

2 pounds fresh halibut cheeks or ling cod

¼ cup gluten-free flour mix

1 tablespoon vegetable oil

3 tablespoons butter

Lemon wedges

4 servings

Lightly dust halibut with gluten-free flour. In a medium skillet, heat oil and butter over moderate high heat. Sauté halibut, turning once, until the center is no longer translucent (about 8-9 minutes per inch of halibut thickness). Serve with lemon wedges.

wine suggestion: Oregon Pinot Gris or Chardonnay

Tartar Sauce: makes 3/4 cup

Combine mayonnaise, vinegar, capers, and herbs. Keep refrigerated.

¾ cup mayonnaise

1 tablespoon distilled white vinegar

2 teaspoons gluten-free capers

2 teaspoons finely chopped fresh chives

1 teaspoon finely chopped fresh dill

1 teaspoon finely chopped fresh
   Italian parsley

Jerk Chicken with Cilantro Mango Salsa

The island of Cayman Brac is a paradise for scuba divers, though, at the time of our visit very few restaurants existed. One evening we found "the" place for locals. They were having a big party, and jerk chicken was the main attraction. It was fabulous! This tasty recipe is quite a faithful interpretation. Try the Cilantro Mango Salsa for a nice foil to the spicy chicken. A serving of brown rice and Sugar Peas (page 143) completes the meal. For a true island presentation, serve with red beans and plantains.

ingredients:

Cilantro Mango Salsa

2 cups peeled, chopped mango

¼ cup chopped red onion

2 tablespoons finely chopped cilantro

Juice from 1 lime

2 whole chicken breasts, boneless,
  skinless, and halved

½ teaspoon crushed red pepper flakes

1 teaspoon garlic powder

1 teaspoon paprika

½ teaspoon ground cloves

½ teaspoon ground cinnamon

½ teaspoon ground allspice

½ teaspoon ground ginger

2 teaspoons salt

1 teaspoon freshly ground pepper

2 teaspoons dried thyme

¼ cup brown sugar, tightly packed

4 servings

Combine mango, onion, cilantro, and lime juice. Keep refrigerated.

Preheat an outdoor grill.

Pound the chicken to ½-inch thickness. Combine spices and sugar in a small bowl and rub the mixture evenly into each chicken breast before grilling. Cook chicken over a medium-hot fire (about 3 minutes per side) until cooked but still plump and juicy.

wine suggestion: Washington Syrah

Grilled Swordfish Steak over Grilled Eggplant Tapenade with Basil Oil

Chef Christian Svalesen, 36° – Dallas, Texas

In the middle of Texas, Chef Christian Svalesen has fresh fish flown in daily to his Net Result seafood market and 36° Restaurant next door. Chris creates some of the finest fare in the region. Most large cities have first-rate fish markets; take the time to find one in your area and savor this wonderful dish! Serve with a side of Creamy Polenta (page 148).

ingredients:

Basil Oil Puree

1 cup basil leaves

2 cloves garlic, roughly chopped

1 cup olive oil

Tapenade

1 small eggplant, sliced ¼-inch thick

1 zucchini, sliced ¼-inch thick

1 yellow squash, sliced ¼-inch thick

1 each red, green, and yellow bell peppers,
    quartered, seeds and veins removed

3 tablespoons olive oil

1 tablespoon fresh oregano or
    1 teaspoon dried oregano

Four 6-ounce swordfish steaks

4 servings

Using a small food processor or blender, puree basil, garlic, and olive oil. Set aside.

Preheat outdoor grill. Brush vegetables lightly with 1 tablespoon olive oil, season with salt and pepper, and grill until tender but still firm. Transfer vegetables from grill to cutting board and cut into ¼-inch dice. Place diced vegetables into a medium bowl and add 1 tablespoon olive oil, oregano, and 1 tablespoon basil oil puree. Stir well and let sit at room temperature. (You can also roast the vegetables in a 400°F. oven on a large baking sheet for 20 minutes.)

Brush swordfish lightly with 1 tablespoon olive oil and season with salt and pepper. Grill for two minutes, then turn over and grill for another 2 minutes, or until swordfish is opaque in the center but still springy and moist.

Serve swordfish on a bed of the tapenade. Finish with a drizzle of the basil oil puree over the swordfish.

wine suggestion: Pinot Noir

Beef Kebabs

ingredients:

2½ pounds Spencer or top sirloin steak
    cut into 1-inch cubes
1-2 tablespoons olive oil
Garlic pepper or garlic salt (to taste)
12 ounces cherry tomatoes
8 ounces button mushrooms
1 green pepper, cut in 1½-inch pieces
1 sweet onion, quartered

4 servings

Using bamboo or metal shish kebab skewers, form kebabs, alternating meat cubes with vegetables and pushing tightly together. Brush kebabs with olive oil and season with garlic salt or garlic pepper. Preheat an outdoor grill. Grill over hot coals for about 5 minutes per side. Use tongs to turn the skewers.

wine suggestion: French Rhône Syrah Grenache Blend

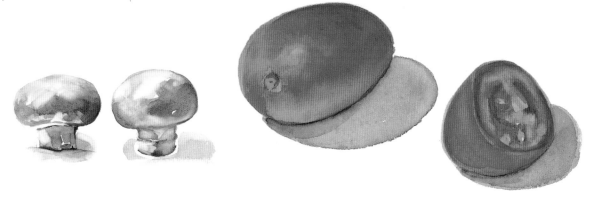

Note: Hot coal test: you will be able to hold your hand above the grate for only 2 seconds.

Red Sauce with Sweet Butter Clams and Pasta

This excellent meal can be made in the time it takes to boil the pasta. If fresh clams are unavailable, you can use a 10-ounce can of baby clams (typically from Thailand, they are fairly consistent in quality). However, if you have access to live clams in the shell, by all means use them; their flavor and visual appeal make this a great meal for entertaining. Serve with Seasonal Greens and Garden Cucumbers (page 128).

ingredients:

½ cup olive oil

½ medium onion, finely chopped

2 tablespoons minced garlic

1 teaspoon red pepper flakes

1 cup dry white wine, room temperature

16 ounces bottled clam juice

1 can (28 ounces) diced tomatoes

2 tablespoons tomato paste

½ cup butter

4 tablespoons finely chopped parsley

2 pounds live butter, Manila, or
   littleneck clams, thoroughly scrubbed

1 pound gluten-free pasta,
   spaghetti or linguine

comment:

If you dig the clams yourself, be sure to clean them well. Place clams in a large bucket of cold water mixed with cornmeal (6 tablespoons for every 4 cups of water) for a few hours. The clams siphon the cornmeal, which purges them of sand. (Salt may be substituted in equal quantities for the cornmeal.)

4 servings

In a large skillet with a lid, sauté onion in olive oil until translucent. Add garlic and red pepper flakes. Cook, stirring frequently, for one minute. (Do not let garlic brown.) Add wine, bring to a boil, and reduce by half. Add clam juice and reduce again by one third. Add tomatoes and tomato paste and stir well. Simmer, covered, for 15 minutes. While sauce is simmering, cook pasta according to package directions. Add butter and parsley to sauce, stirring until butter is incorporated. Add clams and cover for 5 minutes. Clams will open when cooked. (Discard any clams that do not open.) Transfer cooked clams to a bowl. Toss sauce with pasta and divide between 4 plates. Arrange clams on and around the pasta for a striking presentation.

wine suggestion: Vernaccia di San Gimignano

This recipe is adapted from *Pasta & Co. By Request* (1991). Pasta & Co. is Seattle's premier upscale take-out food shop with five locations. They also stock gluten-free pasta.

Notes: If using canned clams, drain and pick over, discarding shell fragments. Add clams to sauce at the same time as butter and parsley. Heat until clams are warmed through.

Yellow Tomato Soup with Avocado, Red Onion, and Mint

Chef Todd Gray, Equinox — Washington, D.C.

Equinox is one of this city's premier fine dining establishments, offering sophisticated, pure American cuisine. Chef Gray uses fresh, local organic ingredients whenever possible. He is a James Beard Award Nominee for Chef of the Year, Mid-Atlantic, in 2001, and has won various "top table" awards from *Condé Nast*, *Bon Appétit*, *Esquire*, and *Gourmet* magazines.

Serve with Red Snapper Fillet with Spaghetti Squash, Saffron, and Tomato Cream (page 82) and Grand Marnier Semifreddo with Bittersweet Chocolate Sauce and Local Blackberries (page 206).

ingredients:

⅓ cup grapeseed oil or olive oil

2 Vidalia onions, peeled and sliced

6 garlic cloves, crushed

10 yellow tomatoes, quartered

3 cups heavy cream

1 quart vegetable stock

3 avocados, peeled and chopped

1 red onion, minced

½ garlic clove, minced

¼ bunch mint, chopped

A few mint leaves for garnish

6 servings

Heat grapeseed oil in a large saucepan until hot. Add onions and garlic. Sauté for 3 minutes. Add yellow tomatoes and cook for five minutes. Season with salt and pepper. Add cream and stock. Simmer for 30 minutes.

To make guacamole, mash avocado in a small bowl. Add red onion, garlic, and mint. Combine well, cover tightly, and chill.

Remove soup from heat, puree in a blender, and pass through a fine mesh sieve. Chill soup for two hours.

Chill six large bowls in the refrigerator.

To serve, ladle soup into chilled bowls and place a large dollop of guacamole in the center. Garnish with a fresh mint sprig. Serve immediately.

Apple Cider-Dijon Salmon

A wonderful meal that requires little effort. Once you have done the minimal prep work for the side dishes, you can devote your attention to grilling the salmon. Serve with Spinach Sautéed with Garlic and Lemon (page 146) and Oven Roasted Baby Red Potatoes (page 139).

ingredients:

2 tablespoons apple cider

1 tablespoon gluten-free Dijon mustard

3 tablespoons brown sugar

4 tablespoons olive oil

2 pounds fresh king salmon fillet

4 servings

Preheat an outdoor grill placing coals eight inches below the cooking grate. Combine apple cider, Dijon mustard, and brown sugar. Slowly drizzle in 2 tablespoons olive oil, stirring constantly with a wire whisk. Brush skin side of salmon with remaining olive oil. Turn fish over and spread cider glaze evenly over the flesh side of the salmon. Season with salt and pepper.

Place salmon flesh side down and cook for 5-7 minutes. Using a large metal spatula, turn salmon over (skin side down) and cook until barely translucent in the center. (Total cooking time is about 8-9 minutes per inch of thickness in the fillet).

wine suggestion: French Chablis

Glaze Variation: Honey Mustard Glaze

makes 1/2 cup of glaze

½ cup honey

½ tablespoon gluten-free Dijon mustard

½ tablespoon lemon juice

2 tablespoons butter

½ teaspoon coriander

½ small garlic clove, finely chopped

In a small saucepan, heat honey, mustard, lemon juice, butter, coriander, and garlic just until the butter melts. Spread mixture on salmon. Cook as directed above.

Note: You may broil the salmon instead if you prefer.

Thyme-Marinated Flank Steaks

Serve with French New Potato Salad with Summer Herb Coulis (page 127).

ingredients:

6 sprigs fresh thyme

2 cloves of garlic, finely chopped or
passed through a garlic press

1 tablespoon freshly ground pepper

¼ cup olive oil

3 tablespoons red wine vinegar

2 pounds flank steak

4 servings

Whisk all marinade ingredients together. Place flank steaks in a nonreactive glass dish and pour marinade over the meat. Cover dish and refrigerate for at least 5 hours, turning meat over several times. Preheat an outdoor grill or prepare a broiler pan. Grill two inches above hot coals or cook under the broiler, 4-5 minutes on each side (until internal temperature is 120°F–130°F for rare meat, 130°F-135°F for medium rare). When serving, cut thin slices across the grain of the meat for a more tender result.

wine suggestion: California Cabernet

Seared Sea Scallop-Green Papaya Salad with Cranberry Essence

Chef Linda Yamada, The Beach House Restaurant — Kauai, Hawaii

The Beach House is a favorite restaurant for our family vacations on Kauai. Consistently voted near the top of the Zagat Restaurant Survey each year, The Beach House offers fresh island flavor by using locally grown ingredients as the focal point of their menu.

ingredients:

Cranberry Essence

2 cups red wine

2 cups sugar

2 cups cranberry juice

1 cup fine julienne green papaya

¼ cup fine julienne carrot

1 teaspoon finely chopped garlic

2 teaspoons finely chopped fresh cilantro

2 tablespoons fresh lime juice

1 teaspoon Thai fish sauce (see Sources)

Pinch of sugar

12 large sea scallops

(about 10 scallops per pound)

3 tablespoons olive oil

5-6 ounces salad greens

Fried corn tortilla strips (optional)

4 servings

In a nonreactive pot, bring wine and 1 cup sugar to a boil. Simmer until mixture achieves a thin syrup consistency (about 230°F. on a candy thermometer). Meanwhile, in a separate nonreactive pot, bring cranberry juice and remaining sugar to a boil and simmer to a thin syrup consistency. Combine the wine syrup and cranberry syrup together. Set aside at room temperature until ready to use. If syrup begins to harden, you can soften it again by placing the pot of syrup in a warm water bath. (Syrups take about 10-15 minutes to make.)

Mix green papaya, carrot, garlic, cilantro, lime, fish sauce, and sugar. Set aside.

Season scallops with sea salt and cracked black pepper. Heat a sauté pan until hot. Add olive oil and sear scallops on both sides until browned and the center is no longer translucent.

Place salad greens in the center of each plate and top with papaya salad. Arrange 3 scallops around plate and drizzle with Cranberry Essence. Fried corn tortilla strips can be used for garnish.

wine suggestion: Loire Valley Sancerre

Note: Be careful not to cook the Cranberry Essence too long, or you will end up with a hard candy.

Pan-Fried Chicken and Black Bean Salad

The chicken recipe is good even without the Marsala, and is quite versatile. Serve it over rice, or as part of a salad as shown here.
The sweetness of balsamic dressed greens complements the heat of the jalapeños in the Black Bean Salad.

ingredients:

One recipe Black Bean Salad (page 130)

2 whole chicken breasts, boneless, skinless,
   and halved

1 tablespoon olive oil

2 small garlic cloves, thinly sliced

1 shallot, finely minced

3 tablespoons Marsala

Juice from one lemon

One head of red leaf lettuce, rinsed and dried

2 tablespoons balsamic vinegar

2 tablespoons olive oil

4 servings

Cut chicken into 2-inch long strips. Heat oil in a large frying pan until medium hot. Sauté garlic and shallots until soft, stirring frequently. Increase heat to high, add chicken, and stir-fry quickly until browned. Add Marsala and lemon juice, and season with salt and pepper. Stir to coat chicken and reduce liquid a bit. Remove from heat. Toss red leaf lettuce with balsamic vinegar and olive oil. Divide salad between four plates. Top each with a serving of chicken and Black Bean Salad.

wine suggestion: French Rhône Valley Red

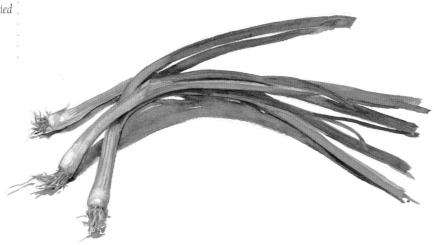

Mexican Green Soup

Chef Christian Svalesen, 36° – Dallas, Texas

36° offers the flavors of modern Texas cooking, combining such ingredients as chile peppers and cilantro with French technique. The result is a wonderfully unique way with Chris' signature fish and seafood dishes. This bouillabaisse-type fish stew is one of Chef Svalesen's best-loved recipes.

ingredients:

12 littleneck clams

12 mussels

12 large scallops

8 large shrimp (peeled and deveined)

1½ pounds assorted fish
   (halibut, salmon, snapper, sole, etc.)

2 Maine lobsters
   (halved, stomach and intestine removed)

1 cup poblano chiles, pureed

½ cup fresh cilantro leaves, stems removed

¼ cup olive oil

2 teaspoons chopped shallots

2 teaspoons chopped garlic

4 cups dry vermouth
   (Note: Use the best quality you can afford)

2 tablespoons butter

4 servings

Thoroughly wash all seafood. Cut assorted fish into 2 ounce pieces.

Roast poblano chiles over a gas flame or under a broiler until blackened on all sides. Peel and remove seeds and veins. Place in the bowl of a food processor and puree.

In the bowl of a small food processor, puree cilantro, olive oil, shallots, and garlic. (Recipe can be prepared in advance up to this point. Refrigerate ingredients until ready to finish the bouillabaisse.)

In a Dutch oven or large heavyweight pan, combine poblano chile puree, cilantro oil mixture, vermouth, and butter. Season with salt and pepper. Bring to a boil over medium heat and reduce liquid by half.

Add seafood, layered in the following order: halved and cleaned lobster, large chunks of fish, shrimp, scallops, mussels, and clams. Bring liquid to a boil again, then simmer just until clams and mussels open (about 8-10 minutes). Discard any unopened clams and mussels. Serve immediately.

wine suggestion: Riesling or Pinot Grigio

Tip: Ask the fish market personnel to split and remove the stomach and intestines from the lobster.

Pizza

This pizza has a good yeast-risen crust that is the closest thing I have tasted to a thick wheat flour crust.
Be sure to make big batches of pesto, tomato sauce, and crusts for freezing; you can then enjoy fresh gluten-free pizza in less time than it takes to have a pizza delivered.
If you are making the pesto, sauce, and crust in one day, prepare each recipe in the order shown for the most efficient use of time.

ingredients:

Homemade Pesto

¼ cup pine nuts

1 cup fresh basil, stemmed

⅛ cup olive oil

½ cup grated Parmesan

6 cloves garlic, finely chopped or
    passed through a garlic press

Scratch Pizza Sauce

¼ cup olive oil

2 medium onions, finely chopped

2 large cloves garlic, finely chopped or
    passed through a garlic press

2 cans (28 ounces each) crushed tomatoes

2 tablespoons sugar

4-5 tablespoons fresh basil leaves,
    finely chopped

Recipe requires an hour or more preparation/cooking time.

Thick Pizza Crust recipe (page 171)

Suggested toppings

(for one 13-inch pizza)

½ cup sun-dried tomatoes, chopped

1 can (14 ounces) whole artichoke hearts,
    well-drained and chopped

3-4 tablespoons homemade pesto

12 ounces mozzarella cheese, grated

¼ cup Parmesan cheese, grated

Note: Muir Glen Organics makes a good pizza sauce. However, if you have the time, try making it yourself and taste the difference. Be sure to cook the sauce down to a thick, rich consistency. (A watery sauce and a gluten-free crust do not go together well at all.)

comment:

Prior to going gluten-free, this pizza was a favorite at our local pizzeria, Romio's. It is called the G.A.S.P., which stands for garlic, artichokes, sun-dried tomato, and pesto. They use much more garlic and it tends to take your breath away (gasp!). This version is much smoother and probably appeals to more people. My daughter said this is the only "adult pizza" she likes. For a spicier pizza, sprinkle with red pepper flakes

Pesto: Finely chop pine nuts in a small food processor. Remove nuts from bowl and set aside. Place basil and olive oil in the food processor. Gently pulse until most of the leaves are chopped. Add Parmesan and garlic and pulse a few more times. Add pine nuts and process until well blended. Let stand for one hour at room temperature. Recipe makes about 1 cup and freezes well.

Sauce: In a large saucepan, heat olive oil over medium-high heat. Add onions and garlic and sauté until onions are translucent. Stir in tomatoes, sugar, and basil. Season with salt and pepper. Cover and simmer for 30 minutes, or until nicely thickened. Makes enough sauce for four 13-inch pizzas and freezes well.

Make pizza crusts and cover each with tomato sauce. Prepare pizza toppings as stated above and arrange on pizza in order listed. Bake for 20 minutes.

wine suggestion: a dry Northern Italian white wine

Sautéed Salmon with Caramelized Onion-Strewn Grits and Portobello Mushroom-Red Wine Sauce

Chef Charlie Trotter, Charlie Trotter's – Chicago, Illinois

Charlie Trotter's offers highly personal cuisine combining impeccable products, French techniques, and Asian influences.
Charlie's restaurant and cookbooks are well known across the country. The restaurant's list of awards ranges from Relais Gourmand to the *Wine Spectator*,
the James Beard Foundation, AAA—the list goes on and on. Recipe with permission from *Charlie Trotter's Seafood*, (Ten Speed Press, 1997).

ingredients:

1 red onion, julienned

3 tablespoons butter

2 tablespoons chopped chives

1 tablespoon lemon juice

2 cups cooked white grits

2 roasted portobello mushrooms (page 150)

½ cup Red Wine Jus (page 71)

Four, 4-ounce pieces salmon, skin on

2 tablespoons canola oil

Recipe requires an hour or more preparation/cooking time.

chef's comments:

Leaving the skin on the salmon in this dish creates a crispy, crackly layer that melts into the flesh with each bite. The buttery, sweet mound of grits with the caramelized red onion makes an interesting textural contrast. To further push this preparation into soul-satisfying territory, it is paired with an earthy yet refined Portobello Mushroom-Red Wine Sauce. This combination of flavors and textures would satisfy even the most avid meat lover.

4 servings

Cook red onion in a sauté pan over moderate heat with 1 tablespoon of the butter for 5-8 minutes, or until golden brown and caramelized. Fold the caramelized onion, chives, and lemon juice into the cooked grits and season to taste with salt and pepper.

Coarsely chop one of the roasted mushrooms. Place in a blender with the Red Wine Jus and puree for 2 minutes, or until smooth. Place the mushroom puree in a small saucepan and warm over medium heat. Whisk in the remaining 2 tablespoons of butter and season to taste with salt and pepper.

Season the salmon with salt and pepper and score the skin side with a sharp knife. Place skin side down in a hot sauté pan with the canola oil and cook for 2-3 minutes per side, or until golden brown and cooked to the medium stage.

continued:
Sautéed Salmon with Caramelized Onion-Strewn Grits and Portobello Mushroom-Red Wine Sauce

Thinly slice the remaining roasted mushroom. Place a small mound of grits in the center of each plate and top with some of the sliced portobello. Place a portion of salmon on top and spoon the Portobello Mushroom-Red Wine Sauce around the plate. Sprinkle with freshly ground black pepper.

wine suggestion: An earthy, aromatic red Burgundy will bring this dish to another level. Vosne-Romanée by producers such as Mongeard-Mugneret or Jean Gros will heighten the flavors of the caramelized onion and mushroom, but still allow the rich salmon to shine through.

Red Wine Jus

This intense reduction is compatible with fish as well as meat and poultry.

ingredients:

1½ cups chopped onions

1 cup chopped carrots

1 cup chopped celery

2 tablespoons canola oil

1 Granny Smith apple, chopped

1 orange, peeled and chopped

6 cups Burgundy wine

3 cups port

makes 1 ¹/₂ cups

In a medium saucepan, cook the onions, carrots, and celery in the canola oil over medium heat, stirring frequently, for 10 minutes, or until golden brown and caramelized. Add the remaining ingredients and simmer over low heat for 1 hour. Strain through a fine mesh sieve and return to the saucepan. Simmer for 30-45 minutes, or until reduced to 1½ cups. Season with salt and pepper.

Mustard Crusted Black Cod with White Asparagus, Black Trumpet Mushrooms, Leek-Potato Puree and Seville Orange Vinaigrette

Chef Dennis Leary, Rubicon – San Francisco, California

Drew Nieporent's Rubicon showcases the culinary talents of Dennis Leary and the formidable wine knowledge of Master Sommelier Larry Stone. Larry is a legend in wine circles. Dennis was named the Best Rising Star Chef in San Francisco, 2001 and was featured as one of the Ten Best New Chefs in *Food & Wine* magazine in 1994. The restaurant has received accolades for food and wine selection from the *Wine Spectator* and the James Beard Foundation.

ingredients:

Mustard Crust

1 egg
¾ cup grapeseed oil
¾ ounce brown mustard seed, ground
   (a little less than 2 tablespoons)
1 ounce hazelnuts, lightly toasted
Juice of ½ lemon
1 teaspoon white wine vinegar
1 ounce water

Seville Orange Vinaigrette

1 Seville orange
1 Valencia orange
1 shallot, peeled and diced
½ cup extra virgin olive oil
3 drops white wine vinegar
2 tablespoons water
Pinch of sugar

Vegetables

16 stalks white asparagus
2 tablespoons salted butter
12 ounces fresh black trumpet mushrooms,
   rinsed thoroughly
2 tablespoons vegetable oil
12 stalks celery

Leek-Potato Puree

10 large leeks (about 1½ pounds)
4 ounces (1 stick) butter
2¼ pounds Yellow Finn potatoes

Four, 6-ounce Black Cod fillets
½ cup finely ground gluten-free
   bread crumbs

Black trumpet mushrooms have a distinct aroma and an elegant buttery flavor. You will find them from midsummer through the middle of fall in specialty produce markets. Seville oranges are typically used to make liqueurs such as Cointreau, Grand Marnier, and Triple Sec. The flesh is tart, bitter, and has a high acid content.

chef's comments:

It is best to make the mustard crust ahead of time (24 hours or more) to allow the flavor to develop. Prepare Seville Orange Vinaigrette six hours prior to serving for better flavor.

4 servings

Mustard Crust: Place egg in a food processor and add oil in a slow stream. Add ground mustard, hazelnuts, lemon juice, vinegar, and water. Season with salt and pepper. The consistency should be that of thin mayonnaise, but still spreadable.

continued:

Mustard Crusted Black Cod with White Asparagus, Black Trumpet Mushrooms, Leek-Potato Puree and Seville Orange Vinaigrette

Recipe requires an hour or more preparation/cooking time.

Seville Orange Vinaigrette: Juice Seville orange into a small bowl. Juice ½ of the Valencia orange into the same bowl and add shallot, olive oil, vinegar, and water. Season with salt and pepper. (The vinaigrette should be pleasantly tangy; add sugar if necessary to adjust acidity.) Set aside.

Vegetables: Peel asparagus, leaving tips intact. Cook in a large pot of salted boiling water until barely tender, about 2 minutes. Brush with butter while still hot and set aside.

Preheat oven to 350°F.

Toss trumpet mushrooms in two tablespoons vegetable oil and a generous pinch of salt. Roast uncovered for 5 minutes, or until some of their moisture has evaporated. Do not overcook, or they will shrink excessively. Drain on paper toweling and set aside.

Peel celery stalks and cut into 2-inch pieces. Cook in generously salted boiling water for 30 seconds until bright green. Immediately plunge celery into a bowl of ice water for 10 seconds. Remove and drain thoroughly. Set aside.

Leek-Potato Puree: Slice leeks in half lengthwise, then chop finely. Rinse well and drain. Place leeks in a shallow sauté pan with half the butter and cook, covered, over low heat until tender. Watch carefully to avoid browning or burning.

Peel potatoes and cook in boiling salted water until soft.

Combine leeks, potatoes, and remaining butter in a food processor. Puree until uniformly smooth. The puree should be slightly stiff but have no traces of fiber, and it should not be gummy. Add a little hot water to correct the consistency if necessary. Set aside in a warm place.

To serve, preheat oven to 375°F. Bake cod fillets for 7 minutes, or until almost cooked through. Remove from oven and brush each fillet with a liberal amount of mustard crust. Briefly warm the asparagus, mushrooms, and celery in the oven. Spoon warm leek-potato puree onto four warmed plates. Arrange vegetables around the puree and drizzle them with a small amount of vinaigrette.

Just before serving, sprinkle cod fillets with gluten-free bread crumbs and brown briefly under the broiler. Place on top of the leek puree and serve at once.

wine suggestion: Duckhorn Vineyards Sauvignon Blanc

73

Slow Barbecue Baby Back Ribs

Some of the best baby back ribs you will taste!
This recipe allows for a ½ rack per person (about a pound). Serve with Tomato Bread Salad (page 131) and Green Beans (page 139).

ingredients:

4 pounds baby back pork ribs

Lawry's Seasoned Salt

2 cups large mesquite wood chips

4 servings

Cover ribs with a light sprinkling of seasoned salt on all sides.

Prepare an outdoor grill by mounding the charcoal about nine inches below the grating at its highest point. Preheat the grill. While grill is preheating, soak wood chips in water. Once coals are hot (you should be able to hold your hand above the grating for only 2 seconds), spread them out in an even layer. Drain wood chips and place a handful on the hot coals. Put grating in place, heat until temperature is 225°F., then clean with a wire brush. Place ribs on grill and smoke for 45-60 minutes (turning ribs once) until well browned on both sides. Remove ribs and wrap tightly in two layers of regular aluminum foil. Return to grill for 30-45 minutes. Remove foil packet from grill and let ribs rest in the foil for 15 minutes before serving.

wine suggestion: California Zinfandel

Recipe requires an hour or more preparation/cooking time.

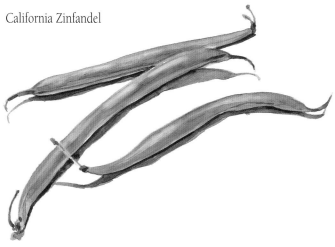

Assorted Sausages and Mustards 76

Leek and Saffron Soup with Sautéed Shrimp 77
  Chef Michael Kornick

Spicy Tomato and Sausage Pasta 78

Cream of Yellow Squash Soup 79
  Chef Erol Tugrul

⊘ Homemade Tacos 80

Roasted Pork Tenderloin...... 81

Red Snapper Fillet with Spaghetti Squash, Saffron, and Tomato Cream 82
  Chef Todd Gray

⊘ Vegetable Tofu Stir-Fry 83

⊘ Tomato Basil Soup 84
  Marcella Rosene, Pasta & Co.

⊘ Pan-Fried Chicken in Marsala 85

Moroccan Chickpea Stew 86
  Chef Tom Douglas

Buttermilk Chicken 87

Simple Sushi 88

Miso Soup 89

⊘ Omelets 90

⊘ Pan-Fried Pork Chops with Lime Juice 91

Coconut Chicken 92
  Chef Thoa Nguyen

"Groovy" Gnocchi with Portobello Mushroom Carpaccio 93
  Chef Ludger Szmania

⊘ – indicates a quick meal

FALL

Assorted Sausages and Mustards

Many butcher shops sell wonderful sausages made without gluten. Find your favorites and try this easy meal. Present it family style so everyone has a chance to sample the variety of sausages. Serve with Garlic Mashed Potatoes (page 140) and Butter Lettuce with Caramelized Nuts (page 122).

ingredients:

2 kielbasa

2 hot (spicy) Italian sausages

2 bockwurst

2 knackwurst

2 cups or more water

2-3 tablespoons butter

Assorted gluten-free mustards

4 servings

Place sausages in a large skillet. Pour 1 cup of water over sausages and cook over medium-high heat until water evaporates. Allow sausages to brown lightly on both sides, then add another cup of water to the skillet. The browned bits stuck to the pan will be released (a process called deglazing). Simmer until water cooks down again and repeat until sausages are cooked through (about 20 minutes). Lower heat to medium. Add butter to the skillet and melt. Brown sausages on all sides. Serve with your favorite gluten-free mustards.

wine suggestion: French Syrah

Note: Not all sausage is gluten-free, check with the manufacturer.

Leek and Saffron Soup with Sautéed Shrimp

Chef Michael Kornick, mk — Chicago, Illinois

Michael is a nationally recognized leader in the culinary arts. His distinguished career began at New York's legendary restaurant, The Quilted Giraffe. Since then, he has received numerous accolades during his tenure as executive chef at Aujord'hui in Boston and various Chicago restaurants including Gordon, Marche, and Red Light. Michael is now consultant/partner of Nine in Chicago and Exec Chef/partner at mk.

ingredients:

½ cup chopped, fresh Italian parsley

½ cup olive oil

4 chopped garlic cloves

18 uncooked medium shrimp, peeled, deveined, and halved lengthwise

6 tablespoons (¾ stick) butter

5 chopped medium leeks, about 3 cups (use pale green and white parts only)

One 8-ounce russet potato, peeled and chopped (about 1½ cups)

¼ teaspoon (scant) crumbled saffron threads

5 cups gluten-free chicken stock or canned low-salt chicken broth

1 tablespoon whipping cream

1 small bunch chives, cut into 1-inch pieces

comment:

This soup is a real treat, with outstanding flavors and a lovely presentation. Serve either as a first course or as a light meal with a salad.

6 servings

Combine parsley, oil, and one garlic clove in food processor. Blend until parsley is coarsely chopped. Transfer ¼ cup parsley-garlic oil to medium bowl. Add shrimp and toss to coat. Pour remaining parsley-garlic oil into a cup. Cover shrimp and remaining oil separately and refrigerate.

Melt butter in a large heavy pot over medium-high heat. Add leeks and sauté until tender and wilted, about 5 minutes. Add potato, remaining 3 garlic cloves, and saffron. Sauté for 2 minutes. Add chicken stock and bring to a boil. Reduce heat to medium-low. Cover and simmer 30 minutes.

Working in batches, puree soup in blender or processor until smooth. Return to pot. Add cream and season with salt and pepper.

Heat a heavy medium skillet over low heat. Add shrimp and sauté until just opaque in center. Ladle soup into heated bowls with 6 shrimp halves per serving. Garnish with chives and several drops of remaining parsley-garlic oil and serve.

wine suggestion: French Sancerre

Notes: If using frozen shrimp, inquire if it was frozen in a wheat slurry
(to prevent individual pieces from sticking to one another).

Spicy Tomato and Sausage Pasta

The spiciness of the pasta dish is nicely complemented by the sweetness of the Gorgonzola–Pear Salad (page 121).
This will not be a high calorie meal if individual servings are moderate in size.

ingredients:

4 large gluten-free Italian sausages
    (2 hot and 2 mild)

1½ cups dry white wine or water

1 medium onion, chopped

2 cloves garlic, finely chopped or
    passed through a garlic press

2 tablespoons olive oil

5 ounces mushrooms, sliced

1 can (28 ounces) crushed tomatoes

1 can (28 ounces) whole tomatoes, chopped
    (use tomatoes only, discarding the juice)

3 tablespoons fresh basil, very finely chopped
    (or 3 teaspoons dried basil)

¾ pound gluten-free penne pasta

Freshly grated Parmesan cheese

4 servings

In a large saucepan, cook sausages in ¾ cup of white wine over high heat until wine evaporates. Add another ¼ cup of wine to deglaze the saucepan. Cook sausages for a few minutes longer, turning occasionally, until lightly browned. Remove sausages and cut in ¼-inch slices (they should be pink inside). Set aside, along with any remaining liquid.

In the same saucepan, sauté onion and garlic in olive oil until onions are translucent. Add mushrooms and cook until limp. Add cooking liquid from sausages and remaining wine to the saucepan. Reduce liquid by half over medium-high heat. Add sliced sausage, crushed tomatoes, chopped whole tomatoes, and basil. Season with salt and pepper. Simmer for about 30-40 minutes, stirring occasionally.

Cook pasta to al dente stage in boiling salted water, drain, and toss with sauce. Serve with Parmesan cheese.

wine suggestion: Valpolicella or Chianti Classico

Notes: Your community very likely has a high quality meat market where you can purchase top-grade gluten-free sausages. An inferior product will translate into a poor sauce.
If finding crushed tomatoes proves difficult,
you may substitute 1 can (28 ounces) diced
tomatoes and 1 can (14 ounces) tomato
sauce for the crushed tomatoes.

Cream of Yellow Squash Soup

Chef Erol Tugrul, Café Margaux — Cocoa, Florida

A recent Zagat Restaurant Survey describes Café Margaux as a "great little French café," and bestows upon it the title of Most Popular Restaurant on the Atlantic Coast.

ingredients:

10 yellow crookneck squash, halved, seeds
    scooped out, chopped

1 large carrot, chopped

3 celery ribs, chopped

1 medium onion, chopped

½ cup chopped leeks

1 tablespoon olive oil

3 quarts gluten-free chicken stock

1 tablespoon butter

1 tablespoon potato starch flour

2 cups heavy cream

comment:

A delicately flavored soup that can be made vegetarian if a quality vegetable stock is substituted for chicken stock. Enjoy this soup either as a first course or as a light meal with a salad.

4 servings

Over medium-high heat, sauté squash, carrot, celery, onion, and leeks in olive oil until softened. Working in batches, puree vegetables in a blender, adding stock as needed. Combine vegetable puree and remaining stock in a heavy pot. Reduce by half over medium heat, stirring occasionally (about 30 minutes).

Meanwhile, melt butter in a small saucepan. Add flour. Cook over low heat, stirring frequently, for about 10 minutes. (This mixture is known as a roux.) Mix some of the soup into the roux, stirring constantly with a wire whisk until smooth, then whisk mixture back into the rest of the soup. Simmer, stirring frequently, until soup is lightly thickened. Add cream, combine thoroughly, and serve.

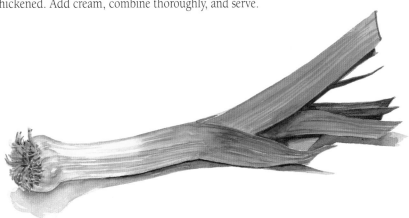

Homemade Tacos

Some version of tacos is served at our house at least once a month. It is a hassle to fry up your own tortillas, but they are much better than anything store bought.
Buy two dozen corn tortillas so that you have extra on hand if a few don't turn out.
Serve with Banana-Pineapple Sauté (page 135) and Homemade Refried Beans (page 153—canned beans can also be substituted).

ingredients:

homemade taco seasoning

2 teaspoons arrowroot

1 teaspoon ground red pepper

2 teaspoons ground cumin

2 teaspoons garlic salt

1 teaspoon paprika

2 pounds ground beef or boneless, skinless
    chicken breast cut into 1-inch pieces

2 ripe tomatoes, sliced

1 cup shredded iceberg lettuce

1 cup grated cheddar cheese

Olives, guacamole, gluten-free sour cream,
    other toppings

1 dozen corn tortillas (experiment until you
    find your favorite brand, as quality varies)

Vegetable oil for frying

4 servings (3 tacos per person)

Combine arrowroot, red pepper, cumin, garlic salt, and paprika in a small bowl.

Brown ground beef and drain excess oil (or pan-fry chicken in a bit of oil). Add taco seasoning and 1½ cups water. Stir well. Bring to a boil, reduce heat, and simmer for 10 minutes. Place prepared tomatoes, lettuce, cheese, and taco toppings in small bowls for serving.

Fry taco shells ten minutes before serving. To prepare, heat ½-inch vegetable oil until shimmering, in a large skillet, over high heat. Using long-handled tongs, submerge a flat tortilla in the oil. Let it cook for about a minute until puffy, turn it over, and cook other side. Pick up one side of the tortilla with the tongs, fold in half to form a taco shell, and cook for about a minute more. Remove to a plate lined with paper toweling to drain. Repeat with remaining tortillas. (Note: The longer you fry the tortillas, the crisper they become. The first tortilla or two may not turn out if the oil is either too hot or not hot enough. It's a bit tricky, but will come more easily with practice.)

Assemble tacos and enjoy!

Roasted Pork Tenderloin

Another very easy, tasty meal! The pork tenderloin may also be grilled for this dish. Serve with Sweet Sautéed Yams (page 142) and Classic Spinach Salad (page 123).

ingredients:

2 pounds pork tenderloin

2 cloves garlic, finely minced or
passed through a garlic press

4 servings

Preheat oven to 400°F. Place tenderloin on a rack in a shallow baking pan. Rub with garlic and season on all sides with salt and pepper. If one side has more fat on it, place the fatty side up.

Roast for about 30 minutes. Be careful not to overcook; the trick is to take it out of the oven while the center is just a bit pink (internal temperature will read 150°F. on a meat thermometer). Cover with foil and let rest for 5 minutes, then slice and serve.

Variation:
Roasted Pork Tenderloin with Pinot Noir Sauce

After tenderloin has finished cooking, remove from roasting pan. Add 2 cups chicken stock to the pan. Reduce by half. Add 1 cup Pinot Noir and reduce again by half. Off the fire, finish by stirring in 2 tablespoons whole grain gluten-free mustard. Serve this sauce with the tenderloin.

wine suggestion: Oregon Pinot Noir

Red Snapper Fillet with Spaghetti Squash, Saffron, and Tomato Cream

Chef Todd Gray, Equinox – Washington, D.C.

Equinox is one of this city's premier fine dining establishments, offering sophisticated, pure American cuisine. Chef Gray uses fresh, local organic ingredients whenever possible. He is a James Beard Award Nominee for Chef of the Year, Mid-Atlantic, in 2001, and has won various "top table" awards from *Condé Nast*, *Bon Appétit*, *Esquire*, and *Gourmet* magazines. Serve with starter Yellow Tomato Soup with Avocado, Red Onion, and Mint (page 63) and for dessert Grand Marnier Semifreddo with Bittersweet Chocolate Sauce and Local Blackberries (page 206).

ingredients:

1 medium spaghetti squash

6 red snapper fillets, cleaned

1 tablespoon grapeseed oil or olive oil

1 cup white wine

1 cup heavy cream

2 tablespoons butter

Juice from ½ lemon

1 teaspoon saffron threads

4 Italian plum tomatoes, diced and seeded
   (or 2 medium beefsteak tomatoes)

6 servings

Spaghetti squash can be steamed quickly in a microwave. Pierce the skin with a fork, cut squash in half down the middle, and cover with plastic wrap. Microwave for 8-12 minutes, or until tender. (To cook in the conventional manner, bake at 400°F. for about 30-40 minutes, or until skin is easily pierced with a knife.) When cool enough to handle, remove seeds. Using a fork, scrape out the flesh, which will have the texture of spaghetti. Divide "spaghetti" among 6 dinner plates.

Season snapper fillets with salt and pepper. Heat grapeseed oil to medium temperature in large sauté pan. Sauté fish skin side down for 2 minutes. Turn fish and finish cooking.

In a saucepan over medium heat, reduce white wine to one quarter its original volume. Add cream and reduce by half. Whisk in butter, then lemon juice and saffron, stirring well to combine. Pass sauce through a fine mesh strainer and return to the saucepan. Add diced tomatoes and stir. Season with salt and pepper.

Divide sauce between six serving plates and place a red snapper fillet in the middle of each plate. Serve immediately.

wine suggestion: Pine Ridge Chenin Blanc Viognier, California 1999

Vegetable Tofu Stir-Fry

Although the list of ingredients seems long, this recipe does not take much time to prepare. Freezing the tofu gives it a chewier texture, which is desirable for this dish. Serve with Master Recipe for Long Grain White Rice (page 151).

ingredients:

1 package traditional firm tofu,
    previously frozen

marinade

2 tablespoons peanut oil
1 tablespoon sesame oil
1 tablespoon grated ginger or ginger juice
    (see Sources)
1 clove garlic, minced or
    passed through a garlic press

1 tablespoon peanut oil
¼ small red onion, chopped
2 scallions, chopped
1 tablespoon grated ginger or ginger juice
1 clove garlic, thinly sliced
2 medium carrots, peeled and
    sliced diagonally ¼-inch thick
½ medium cauliflower, cut in 1-inch pieces
1 cup asparagus, cut in 2-inch long pieces
4-6 large leaves bok choy, chopped
1 tablespoon sesame oil
½ cup peanuts, toasted
Gluten-free tamari to taste

4 servings

Drain tofu by placing it on a plate, resting another plate on top, and setting a 1-pound weight atop the second plate. After 10 minutes or so discard excess water. Chop tofu into ½-inch cubes and place in a glass dish. Combine marinade ingredients and pour over tofu cubes. Cover and refrigerate for an hour or so.

Preheat oven to 400°F.

Remove tofu cubes from marinade. Spread in a single layer on a baking sheet. Bake for 10-15 minutes.

Heat peanut oil in a wok over medium-high heat. Add red onion and scallions. Cook, stirring, for 1 minute, then add ginger and garlic. Cook, stirring, for 1 minute more. Add carrots and cauliflower. Stir-fry for 3 minutes. Add asparagus, bok choy, and sesame oil. Stir-fry until vegetables are crisp tender. Add peanuts and season with salt and pepper. Mound stir-fried vegetables on a bed of rice. Top with baked tofu.

Tomato Basil Soup

This soup is a great way to preserve the wonderful taste of summer with fresh tomatoes and basil. You may need to add a tablespoon of tomato paste when using fresh tomatoes. Serve with Baked Cheese Wafers (page 28) and spinach greens topped with Tomatillo Salsa (page 32).

This recipe is adapted from *Pasta & Co. By Request* by Marcella Rosene (Pasta & Co., 1991). Pasta & Co. is Seattle's premier, upscale take-out food shop with five locations.

ingredients:

¼ cup olive oil

1 large onion, chopped

2-3 garlic cloves, chopped or
    passed through a garlic press

1 can (28 ounces) crushed tomatoes (or 4
    garden tomatoes, skinned and chopped)

1 can (15 ounces) whole tomatoes (or 2
    garden tomatoes, skinned and chopped)

2 cans (14.5 ounces each) low salt,
    gluten-free chicken stock

3 ounces fresh basil leaves, finely chopped

¾ teaspoon sugar

½ teaspoon pepper

½ teaspoon thyme

makes 8 cups

Heat olive oil in a large soup pot. Add onions and garlic. Cook until soft without letting garlic brown. Stir in tomatoes, stock, basil, sugar, pepper, and thyme. Simmer for 20 minutes. Remove from heat and puree in a food processor in small batches to avoid splattering.

wine suggestion: Italian Chianti Classico

Notes: A quick way to remove the skins of fresh tomatoes is to briefly blanch the tomatoes in boiling water. Once skin splits, remove from boiling water and immerse in cold water for a few minutes. Skins should slip off easily.

Pan-Fried Chicken in Marsala

We enjoy the simplicity of this dish. Serve with Roasted Asparagus (page 137) and gluten-free pasta tossed with butter and Parmesan.

ingredients:

2 whole chicken breasts, boneless, skinless,
    and halved

1 cup gluten-free flour mix

1 teaspoon salt

½ teaspoon pepper

3 teaspoons olive oil

½ medium onion, chopped

2 cloves of garlic, finely chopped or passed
    through a garlic press

¼ cup dry white wine

½ cup sweet Marsala wine

4 servings

Place chicken between two pieces of plastic wrap and pound to ¼-inch thickness. (If breast is fairly thick, use a sharp knife to cut slits into the underside of breast to flatten it out a bit first, as it is important to pound it out very thinly.) Place gluten-free flour mix, salt, and pepper in a plastic bag or on a plate. Dredge chicken pieces in the flour to coat evenly, shaking off excess.

In a large, heavy skillet, heat 1 teaspoon olive oil and add onions and garlic. Sauté until onions are translucent but not browned. Remove onions from skillet. Add wine to skillet, deglaze, and pour wine over onions. Set aside. Rinse skillet or wipe out with a paper towel.

Replace skillet over high heat. When hot, add 1 teaspoon olive oil and half the chicken pieces. Cook quickly on both sides until they begin to brown. Remove to a warm plate and cook remaining chicken in another teaspoon of oil. Remove chicken, add Marsala to skillet, and reduce briefly. Return chicken to skillet, add reserved onions with their liquid and coat chicken with the sauce. Serve immediately.

wine suggestion: Salice Salentino

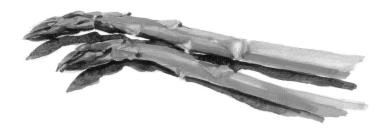

Moroccan Chickpea Stew

Chef Tom Douglas, Dahlia Lounge, Etta's Seafood, and Palace Kitchen — Seattle, Washington

Tom Douglas is a winner of the James Beard Award, considered the Academy Award of the culinary world! He is known for his wonderful restaurants and his Rub with Love meat rubs that add great flavor to salmon, pork, and chicken (see Sources).

ingredients:

2 tablespoons olive oil

1 medium onion, peeled and sliced

1 teaspoon minced garlic

½ teaspoon ground cumin

½ teaspoon ground coriander

1 tablespoon curry powder

1 cinnamon stick

2 cups canned crushed tomatoes

⅓ cup dry white wine

1 red bell pepper, roasted, peeled,
    seeded, and chopped

¼ teaspoon gluten-free harissa (or to taste),
    or substitute Tabasco

1 cup cooked chickpeas (garbanzo beans)

chef's comment:

This Moroccan-inspired vegetarian stew is seasoned with a little harissa, which is a traditional Moroccan hot sauce. (Try the "Dea" brand.) Tabasco is a fine substitution for harissa; you can also use cayenne pepper or red chili flakes. At the Dahlia Lounge, this stew is served with couscous, but brown rice is used to make the dish gluten-free. Serve with Curry Roasted Vegetables (page 143) and Brown Rice with Pine Nuts and Currants (page 152).

4 servings

Heat olive oil in a large skillet over medium heat and sauté onions until soft and caramelized, about 15-20 minutes. Add garlic, cumin, coriander, curry powder, and cinnamon stick, and sauté for a couple of minutes. Add tomatoes, white wine, and red bell pepper. Simmer for 15-20 minutes. Remove mixture from skillet and discard cinnamon stick. Puree the stew semi-smooth in a food processor or blender, working in batches if necessary. (Leave a little bit of a chunky texture). Return stew to skillet and season to taste with harissa (or Tabasco), salt and pepper. Add chickpeas and reheat the stew. Serve hot.

wine suggestion: Washington Lemberger or a Zinfandel

Note: Canned roasted red bell pepper and chickpeas are perfectly acceptable, and will save you much preparation time.

Buttermilk Chicken

This is the very best "fried chicken" we have ever had. It is less caloric than regular fried chicken, since the recipe uses skinless white meat (although you may use dark meat if you wish). A year-round favorite, it makes great picnic and back yard fare. Serve with Spinach Basil Kumquat Salad (page 124) and a wild rice mix (see Sources).

ingredients:

3 large, whole, boneless, skinless
   chicken breasts, cut into 2-inch pieces
1 quart buttermilk
3-4 cups vegetable oil for frying
2-3 cups gluten-free flour mix or rice flour
2 teaspoons salt
1 teaspoon pepper

4 servings (with leftovers)

In a large glass dish, soak chicken overnight in the buttermilk.

The next day, preheat frying oil to 400°F. in a deep fryer or heavy skillet. Mix flour with salt and pepper. Put flour mixture on a plate or in a large plastic bag. Dredge chicken pieces in flour, shaking off excess. Fry chicken in batches so as not to overcrowd the fryer. (Doing so will lower the temperature of the oil and make the chicken greasy.) Each batch will cook to a nice golden brown in approximately 5-7 minutes. (You might want to test a piece for doneness by cutting into the center.) Drain on paper toweling. Serve either hot or cold.

wine suggestion: Spanish Rioja

Simple Sushi

This is a fun family project. You may choose your favorite ingredients from the list below, or substitute if you wish.
Serve with pickled ginger, tamari, and Miso Soup (opposite page). Have all ingredients ready before making rice.

ingredients:

2½ cups hot, cooked sushi rice or
   short grain white rice
¼ cup seasoned rice vinegar
5 nori sheets, cut 4 x 6½-inches
Wasabi, gluten-free
¼ pound cooked shrimp or prawns
¼ pound cooked crabmeat,
   picked over for shells
2 large carrots, thinly sliced in 6-inch strips
1 large cucumber, thinly sliced in
   6-inch strips
1 medium avocado, thinly sliced lengthwise
Pickled ginger, gluten-free
Bamboo rolling mat
Tamari, gluten-free

Note: Some fish markets have sashimi grade ahi (yellow fin tuna), albacore, and other top-grade raw seafood; however, I prefer to put cooked seafood in our sushi when feeding the children.

comment:

Bamboo rolling mats, nori (sheets of seaweed for making rolls), pickled ginger, and wasabi (Japanese horseradish) can all be found in the Asian food section of most supermarkets.

4 servings (with leftovers) – 10 rolls (60 pieces)

Place cooked rice in a large, flat-bottomed, nonmetallic bowl. Using a flat rice paddle or rubber spatula, spread an even layer of rice on the bottom of bowl. Make a hollow in the center and pour some, but not all, of the vinegar into the hollow. Using a slicing motion, lift and mix the rice (as opposed to stirring); this technique is known as folding. Your goal is to evenly blend the vinegar into the rice so that the rice is slightly sticky. Gradually add remaining vinegar if needed. (Do not add too much, or the rice will become mushy.)

Once rice and vinegar are combined and have cooled to body temperature, cover with a warm, damp towel to hold rice at this temperature. If rice becomes colder, it will harden and become difficult to work with.

rolling sushi:

Position nori in the middle of the bamboo rolling mat. (Lower edge of nori should be about 1-inch from the bottom edge of the mat.) With damp hands, take a golf ball-sized handful of sushi rice and spread evenly from left to right in the center of the nori, forming a log shape. (Be sure to leave a ¾-inch strip of nori uncovered on the upper edge of the sheet.) Form a channel down the center of the rice to help keep the filling in place. Spread ⅛ teaspoon of wasabi from left to right across the surface of the rice. Place a few tablespoons of seafood and vegetables (from ingredient list) in the channel. While holding filling in place with your fingers, use your thumbs to lift up the edge of the bamboo rolling mat closest to you. Wrap mat around nori and roll away from you while pressing down evenly. The ¾-inch strip of nori at the end of the sheet will adhere to the outside of the roll and form a seal. Apply firm pressure down the length of the roll to seal end to end, then gently roll once more to restore a cylindrical shape. With a sharp, clean knife, slice roll into six equal pieces to form bite size pieces of sushi.

wine suggestion:

Sake or Italian Soave

Miso Soup

This recipe is from Cynthia Lair's cookbook, *Feeding the Whole Family* (Moon Smile Press, 1997), a whole foods cookbook for babies and young children (and their parents). It is a great book for anyone interested in getting their children off to a healthy start in life. The book includes good vegetarian meals, recipes to incorporate more legumes into your diet (providing nutrients that the typical gluten-free diet lacks), and ideas for using quinoa, brown rice, tofu, sea vegetables, greens, and alternative sweeteners.

ingredients:

4-inch piece of wakame
   (a sea vegetable found in the Asian
   section of most supermarkets)
6 cups water
1 tablespoon grated gingerroot
¼ pound firm tofu, cut in cubes
4 tablespoons light or
   mellow unpasteurized miso
1-2 scallions, thinly sliced for garnish

comment:

4 servings

for babies
10 months and older:

Miso is a salted paste made from cooked and aged soybeans. The soybeans are mixed with various grains and other ingredients to produce a variety of flavors. Be sure you buy a miso that is gluten-free. Look for it in the refrigerated section of your store.

Place wakame in a small bowl of water. Soak for 5 minutes. Put 6 cups of water in a 3-quart pot and bring to a simmer. Remove wakame from water and chop into small pieces, removing the spine. Add chopped wakame to water. Simmer for 10 minutes, adding gingerroot and tofu cubes during the last minute or two of cooking time. Pour a bit of broth into each serving bowl and dissolve 1 tablespoon (or less, according to taste) of miso into each bowl. Fill bowl with soup, stirring gently. Garnish each bowl with a light sprinkling of sliced scallions.

Remove a little of the cooked wakame from the soup. Chop very finely and add to pureed cereal or vegetables you are serving the baby. Wakame is a source of calcium and other minerals.

Omelets

This recipe makes one large omelet to split between two people. Though this is an unconventional way to make an omelet, it is ultimately quicker and allows the family to sit down to eat together. Serve with Apple Sauté (page 135).

ingredients:

4-5 large eggs
½ tablespoon butter
⅓- ½ cup grated cheddar cheese
⅛ cup chives or scallions, chopped

comment:

2 servings

To this basic omelet recipe you may add any number of ingredients. I like to add crumbled cooked bacon inside the omelet and top it with avocado slices and tomato salsa. Try your own combinations with mushrooms, onions, sausage, peppers, herbs, etc. For a fluffy omelet, beat the yolks and whites separately until light and airy (the whites should stand in firm but not stiff peaks), and fold together before cooking.

In a small bowl, lightly whisk the eggs. Over medium heat, melt butter in a non-stick skillet. When butter is fragrant and sizzling, pour eggs into pan. As eggs begin to set, use a plastic spatula to gently move the cooked eggs away from the edges of the skillet and let the uncooked eggs run underneath. When eggs are almost completely set, add cheese, scallions, and other fillings. Continue to cook over medium heat while cheese melts then flip one side of omelet over onto the other side so it is folded in half and serve.

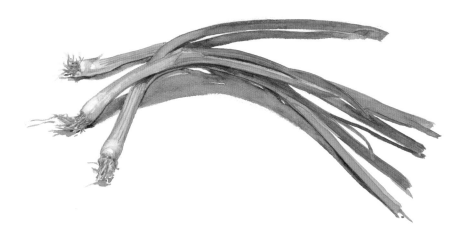

Pan-Fried Pork Chops with Lime Juice

A quick, flavorful meat entrée. Serve with brown rice and Baby Lettuces with Beets, Pumpkin Seeds, and Pesto (page 123).

ingredients:

1-2 teaspoons vegetable oil

Four pork chops, cut ¾-inch thick

Juice of 1 lime

4 servings

Heat oil in a large skillet over high heat, sear the chops 4-5 minutes per side until browned and cooked through. (Be careful not to overcook; chops should still be juicy in the center.) Add lime juice to deglaze the pan. Pour over the chops.

wine suggestion: French Red Burgundy

Coconut Chicken

Chef Thoa Nguyen, Chinoise Café – Seattle, Washington

Chinoise is an Asian grill and sushi bar that has become a weekly destination for many Seattleites. Although the entire menu is mouth-watering, this dish has become my personal favorite. I am grateful to Thoa for taking so much time to adjust the recipe for home use. Fish sauce and coconut milk can be found in the Asian food section of most supermarkets. Serve with Edamame (page 152), jasmine rice, or sliced fresh cucumbers.

ingredients:

marinade

⅓ cup fish sauce (see Sources)

⅔ cup coconut milk

1½ tablespoons yellow curry powder

½ cup sugar

⅓ cup water

1 tablespoon vegetable oil

3 pounds chicken thighs (boneless and
    skinless), pounded to ¼-inch thickness

Coconut Dipping Sauce

14 ounces coconut milk

⅓ cup creamy peanut butter

½ teaspoon yellow curry powder

2 tablespoons sugar

2 tablespoons fish sauce

serves 6

Combine all marinade ingredients in a large bowl and mix well. Submerge chicken thighs in marinade, cover, and refrigerate for at least 2 hours.

Preheat oven to 425°F. Remove chicken from marinade and arrange in a single layer in a shallow baking pan. Reduce oven to 375°F. and bake chicken for about 20 minutes, or until golden brown. (If you prefer, you may grill the chicken instead.)

While chicken is cooking, bring all sauce ingredients to a boil and mix well. Serve in small warm bowls, presenting one with each plate for dipping.

Instead of wine, try green tea with this dish.

"Groovy" Gnocchi with Portobello Mushroom Carpaccio

Chef Ludger Szmania, Szmania's — Seattle, Washington

Szmania's is a warm, inviting neighborhood restaurant in Seattle that has earned accolades in *Zagat*, *Gourmet* magazine, and *Food & Wine* magazine. Ludger is such a talented chef, and we are thankful to have his excellent restaurant in our neighborhood! The gnocchi is "groovy" because of the grooves impressed upon each one with a fork or gnocchi board. Make a double or triple batch of gnocchi if you wish to freeze some for quick weekday meals.

ingredients:

Gnocchi

2 large russet potatoes,
   unpeeled and scrubbed

1½ cups gluten-free flour mix

½ teaspoon xanthan gum

2 egg yolks

Dash of nutmeg

Portobello Mushroom Carpaccio

3 large portobello mushrooms

¼ cup olive oil

¼ cup red wine vinegar

2 tablespoons butter

2 tablespoons shallots, finely chopped

1 cup white wine

½ cup gluten-free chicken stock

2 tablespoons chèvre (goat cheese)

4 tablespoons herbs (parsley and chives),
   finely chopped

Olive oil

Asiago cheese, grated, to taste

4 servings

Gnocchi: Bake the potatoes in a 400°F. oven for 45 minutes. Let cool and cut in half. With a spoon, scoop the soft cooked flesh into a bowl. Pass cooked potato through a potato ricer. Combine the "riced" potato with the flour, egg yolks, and nutmeg. Season with salt and pepper. Blend with a wooden spoon, dusting with flour every so often to prevent the dough from sticking.

On a smooth, floured surface, roll out the dough into a long ½-inch cylinder. Cut lengthwise into 1-inch pieces and "groove" the gnocchi with either fork or gnocchi board. It's a good idea to do this over a floured tray so the gnocchi do not stick to the counter or to each other. Once formed, boil gnocchi in salted water until they float. Remove from heat, drain, and shock in an ice water bath.

(To freeze, spread uncooked gnocchi in a single layer on a lightly floured baking sheet. Wrap tightly and freeze until gnocchi are hard, then package in freezer bags.)

Portobello Mushroom Carpaccio: Marinate the mushrooms with olive oil and vinegar. Cook either on the grill or in a skillet over low to medium heat. Cool.

Heat butter in a skillet over low heat. Sauté shallots until brown. Add white wine and reduce by half. Add chicken stock and again reduce by half. Lastly, add the goat cheese and herbs, mixing well.

Slice the cooked portobellos very thinly on the bias and arrange on each plate. Sauté the gnocchi in a bit of olive oil, adding salt, freshly ground pepper, and Asiago. Place atop sliced mushrooms and drizzle with the sauce.
Garnish with fresh herbs and enjoy.

wine suggestion: French White Burgundy

> *Recipe requires an hour or more preparation/cooking time.*

⏱ Caramelized Cremini Mushroom Soup with Fresh Rosemary 97
   Chef Gerry Hayden

⏱ Pan-Roasted Pork Tenderloin with Fennel, Radish,
   and Arugula Salad 98
   Chef Gerry Hayden

⏱ Bathing Rama 99

   Supper Nachos with Homemade Corn Tortilla Chips 100

   Meat Loaf 101

   Stuffed Quail with Spinach, Pine Nuts, and
   Fresh Chanterelle Mushrooms 102
   Chef Ludger Szmania

   Gnocchi Sautéed with Rosemary, Sage, and Almonds 104
   Chef Lynne Vea

   Apricot Pecan Chicken 105

   Cannelloni in Marinara Sauce 106

   Butternut Squash Soup with Roasted Chestnuts 107
   Chef Hans Bergmann

⏱ Pork Tenderloin with Pancetta and
   Brussels Sprouts in Madeira 108

⏱ Cumin-Seared Tofu with Corn and Baby Lettuces 109

(continued on next page)

⏱ – *indicates a quick meal*

WINTER

Minestrone Genovese 110
  Marcella Rosene, Pasta & Co.

Beef Fajitas with Pico de Gallo 111

**Roasted Root Vegetables over
Warm Goat Cheese Medallions** 112
  Chef Lynne Vea

○ **Enchiladas Cazuela** 113

Hearty Spaghetti Sauce 114

**Sautéed Lamb Chops with Goat Cheese on a Roasted
Bell Pepper Sauce with Sun-Dried Tomatoes** 115
  Chef Hans Bergmann

Chicken a la Margaux 116
  Chef Erol Tugrul

**Sunday Slow-Cooked Roast Beef with Half a Bottle of Wine and
a Cup of Garlic** 117
  Chef Kathy Casey

Caramelized Cremini Mushroom Soup with Fresh Rosemary

Chef Gerry Hayden, Aureole – New York, New York

This starter complements Gerry's Pan-Roasted Pork Tenderloin with Fennel, Radish, and Arugula Salad (following page) and his dessert
Floating Islands with Caramel Blood Oranges (page 212).

ingredients:

2 tablespoons butter

1 pound cremini mushrooms, cleaned
    and sliced

½ cup shallots, sliced

2 cups water or gluten-free chicken stock

½ tablespoon finely chopped rosemary

2 tablespoons extra virgin olive oil (optional)

Freshly ground white pepper

4 servings

In a heavy-bottomed soup pot, heat butter to a light brown color. Stir in mushrooms, reserving a few nice slices for garnish. Add sliced shallots and continue to cook until mushrooms and shallots are a deep golden brown. Pour in water or chicken stock and add rosemary. Season with salt and freshly ground white pepper. Simmer for 10 minutes.

Puree mixture in a blender until very smooth and adjust seasoning. Ladle soup into heated bowls and garnish with reserved mushroom slices and a drizzle of olive oil. A fresh grind of white pepper completes the dish.

Pan-Roasted Pork Tenderloin
with Fennel, Radish, and Arugula Salad

Chef Gerry Hayden, Aureole - New York, New York

Charlie Palmer's Aureole is revered as a paradigm of progressive American cuisine. It is one of New York's finest restaurants. Restaurant critic Bob Lape says of Aureole, "An elegant dining experience packed with punch … boldly flavored seasonal dishes … theatrically inspired three-dimensional desserts serve to delight all the senses." Chef de cuisine Gerry Hayden taps his experience from some of the finest kitchens in America: the critically acclaimed River Café, Marguery Grill, Tribeca Grill, and Aqua.

ingredients:

¼ cup balsamic or red wine vinegar

¼ cup extra virgin olive oil

1 fennel bulb, trimmed, washed,
    and sliced thin

1 bunch arugula, washed and julienned

10 red radishes, washed and sliced into circles

1½ pounds fresh pork tenderloin

2 tablespoons canola oil

3 tablespoons butter

¼ cup water

chef's comments:

Serve Caramelized Cremini Mushroom Soup with Fresh Rosemary (previous page) as a first course, and serve Floating Islands with Caramel Blood Oranges (page 212) for dessert.

4 servings

In a small bowl, whisk together 1 tablespoon of the vinegar and 3 tablespoons of the olive oil. Season with salt and pepper. Set aside. In a separate larger salad bowl, combine the fennel, arugula, and radishes.

Season the pork tenderloin with salt and freshly ground pepper. In a heavy bottomed sauté pan over medium-high heat, sear tenderloin in canola oil until light brown on all sides. Lower heat slightly and add 2 tablespoons butter to pan. Baste tenderloin with butter for 3-4 minutes (internal temperature 150°F.) Remove tenderloin from pan, cover with foil, and let rest on cutting board for 5-8 minutes.

Pour excess grease out of pan and return to heat. Pour in water to deglaze any pan drippings, scraping them up with a wooden spoon if necessary. Pour in remaining vinegar and reduce by half. Whisk in 1 tablespoon butter and 1 tablespoon olive oil. Remove pan from heat and adjust seasoning of sauce.

Toss vegetables with the reserved vinaigrette and adjust seasoning. Arrange salad on plates. Slice pork and arrange on top of each salad, spooning sauce around the plate.

wine suggestion: 1998 Frog's Leap Sauvignon Blanc

Bathing Rama

This dish's curious name is of Thai origin. Essentially, it consists of pan-fried chicken strips with a peanut sauce, served over rice and spinach. This quick, satisfying meal is ideal for a busy schedule.

ingredients:

¾ cup coconut milk

2 teaspoons ginger juice or grated fresh ginger

¼ cup gluten-free tamari or
 gluten-free soy sauce

2 teaspoons brown rice vinegar

¼ cup chili oil

2 tablespoons sesame oil

1 cup peanut butter (cashew or almond
 butter may be substituted)

½ cup (or less) water

2 whole chicken breasts, boneless and skinless

2 teaspoons peanut oil

1-2 cloves garlic, minced

4 servings hot, cooked white rice
 (try sushi or pearl rice)

4 handfuls of washed spinach leaves

4 servings

Combine coconut milk, ginger, tamari, vinegar, chili oil, sesame oil, and peanut butter in a blender. With motor running, add water gradually until mixture reaches desired consistency. (The heat from the rice is enough to warm this sauce, but, if you prefer, you may heat the sauce briefly in a saucepan before serving.)

Cut chicken into strips ½-inch wide. Heat oil in a skillet over medium-high heat; when hot, add chicken and garlic. Season with salt and pepper. Cook, stirring, until chicken is nicely browned. (It should be moist and not overcooked.)

To serve, make a bed of the rice and spinach leaves on four warmed dinner plates. Heap chicken strips on the rice and spinach. Top with peanut sauce and serve immediately.

Green tea, rather than wine, is recommended for this dish.

Note: Ginger juice is a great item to keep on hand.
Made by The Ginger People, it can be substituted for fresh grated ginger
in the same quantities without the extra work. (see Sources)

Supper Nachos with Homemade Corn Tortilla Chips

This is a family recipe that is especially appealing when prepared in a baking dish made of glazed Mexican pottery. This one-dish meal lends itself to preparing ahead for parties. If time is short, you may prefer to use your favorite gluten-free packaged tortilla chips instead of making them yourself.
Serve with margaritas; many margarita mixes are gluten-free, as is most tequila.

ingredients:

½ pound ground beef

½ pound gluten-free pork sausage

1 large onion, chopped

1 can (12 ounces) gluten-free refried beans
    (or recipe on page 153)

1 can (7 ounces) chopped green chilies

2 cups of grated cheddar and
    Monterey Jack cheese

8 ounces gluten-free green or red taco sauce

10-15 corn tortillas

¾ cup vegetable oil

Garnishes:

(choose several to suit your taste)

⅛ cup chopped fresh chives

⅛ cup chopped black olives

Avocado, sliced or made into guacamole

Gluten-free sour cream

6 servings

Preheat oven to 400°F.

In a large skillet, brown the ground beef and sausage over medium-high heat. Add chopped onion and cook, stirring frequently. Drain fat and season meat with salt and pepper to taste. Using the back of a spoon, spread the refried beans evenly in a shallow 13 x 9-inch baking dish. Spread meat mixture over the beans and sprinkle with the chopped green chilies. Cover evenly with grated cheese. Drizzle taco sauce over the cheese. Bake uncovered for 20-25 minutes.

While the supper nachos are baking, stack 4-5 corn tortillas on top of each other and slice through the stack to cut each tortilla in half, then slice each half stack of tortillas into thirds (triangular-shaped chip size). Heat oil on high heat until very hot (shimmering) in a large, heavy, skillet. Oil should be deep enough to cover tortilla chips as they cook. Add about 8 tortilla chips to the oil. Cook quickly until they firm up. Using long-handled tongs, remove chips to a bowl lined with paper towels. Drain briefly.

Top supper nachos with your choice of garnishes and serve with homemade chips.

Meat Loaf

Great comfort food to have from time to time. Although it is not necessary to sauté the onions first, it will lightly caramelize them, thereby enhancing their flavor. My mom always covered the top lightly with ketchup, which may seem quirky, but old habits and memories die hard. Serve with Potato Pancakes (page 144) and Sugar Peas (page 143).

ingredients:

1 tablespoon olive oil

1 clove garlic, finely chopped or
    passed through a garlic press

½ large onion, chopped

1 tablespoon chopped fresh sage (optional)

1 pound ground beef

1 tablespoon Worcestershire sauce

1 tablespoon gluten-free Dijon mustard

1 egg, slightly beaten

¾ teaspoon salt

¼ heaping teaspoon pepper

½ cup gluten-free bread crumbs

Ketchup (optional)

4 servings

Preheat oven to 350°F.

Sauté garlic and onion in olive oil until onions are translucent. If using sage, add and cook for 1 minute more. Let cool completely. Butter a 5 x 9-inch baking dish. In a large bowl combine ground beef, cooled onions, Worcestershire, Dijon mustard, egg, salt, pepper, and bread crumbs. Mix ingredients well with your hands, taking care to avoid overworking the mixture. Place meat in prepared baking dish and form into a loaf shape. Using the back of a spoon, spread ketchup over the top of the meat loaf. Bake for 35-40 minutes, until internal temperature is 135°F., medium rare. Slice and serve.

wine suggestion: California Syrah

Stuffed Quail with Spinach, Pine Nuts, and Fresh Chanterelle Mushrooms

Chef Ludger Szmania, Szmania's – Seattle, Washington

Szmania's is a warm, inviting neighborhood restaurant in Seattle that has earned accolades in *Gourmet* magazine, the *Zagat* survey, and *Food & Wine* magazine. I enjoy stopping in for a seat at the counter to watch the chef and learn new techniques. Serve this meal with wild rice or Creamy Polenta (page 148).

ingredients:

1 bunch spinach

3 tablespoons olive oil, plus additional
   for roasting quail

½ large onion, finely diced (reserve
   2 tablespoons for chanterelles)

1 clove garlic, finely chopped

½ cup Asiago cheese, grated

½ cup pine nuts, toasted

4 boneless quail (all bones are removed
   except those in the wings and legs)

4 tablespoons butter, softened

3 cups fresh chanterelle mushrooms,
   cleaned and sliced

¾ cup dry white wine

2 tablespoons parsley, coarsely chopped

chef's comments:

The quail for this recipe are available in many grocery stores, but you may need to place a special order a few days in advance. They are very small, so if you are serving big eaters, you may want to prepare two quail per portion.

4 servings

Preheat oven to 350°F.

Cut off root end of spinach, leaving stems on, and wash thoroughly. Blanch for a few seconds in boiling water, then immerse in ice water to stop it from cooking further. Drain spinach and dry on paper toweling. Cut up coarsely.

In a medium skillet, heat 3 tablespoons of olive oil over moderate heat. Add diced onions (reserve 2 tablespoons) and sauté until golden brown. Add the garlic and spinach. Sauté for 3-4 minutes more. If the pan gets too dry, add a little olive oil.

Remove spinach from skillet and put on a plate, pouring any excess liquid back into skillet. Reduce liquid to a honey-like consistency. Add the spinach, Asiago, and pine nuts to the reduction.

Stuff the quail with the spinach mixture. (If preparing in advance, allow the stuffing to cool thoroughly in the refrigerator before stuffing). Using cooking twine, tie legs together to secure the stuffing. Season with salt and pepper.

continued:
Stuffed Quail with Spinach, Pine Nuts, and Fresh Chanterelle Mushrooms

In a large skillet over high heat, sear the stuffed quail on all sides in a bit of olive oil. Turn quail on their backs and roast in the oven for 15 minutes (they should be pink within when finished). Remove from oven and let stand for a few minutes before serving.

While quail is roasting, heat 1 tablespoon of the butter in a medium skillet over moderate heat. Add the reserved 2 tablespoons of onion and sauté until golden brown. Add chanterelles and sauté (a lot of moisture will come out). Cook until pan is almost dry, then add white wine. Turn heat to high and reduce liquid by half, seasoning with salt and pepper. Add parsley and remaining butter, mixing thoroughly.

To serve, remove twine from quail. Ladle chanterelles onto center of each serving plate and place quail on top.

wine suggestions: Pinot Noir or Syrah

Tips: Toasting pine nuts: Preheat oven to 325°F. Spread pine nuts out in an even layer on a baking sheet. Bake for 5-10 minutes, or until light golden in color. Watch carefully to avoid burning.

Cleaning mushrooms: Never soak mushrooms in water to clean them, as they will absorb it like a sponge. Use a damp paper towel to wipe them, or, if absolutely necessary, rinse quickly and dry immediately.

Gnocchi Sautéed with Rosemary, Sage, and Almonds

Chef Lynne Vea – Seattle, Washington

Lynne is a talented rising star in the culinary world. Her years as a chef on the Pacific Coast have given her the opportunity to explore and celebrate the diversity of the culinary world. Lynne's creations are a taste sensation, and I always look forward to attending her cooking classes in the Seattle area. She is a food stylist and also works with Chef John Sarich (of Chateau Ste. Michelle winery fame) as his production assistant for the television show, *Best of Taste*.

ingredients:

½ cup Italian Bread Crumbs (page 168)

½ teaspoon gluten-free celery salt

¼ teaspoon ground white pepper

1 recipe of Ludger's Groovy Gnocchi
   (page 93), made in advance and frozen

2 tablespoons butter

1 tablespoon olive oil

¼ cup slivered almonds

2 cloves garlic, minced

4-5 fresh sage leaves, finely sliced

1 sprig fresh rosemary

2 tablespoons chopped Italian parsley

Spicy Winter Tomato Salad (page 129)

Lemon wedges or Truffle Oil with
   Capers (page 129)

chef's comments:

Gnocchi, little poached pillows made of potato and flour, make a perfect alternative to the usual pasta dish. Sage is a classic Tuscan addition. This dish is made especially appealing when arranged on rustic plates around a bed of spicy Winter Tomato Salad.

4 servings

In a small bowl combine the bread crumbs, celery salt, and white pepper. Set aside.

Bring a large pot of salted water to a boil. Drop in handfuls of gnocchi and cook until they float. Remove with a slotted spoon and shock in an ice water bath. Drain and set aside.

In a non-stick skillet, heat the butter and oil. Add the almonds and cook, stirring, for 1-2 minutes, or until lightly golden. Add the garlic and herbs and stir briefly. Toss in gnocchi and stir to coat. Sprinkle in the bread crumb mixture evenly and stir-fry until each little pillow is crusty and lightly browned, 3-4 minutes. Keep warm.

To serve this meal, place about ⅓ cup of Spicy Tomato Salad in a tight mound in the center of each plate. Arrange the gnocchi in a spiral pattern around the salad. Sprinkle the almonds around the plate. Drizzle lightly with lemon juice (or Truffle Oil with Capers) and garnish with fresh herbs and shaved pecorino cheese if desired.

wine suggestion: a good Italian Chianti

Note: If you can find gluten-free frozen gnocchi, buy them; otherwise try Ludger's "Groovy" Gnocchi. Take some time on the weekend to double the batch and freeze it so you can make this a quick meal during the week. Kids love to make this, so you can turn production into a fun family project.

Apricot Pecan Chicken

This is an excellent, nutty chicken dish. Serve with Mushroom Mélange (page 146) and Spinach Sautéed with Garlic and Lemon (page 146). Recipe adapted from *Bay and Ocean: Ark Restaurant Cuisine,* Main and Lucas, (Ladysmith Limited, 1986).

ingredients:

½ cup white wine

½ cup thinly sliced dried apricots

2 whole chicken breasts, boneless, skinless, and halved

2 cups pecans, finely chopped

¼ teaspoon paprika

½ teaspoon white pepper

1 teaspoon curry powder

1 egg

¼ cup milk

¼ cup gluten-free flour mix

2 tablespoons butter

2 tablespoons olive oil

1 teaspoon minced garlic

Juice of ½ lemon

Few dashes of Tabasco or chili oil

½ cup Madeira

½ cup gluten-free chicken stock

½ cup heavy cream

4 servings

Cover apricots with wine and set aside.

Remove tenderloins from chicken breasts and pound chicken to ¼-inch thickness.

Mix together pecans, paprika, white pepper, and curry powder in a shallow bowl. Lightly beat egg and milk in another shallow bowl to make an egg wash. Dredge chicken breasts lightly in flour. Dip floured chicken breasts in egg wash, allowing excess to drip off, then roll in pecan mixture, coating thoroughly.

Simmer apricots and wine in a small nonreactive saucepan until apricots are tender. Meanwhile, in a large, heavy skillet over medium heat, melt butter and olive oil. Add pecan coated chicken and cover. Cook until browned (about 3 minutes per side). Remove chicken to a warmed serving dish.

Add garlic, lemon juice, Tabasco, Madeira, and chicken stock to the skillet and reduce by half. Add cream and reduce a bit until well blended. Pour sauce over chicken and garnish with apricots.

wine suggestion: California Pinot Noir

Cannelloni in Marinara Sauce

Part of this recipe was adapted from Amy Bogino Eernissee's collection of old family recipes that she compiled into a book and gave to friends one year during the holidays. I use her wonderful little book a lot. Serve with a green salad.

ingredients:

1 recipe Marinara Sauce (page 37)

6 ounces gluten-free lasagna noodles
   (see Sources)

15 ounces gluten-free ricotta cheese

¾ cup grated Parmesan cheese

¾ cup finely chopped flat leaf
   Italian parsley (about ½ bunch)

1 egg, lightly beaten

Grated Parmesan cheese

4 servings

Preheat oven to 350°F.

If you have the marinara sauce prepared and frozen, this recipe can be made more quickly. Defrost the sauce in a medium saucepan on low heat. (You can also make the sauce and plan on adding 30 minutes or so to your preparation time.)

Cook lasagna noodles until they are al dente (offer some resistance when bitten into), as pasta will cook further when placed in the oven later on. Drain in colander and rinse in cold water. Drain well. Remove lasagna noodles from colander and lay side by side on a clean work surface.

Combine ricotta, ¾ cup Parmesan, parsley, and egg in a medium bowl, seasoning with salt and pepper. Cover the bottoms of two 9 x 12-inch baking dishes with a thin even layer of the sauce. Place a few tablespoons of ricotta mixture on top of each lasagna noodle, roll up into a tube shape. Place "cannelloni" in baking dishes. Cover with remaining marinara sauce. Bake for 20-25 minutes. Remove from oven and top with grated Parmesan cheese. Return to oven for an additional 5 minutes.

wine suggestion: Chianti Classico

Comments: Amy's original recipe is for stuffed shells but I have yet to find gluten-free pasta in a large shell form. With this recipe lasagna noodles are wrapped around the cheese filling to make little cannelloni. If you are able to find large gluten-free shell pasta, use that instead, as it will be easier! Although homemade gluten-free pasta is time consuming, and the results often leave much to be desired, Bette Hagman's Bean Flour Pasta from the Gluten-Free Gourmet (Revised Edition) is well worth trying. I have had success using her recipe to make both ravioli and this dish.

Butternut Squash Soup with Roasted Chestnuts

Chef Hans Bergmann, Cacharel - Arlington, Texas

Cacharel is a great restaurant situated between Dallas and Fort Worth. The restaurant has received top restaurant status in *Zagat*, *Condé Nast Traveler*, and *Gourmet* magazine.

This is by far the best butternut squash soup we have ever had. It is very smooth and creamy, a wonderful addition to many fall and winter meals.
Double the recipe and freeze it for future meals. To serve this on a weeknight as a quick soup, bake the squash the day before.
Enjoy this soup either as a first course or as a light meal with salad or Breadsticks (page 165).

ingredients:

1 small butternut squash (about 20 ounces)

2 tablespoons butter

1 small onion, diced

½ stalk celery, diced

1 small piece of leek, diced (white part only)

2 garlic cloves, peeled

4 thyme sprigs

½ bay leaf

4½ cups gluten-free chicken stock

10 fresh chestnuts

¾ cup whipping cream

Dash of allspice

4 servings

Preheat oven to 375°F.

Poke a few holes in the squash with a knife or fork, place on a baking sheet, and bake for 45 minutes to one hour, or until soft. Cut cooked butternut squash in half. Using a spoon, remove seeds and discard. Spoon out all meat and discard skin.

Melt butter in a soup pot over medium heat. Add onions, celery, leeks, garlic, thyme, and bay leaf. Sweat vegetables by placing a sheet of foil or parchment directly on top and tightly covering the pot (a procedure which allows the vegetables to soften without browning) for two minutes. Add cooked butternut squash and chicken stock. Bring to a boil, then lower heat and simmer for 30 minutes.

Meanwhile with a small sharp knife, slash a deep X through the tough skin of the chestnuts. Spread out on a baking sheet, sprinkle with water, and roast in the preheated oven for 15-20 minutes, or until they can be easily pierced with a small knife. Remove chestnuts from the oven and pull the skins off while they are still hot. (If you have a rubber garlic peeler, it will make the job easier.) Roughly chop peeled chestnuts.

Remove thyme and bay leaf from soup and process soup in a blender until smooth. Bring soup back to a boil, add whipping cream, and season with allspice, salt, and pepper. Add chopped roasted chestnuts and simmer for one more minute. Ladle soup into heated bowls and serve with a salad.

Notes: You may pressure cook the butternut squash rather than baking it, which will take considerably less time. An alternative to sweating the vegetables is roasting them in the oven, which allows their natural sugars to caramelize and enhances the flavor of the soup. If you plan to freeze the soup for later consumption, do not add the chestnuts until ready to serve.

Pork Tenderloin with Pancetta and Brussels Sprouts in Madeira

Fuller's Restaurant in the Sheraton Seattle Hotel and Towers teamed up with McCarthy and Schiering Wine Merchants one evening to present a winemakers' dinner. The meal was delicious, and inspired me to try to duplicate the entrée. It is a fairly accurate interpretation, although pork tenderloin (which is both more readily available and less expensive) has been substituted for the veal loin served at Fuller's. Serve with Garlic Mashed Potatoes (page 140).

ingredients:

2 pounds boneless pork tenderloin

2 cloves garlic, finely minced or
    passed through a garlic press

½ ounce pancetta

2 teaspoons olive oil

2 shallots, finely minced

1½ cups Madeira

1 cup gluten-free chicken stock

12 small Brussels sprouts, quartered

4 servings

Preheat oven to 400°F.

Rub pork tenderloin with garlic on all sides, seasoning with salt and pepper. Place on a rack in a shallow roasting pan with the fatty side up.

Roast for 30 minutes, or until the internal temperature reads 150°F. on a meat thermometer. Remove from oven, cover with foil, and let rest for 5 minutes.

While the tenderloin is cooking, sauté pancetta until crisp. Remove from pan and drain on paper toweling, then chop and set aside. Over medium-high heat, add olive oil and shallots to the pan and cook until translucent. Increase heat to high and add Madeira. Reduce by half. Add chicken stock and reduce again until rich and flavorful. Strain the Madeira sauce through a small sieve and keep warm.

Meanwhile place Brussels sprouts in a steamer basket over a pot of boiling water. Steam until tender when pierced with a thin sharp knife, being careful not to overcook.

To serve, slice tenderloin and place a few slices on each plate with some pancetta and Brussels sprouts. Ladle sauce over and around the pork.

wine suggestion: Oregon Pinot Noir

Cumin-Seared Tofu with Corn and Baby Lettuces

Tofu is low in calories, high in protein, and has a slightly nutty taste. We try to have one meal a week in which tofu is substituted for meat.
The flavors and colors of this meal have a bright Southwest flair, lending both visual and taste appeal.

ingredients:

2 pounds firm tofu, drained

3 tablespoons vegetable oil

3 cloves of garlic, halved

½ teaspoon ground cumin

2 tablespoons Worcestershire sauce,
  or more to taste

2½ cups frozen corn

5-6 ounces mixed baby lettuces

3 tablespoons olive oil

1 tablespoon rice wine or brown rice vinegar

2 tablespoons chives, cut into 1-inch lengths

Squeeze of lime (optional)

4 servings

Drain tofu by placing it on a plate, resting another plate on top, and setting a 1-pound weight atop the second plate. After 10 minutes or so discard excess water.

Slice tofu into twelve, ¼-inch thick triangle shaped pieces. Heat oil in a large skillet. Sauté garlic for a minute. Add tofu triangles, cooking in batches until nicely browned. (Add more oil if needed to prevent sticking.). Season tofu with cumin and Worcestershire.

Remove tofu to a warm plate. Add corn to skillet and heat through, scraping up and incorporating the browned bits on the bottom of the pan. Season with salt and pepper. Remove corn from heat.

Toss lettuce with oil and vinegar. Divide lettuce equally between serving plates and top with several tofu triangles and corn. Garnish with chopped chives. Try a squeeze of lime juice over the plate for a little extra zip.

wine suggestion: California Sauvignon Blanc

Note: If you have a Trader Joe's near you, try their pre-washed bag of baby spring mix.
It contains a great variety of young lettuces: red and green romaine, oak leaf, lollo rosa, tango, frisée, radicchio,
mizuna, arugula, red chard, and spinach. Any combination from among these options will work fine.

Minestrone Genovese

Minestrone soup is satisfying; this version is quite fresh and is superb when made with a bounty of garden vegetables at their peak. Enjoy this soup either as a first course or as a light meal with salad or Breadsticks (page 165).

ingredients:

⅓ to ½ cup basil leaves, washed, dried, and finely chopped

⅓ cup freshly grated Parmesan cheese

¼ cup tomato paste

3 cloves garlic, finely chopped or put through a garlic press

¼ cup extra virgin olive oil

½ cup gluten-free orzo (see Sources)

½ cup freshly grated Romano cheese

6 cups water

2 teaspoons salt

2 cups carrots, peeled and cut into ¼-inch dice

1 cup onion, cut into ¼-inch dice

1 cup celery, cut into ¼-inch dice

2 cups red potatoes, skins on and cut into ½-inch dice

½ cup green bell pepper, cut into ¼-inch dice

½ cup zucchini, unpeeled, cut into ¼-inch dice

¼ cup gluten-free bread crumbs

½ teaspoon hot paprika

10 grinds fresh black pepper

Very small pinch saffron (optional)

2 cups water

1 can (8 ounces) kidney beans, well rinsed and drained, or 3 cups fresh green beans, washed and cut diagonally into 1-inch pieces

1 can (14.5 ounces) diced tomatoes in rich puree, or 2 cups fresh tomatoes, diced (including juice)

½ cup frozen peas or corn (add to soup frozen) or fresh corn cut from the cob

½ cup finely chopped Italian parsley

Parmesan cheese, grated by hand at the table (Parmigiano-Reggiano if possible)

comment:

Pasta & Co. is Seattle's premier, upscale take-out food shop with five locations in the area. They feature unique food items from all over the world and carry gluten-free pasta as well. This recipe is from *Pasta & Co. By Request* (Pasta & Co., 1991)

makes 13 cups

In a medium bowl, whisk together basil, Parmesan, tomato paste, and garlic into a thick paste. Slowly drizzle in olive oil until incorporated. Set aside.

Cook orzo in a large amount of boiling water until al dente. Drain well and fold into olive oil mixture. Fold in Romano and set aside.

In a large soup pot, bring 6 cups of water and salt to a boil. Add carrots, onion, and celery. Cook 5 minutes. Add potatoes and cook 5 minutes more. Add bell pepper, zucchini, bread crumbs, paprika, black pepper, and saffron and cook 5 minutes more.

Turn off heat and ladle a couple of cups of the soup into orzo mixture. Stir well and pour back into the soup pot. Add 2 cups water, kidney beans, tomatoes, frozen peas or corn, and parsley. Stir to mix.

Serve topped with additional freshly grated Parmesan.

wine suggestion: Vernaccia di San Gimignano

Beef Fajitas with Pico de Gallo

It is great to be able to enjoy flour tortillas again! With a little practice you can roll out and cook 8 flour tortillas in about 15 minutes.
In order to complete this meal within the 45-minute preparation time frame, you will need to pulse the pico de gallo ingredients in a food processor
rather than chopping them with a knife, and the marinade will need to be made the night before. It also helps if you have someone else working the grill,
but it is not critical. Serve everything family style so you can enjoy the bright display of colors created by this bountiful meal.

ingredients:

4 skirt steaks (about 2 pounds)

Marinade:

¼ cup lime juice
1 cup olive oil or cilantro oil
6 garlic cloves passed though a garlic press
1 teaspoon freshly ground pepper

Pico de Gallo:

6 medium roma tomatoes, chopped
½ medium onion, chopped
¼ cup finely chopped cilantro
Juice of one lemon
Juice of one lime
Salt and freshly ground pepper to taste
3-4 jalapeño peppers, chopped

Other ingredients:

1-2 avocados, mashed in a bowl with a
    dash of lemon juice
Gluten-free refried beans, either canned
    or homemade (page 153)
Homemade Flour Tortillas (page 167)

4 servings

Place meat in a nonreactive bowl. Combine marinade ingredients and pour over meat. Marinate for at least 5 hours, and up to 24 hours.

Combine pico de gallo ingredients in a medium-sized, nonreactive bowl and set aside. Refrigerate if preparing ahead.

Preheat an outdoor grill; while the coals are heating, make the flour tortillas.

Once tortillas are made and warming in the oven, remove meat from marinade. Grill 1-2 minutes per side, or to desired doneness. Slice into bite sized pieces. Wrap meat in a flour tortilla together with pico de gallo and avocado. Serve with refried beans.

wine suggestion: California Zinfandel

Roasted Root Vegetables over Warm Goat Cheese Medallions

Chef Lynne Vea – Seattle, Washington

ingredients:

2 Dungeness or other sweet carrots, peeled

2 parsnips or beets, peeled

1 sweet onion, peeled

4-5 Jerusalem artichokes, peeled

4-5 small potatoes (baby reds, yellow Finn,
   Yukon gold), scrubbed

1 red bell pepper, seeded and
   membranes removed

½ cup hazelnuts, with skin on

¼ cup extra virgin olive oil, divided

Juice of ½ lime

Splash of Tabasco

3 tablespoons chopped fresh basil and
   Italian parsley

¼ cup dried sour cherries

1 tablespoon maple syrup

2 tablespoons sherry wine vinegar

Cheese Medallions:

6 ounces creamy goat cheese

4 ounces cream cheese, softened

½ cup fine Italian Bread Crumbs (page 168)

Olive oil

chef's comments: Roasting brings out the natural sweetness of vegetables and deepens and enhances their colors. To complement this transformation, I have added earthy hazelnuts and bright sour cherries in a slightly sweet vinaigrette base. The creamy cheese medallions add the touch of elegance that this beautiful mixture deserves.

4 servings

Preheat oven to 425°F. Coarsely chop all vegetables into ¾-inch cubes. Toss vegetables and hazelnuts with 2 tablespoons olive oil, lime juice, Tabasco, salt and pepper. Spread the mixture in an even layer on two large baking sheets and roast for 15-20 minutes or until the potatoes are tender and the vegetables are caramelized around the edges.

Place roasted vegetables into a large metal bowl and add chopped herbs, sour cherries, maple syrup, sherry vinegar, and remaining olive oil. Season to taste with salt and pepper. Keep in a warm oven while preparing the cheese medallions.

Mix goat cheese and cream cheese together. (*Note: You may use only goat cheese if you wish, substituting 10 ounces of goat cheese for the quantities given.*) Form cheese into 8 equal balls, then flatten until each is a ½-inch thick disk. Press firmly into the bread crumbs on both sides. Let rest in the refrigerator until ready to cook. (*As the warmth from your hands may make the cheese quite soft, you can place the medallions in the freezer for a few minutes to firm them up before cooking.*)

Heat a little olive oil in a heavy skillet over medium heat. Sear the cheese medallions quickly on each side until golden and hot.

Place 2 medallions on each plate. Scatter the roasted vegetables over and around the medallions. Top with sprigs of fresh herbs or a garnish of thinly sliced red peppers.

variation: Place Braised Winter Greens with Garlic (page 147) in a tight mound in the center of each plate and prop the goat cheese medallions at a rakish angle against them. What a gorgeous foil for the more subdued tones of the roasted vegetables.

wine suggestion: a bold Washington Chardonnay

Enchiladas Cazuela

A family favorite and easy one-dish meal that travels well to parties.

ingredients:

½ pound pork sausage

½ pound ground beef

1 can (16 ounces) tomato sauce

1 cup water

1 tablespoon chili powder

½ teaspoon ground cumin

½ teaspoon salt

8 corn tortillas

Vegetable oil for frying

2 cups grated cheddar cheese

½ cup scallions, chopped

1 can (2¼ ounces) sliced black olives

1 cup gluten-free sour cream

4–6 servings

Preheat oven to 350°F.

Brown sausage and ground beef in a large skillet, draining excess fat. Stir in tomato sauce, water, chili powder, cumin, and salt. Simmer for 10 minutes.

Over high heat in another large skillet, heat ¼-inch oil until hot and shimmering. Fry tortillas until soft and puffed. Drain on paper toweling.

In a 10 x 7 x 3-inch baking dish, layer ingredients (reserving ¼ cup cheese) as follows: tortillas, meat sauce, cheese, scallions, and olives. Repeat layers until all tortillas are used. Sprinkle reserved cheese on top.

Bake uncovered for 20-25 minutes.
Top with sour cream.

wine suggestion:

California Zinfandel

Hearty Spaghetti Sauce

This was recorded as my husband was creating his favorite sauce, a concoction designed to please hearty eaters.
You will want to make plenty to freeze for another meal. Serve with Tinkyada or Bi-Aglut pasta.

ingredients:

¾ pound ground beef

¾ pound ground gluten-free Italian sausage

5 cloves garlic, finely chopped or
    passed through a garlic press

1 medium onion, chopped

2 tablespoons olive oil

10 white or button mushrooms, sliced

1 can (28 ounces) whole tomatoes,
    drained and chopped (reserve liquid)

1 can (15 ounces) tomato sauce

1 can (12 ounces) tomato paste

1½ tablespoons dried oregano

1 tablespoon dried basil

¾ cup red wine

¾ cup Parmesan cheese

**Recipe requires an hour or more
preparation/cooking time.**

4 servings

Over high heat in a large deep skillet with a cover (or a Dutch oven) brown the meat. Remove meat from pan, drain well, and set aside. In the same skillet over medium-high heat, sauté garlic and onion in oil until onions are translucent. Add mushrooms. Cover and cook until slightly softened. Add tomatoes, tomato sauce, tomato paste, oregano, basil, red wine, and Parmesan. Season with salt and pepper. If additional liquid is needed, use the reserved liquid from the tomatoes. Simmer for several hours, checking seasoning about 10 minutes from end of cooking time. Serve over gluten-free pasta.

wine suggestion: Italian Sangiovese or Chianti

Sautéed Lamb Chops with Goat Cheese on a Roasted Red Bell Pepper Sauce with Sun-Dried Tomatoes

Chef Hans Bergmann, Cacharel – Arlington, Texas

Cacharel is a great restaurant situated between Dallas and Fort Worth.
The restaurant has received top restaurant status in *Zagat Restaurant Survey* as well as in *Condé Nast* and *Gourmet* magazines.

Serve with Butternut Squash Soup with Roasted Chestnuts (page 107), Turnip Timbale Soufflé (page 141), and Cranberry Soufflé (page 208).
Although these recipes comprise a complete menu, the fledgeling cook may want to start by trying one at a time with simple accompaniments.

ingredients:

2 red bell peppers
3 ounces olive oil
½ onion, diced
2 garlic cloves
1 thyme sprig
1 bay leaf
2 cups gluten-free chicken stock
4 tablespoons sun-dried tomatoes
Cayenne pepper
2 racks of lamb (ask butcher to scrape the
    bones and cut them into 12 chops)
2 ounces goat cheese,
    rolled into 12 balls of equal size

> **Recipe requires an hour or more preparation/cooking time.**

4 servings

Split red bell peppers in half lengthwise. Remove the core, seeds, and white membrane. Cut into 1-inch dice. Heat a sauté pan, pour in 2 ounces olive oil and heat until almost at the smoking point. Add red bell pepper and sauté for 1 minute. Add onion and garlic cloves. Sauté for another 3 minutes, stirring occasionally. Add thyme and bay leaf, deglaze pan with chicken stock, and simmer for 10 minutes. Remove thyme and bay leaf. Pour sauce into blender, blend until smooth, and strain through a sieve.

Cut sun-dried tomatoes into strips and sauté in 1 tablespoon olive oil for 1 minute then add red bell pepper sauce and simmer for 2 minutes. Season with salt, pepper, and cayenne to taste.

Preheat oven to 500°F. Season lamb chops with salt and pepper. In an oven-safe pan over high heat, add one tablespoon olive oil, then quickly sear chops on both sides. Press a goat cheese ball on top of each lamb chop. Place pan in the oven and cook to desired doneness (see below). Ladle sauce onto warmed plates, arrange 3 lamb chops on top of sauce, and serve.

Doneness of Lamb Chops: Europeans prefer rare lamb, which is very tender and full of delicious juices. In America, doneness is more a matter of personal preference. When using a meat thermometer, lamb is medium rare at 135°F. and well done at 170°F. As it is difficult to use a meat thermometer with small chops, you may use this rule of thumb instead: Medium Rare 1-inch chops, 3-4 minutes per side; 1½-inch chops, 5-6 minutes per side.

wine suggestion: Cain 5, a California meritage, or wine made from a proprietary blend of various grapes (this excellent example includes five varietals).

Chicken a la Margaux

Chef Erol Tugrul, Café Margaux – Cocoa, Florida

Café Margaux is a recommended restaurant that is frequented by Gluten Intolerance Group members when attending conferences in Florida. *Zagat* consistently awards Café Margaux with "Top Restaurant" status as well.

Serve with Grilled Garlic-Studded Portobello Mushrooms with Roasted Tomato-Basil Sauce (page 136) and Cream of Yellow Squash Soup (page 79).

ingredients:

Six 5-ounce chicken breasts (skinless
   and boneless), pounded ¼-inch thick
6 slices smoked ham, very thinly sliced
6 medium asparagus stalks, blanched
1 large carrot, cut in 3-inch julienne
6 ounces spinach, steamed
12 thin slices gluten-free bacon

Wild Mushroom Sherry Sauce

1½ cups wild mushrooms, sliced (cèpes, also
   called boletus mushrooms or porcini, work well)
1½ tablespoons olive oil
1½ tablespoons amontillado sherry
6 small bouquets of fresh sage, dill,
   and bay leaves
1½ tablespoons chopped fresh sage
   and parsley

> **Recipe requires an hour or more preparation/cooking time.**

6 servings

Preheat oven 350°F.

Place one slice of ham, one asparagus stalk, a few julienned carrots, and 1 ounce of spinach onto a flattened chicken breast and roll chicken tightly around filling. Wrap 2 slices of raw bacon around rolled chicken so that the chicken is completely covered. (The rolled chicken bundle is called a roulade.) Repeat procedure with remaining chicken breasts. Season with salt and pepper.

Place roulades in a large skillet and cook over medium heat, rotating each roulade at least four times to crisp bacon on all sides. Strain rendered bacon fat by straining through a paper filter or a double thickness of cheesecloth, set aside. Bake roulades in oven for 20 minutes while preparing sauce.

Sauté mushrooms in olive oil, adding sherry toward the end. Season with salt and pepper.

Slice the chicken roulades and place three slices on each plate. Top with cèpes and ladle some of the natural chicken juices and clear rendered bacon fat over both the chicken and mushrooms. Garnish the dish with a bouquet of herbs and a sprinkling of the chopped herbs.

wine suggestion: Beaux Freres Pinot Noir-Oregon

Sunday Slow-Cooked Roast Beef
with Half a Bottle of Wine and a Cup of Garlic

Chef Kathy Casey, Kathy Casey Food Studios® – Seattle, Washington

Kathy Casey is celebrated as a pre-eminent chef who has paved the way for the emergence of women chefs and Northwest cuisine on a national level. She received her first acclaim as executive chef of Fuller's restaurant in Seattle, where *Food & Wine* magazine named her as one of the 25 "hot new American chefs." Casey's talent for innovation continues to be recognized today. As owner of Kathy Casey Food Studios®, a culinary mecca for food, beverage, and concept consulting, she opens her doors to the public for classes and special events. In addition to running her business, she pens a monthly feature column called "Dishing" for *The Seattle Times*.

Serve with Yukon gold mashed potatoes and Buttermilk Biscuits (page 170).

ingredients:

3-3½ pounds beef chuck roast
1 tablespoon kosher salt
½ teaspoon black pepper
2 tablespoons vegetable oil
1 large onion, peeled and cut into 8 wedges
1½ cups sliced mushrooms
½ bottle (about 1½ cups) red wine

3 tablespoons sweet rice flour
20 peeled cloves garlic
5 sprigs of fresh thyme
4 carrots, cut in 1½-inch pieces
4 celery ribs, cut in 1½-inch pieces
1 tablespoon chopped fresh basil (optional)

Recipe requires an hour or more preparation/cooking time.

makes about 6-8 generous servings

Preheat oven to 325°F. Pat roast dry with paper towels. Rub with salt and pepper.

Heat oil in a large Dutch oven or other heavy pot over a high flame. Add roast. Sear on all sides until well browned. Remove meat to a platter. Add onions and mushrooms to the pot. Cook, stirring, for a few minutes, or until onions and mushrooms are softened. Set roast back in the pot, pulling the onion and mushroom mixture up from under the roast.

Whisk together the wine and flour until smooth (add wine gradually to the flour to avoid clumps) and add to the Dutch oven along with the garlic and thyme. Bring to a simmer. Cover and transfer to the preheated oven. Add carrots and celery during the last 45 minutes of cooking time. Roast for about 2½ to 3 hours, turning roast occasionally, or until meat is fork-tender.

Stir basil into sauce and serve.

Note: If you desire a thicker sauce, make a cornstarch slurry with 1 tablespoon cornstarch mixed with 2 tablespoons water. Drizzle and whisk the slurry into simmering sauce a little at a time until desired thickness is reached.

Salads

Basil Spinach Salad 121

Gorgonzola-Pear Salad 121

Butter Lettuce with Caramelized Nuts 122

Classic Spinach Salad 123

Baby Lettuces with Beets, Pumpkin Seeds, and Pesto 123

Spinach Basil Kumquat Salad
with Raspberry Vinaigrette 124

Warm Winter Scallop Salad
with Shiitake Mushrooms and Apples 125
   Chef Lynne Vea

Pasta Salad 126

French New Potato Salad with Summer Herb Coulis 127
   Chef Lynne Vea

Seasonal Greens and Garden Cucumbers 128

Cole Slaw 128

Spicy Winter Tomato Salad 129
   Chef Lynne Vea

Black Bean Salad 130

Tomato Bread Salad 131

Spinach Salad with Dried Cranberries
and Roasted Pumpkin Seeds 132

Warm Beet Salad with Walnuts 133

Jicama Slaw 134
   Chef Bob Kinkead

(continued on next page)

ACCOMPANIMENTS

Fruit Sides

Banana-Pineapple Sauté 135

Apple Sauté 135

Vegetables

Grilled Garlic-Studded Portobello Mushrooms with Roasted Tomato-Basil Sauce 136
Chef Erol Tugrul

Roasted Asparagus 137

Fresh Artichokes 138

Oven Roasted Red Potatoes 139

Fried Sage Green Beans 139

Garlic Mashed Potatoes 140

Oven Roasted Butternut Squash 140

Turnip Timbale Soufflé 141
Chef Hans Bergmann

Sweet Sautéed Yams 142

Roasted Beets 142

Sugar Peas 143

Curry Roasted Vegetables 143
Chef Tom Douglas

Potato Pancakes 144

Caramelized Ginger Carrots 144

Green Beans with Pecan Paste 145
Chef Lynne Vea

Mushroom Mélange 146

Spinach Sautéed with Garlic and Lemon 146

Braised Winter Greens with Garlic 147
Chef Lynne Vea

Corn on the Cob 147

Creamy Polenta 148

Homemade Fries 148

Roasted Vegetables 149

Roasted Mushrooms 150
Chef Charlie Trotter

Rice, Beans, and Pasta

Master Recipe for Long Grain White Rice 151
Chef Christopher Kimball

Brown Rice with Pine Nuts and Currants 152
Chef Tom Douglas

Edamame 152

Homemade Refried Beans 153

Macaroni and Cheese 154

Basil Spinach Salad

ingredients:

¼ bunch fresh spinach

¼ head red leaf lettuce

1 medium tomato, sliced

12 fresh basil leaves, finely chopped

2-3 tablespoons olive oil or basil oil
   (page 60)

2 tablespoons balsamic vinegar

4 servings

Wash and dry spinach and lettuce. Tear into bite size pieces and place in salad bowl. Add tomato and chopped basil to bowl. Drizzle basil oil and balsamic vinegar over salad and toss well, seasoning with salt and pepper.

Gorgonzola-Pear Salad

An excellent recipe from talented home cook Amy Bogino Eernissee.

ingredients:

1 head of bibb lettuce

2 ripe pears, cut into bite size pieces
   (Bosc or Anjou pears are recommended)

2-4 ounces crumbled Gorgonzola,
   French feta, or chèvre goat cheese

¼ cup olive oil

3 tablespoons balsamic vinegar (or to taste)

¼-½ cup walnut halves

4 servings

Wash and dry lettuce. Tear into bite size pieces. Combine lettuce, pears, and cheese with oil and vinegar, tossing well. Top salad with walnuts and a grating of fresh black pepper.

Butter Lettuce with Caramelized Nuts

Butter lettuce can yield small heads under certain growing conditions. Adjust oil and vinegar accordingly.

ingredients

1 cup pecans or walnuts

½ cup confectioners' sugar

⅓-½ cup vegetable oil

2 tablespoons brown rice vinegar

3 tablespoons olive oil

1 head butter lettuce, washed, dried, and torn in bite-size pieces

4 servings

Place nuts in a steamer basket over boiling water and steam for 3 minutes. In a medium bowl mix sugar and steamed nuts, stirring well to coat the nuts with sugar. Heat ½-inch of vegetable oil in a small skillet and place half the sugared nuts in the oil. Cook until sugar caramelizes (about 30 seconds). Remove nuts with a slotted spoon. Repeat steps with remaining nuts. Let dry, spread out in a single layer, before serving.

Whisk the vinegar and olive oil together, seasoning with salt and pepper. Toss with lettuce. Serve sprinkled with caramelized nuts.

Note: This recipe works well for pecans or walnuts. Make an entire batch, and store the extra in an airtight container in the refrigerator. They are so tasty you may end up serving them as a snack.

Classic Spinach Salad

This salad involves some prep work. It is a good one to try on a night when the rest of the meal is easy.

ingredients:

½ bag of washed spinach greens
   (about 3 ounces)
2 hard-boiled eggs
4 strips of thick sliced bacon,
   cooked and crumbled
3 tablespoons olive oil
1 tablespoon balsamic,
   raspberry or red wine vinegar

4 servings

Place all prepared ingredients in a salad bowl, seasoning with salt and pepper.

Toss gently but thoroughly and serve.

Tip: To make a perfect hard-boiled egg, place egg in a small saucepan and cover with cold water by about 1-inch. Bring to a boil, then simmer for 12 minutes. Plunge egg into cold water. Once cooled, peel shell and chop up egg for salad.

Baby Lettuces with Beets, Pumpkin Seeds, and Pesto

If you have a Trader Joe's near you, try their pre-washed bag of baby spring mix. It contains a great variety of young lettuces: red and green romaine, oak leaf, lollo rosa, tango, frisée, radicchio, mizuna, arugula, red chard, and spinach. Any combination from among these options will work fine.

ingredients:

1 tablespoon pesto, (page 69)
3 tablespoons olive oil
2 tablespoons balsamic vinegar
5 ounces mixed baby lettuces
1 medium roasted beet (page 142)
½ cup roasted pumpkin seeds (page 28)

4 servings

Whisk pesto, olive oil, and balsamic vinegar together to make a dressing, seasoning with salt and pepper. Mix remaining ingredients in a salad bowl. Add dressing. Toss together and serve.

Spinach Basil Kumquat Salad with Raspberry Vinaigrette

The kumquat is a small orange citrus fruit, either oval or round in shape. The entire fruit is edible, and can be sliced and served raw in salads.
Kumquats are a good source of potassium, vitamin A, and vitamin C. If you are unable to find them, substitute thinly sliced oranges with the skin and pith removed

ingredients

Raspberry Vinaigrette

⅓ cup olive oil

4 tablespoons raspberry vinegar

3 tablespoons crème frâche (page 209)

½ bunch spinach or ½ bag prewashed
    spinach (about 2 ounces)

2 tablespoons fresh basil,
    leaves torn into pieces

¼ small red onion, thinly sliced

3 kumquats, thinly sliced

½ cup roasted pumpkin seeds
    (page 28) or toasted pine nuts

4 servings

Raspberry Vinaigrette:

Whisk oil, vinegar, and creme frâche together until smoothly combined. (Note: Chilling the ingredients, bowl, and whisk will help keep the vinaigrette emulsified and prevent separation.) Season with salt and pepper.

Combine spinach, basil, onion, kumquats, and pumpkin seeds in a salad bowl. Add just enough vinaigrette to lightly coat the spinach leaves. Toss gently but thoroughly. Serve on room temperature plates.

Warm Winter Scallop Salad with Shiitake Mushrooms and Apples

Chef Lynne Vea – Seattle, Washington

Lynne is a talented rising star in the culinary world. Her years as a chef on the Pacific Coast have given her the opportunity to explore and celebrate the diversity of the culinary world. Lynne's creations are a taste sensation, and I always look forward to attending her cooking classes in the Seattle area.

She is also working with Chef John Sarich (of Chateau Ste. Michelle winery fame) as his production assistant for the television show, *Best of Taste*.

ingredients:

2 tablespoons olive oil combined with
   1 teaspoon sesame oil

1 pound sea scallops (20-24 size)

1 cup rinsed leeks, cut into thirds, halved
   horizontally, and sliced lengthwise
   in julienne strips

4 ounces shiitake mushrooms
   (stems removed), sliced

1 teaspoon fresh rosemary, finely chopped

2 Pink Lady or Braeburn apples,
   cored and thinly sliced

½ cup gluten-free chicken broth

½ cup gluten-free hard cider or
   fresh pressed cider

¼ cup rich coconut milk

½ teaspoon red curry paste (see Sources page)

1 tablespoon gluten-free cranberry chutney

1 tablespoon sherry wine vinegar

4-6 cups loosely packed bright
   winter lettuces, washed and dried

Snipped chives and fresh rosemary for garnish

chef's comment:

Although this seems an unlikely combination, you will be amazed at how the earthy and fruity flavors complement each other.

4 servings

Preheat oven to 200°F.

In a large, heavy, non-stick skillet, heat the oil over a medium-high heat until quite hot. Carefully add the scallops. Cook 3-4 minutes on each side until golden and just cooked through (they will appear opaque). Remove to an ovenproof platter and keep warm in the oven.

Place the pan back on the heat. Add the leeks, mushrooms, and rosemary. Cook, stirring, for one minute. Add apples. Cook, stirring, for 3 minutes. (You may need to add a little oil to the pan if it is too sticky from the scallops.) Turn the heat to high and stir in the broth and cider. Cook, stirring and scraping to deglaze the pan juices, until reduced by half. Add the coconut milk, curry paste, chutney, and sherry wine vinegar. Season with salt and freshly ground black or white pepper. Simmer for 1 minute, blending the curry paste well into the mixture.

To serve, divide the greens between four large plates, piling the greens in a tight mound in the center of the plate. Arrange the scallops around the outside of the lettuces and top each one with a tiny rosemary sprig. Drizzle the dressing over the greens and around the scallops. Garnish with snipped chives.

Substitutions: You may use mango chutney instead of cranberry chutney, in which case you will want to substitute basil or cilantro for the rosemary.

wine suggestion: Oregon Pinot Noir

Note: 20-24 is "fish lingo" for the size of the scallops. It translates as 20-24 scallops per pound.

Pasta Salad

The key to this recipe is the quality of the gluten-free pasta; we like the brand Tinkyada.

ingredients:

8 ounces rotelle (or other spiral shape)
   or penne gluten-free pasta

12 ounces mozzarella, cut into ½-inch cubes

4 ounces gluten-free salami,
   cut into ½-inch cubes

14 ounces whole artichoke hearts,
   cut into 1-inch pieces

10 oil cured, sun-dried olives, finely chopped

½ cup sun-dried tomatoes, chopped

1 teaspoon roasted garlic or
   granulated garlic (or to taste)

4 tablespoons olive oil

2 tablespoon balsamic or red wine vinegar

1-2 teaspoons fresh oregano or basil,
   finely chopped

comment:

Mariani makes sun-dried tomatoes, packaged in a resealable bag, that are soft and ready to use. They are very good and worth the search. See Sources in the Appendix for Mariani's address and ask your local grocer to stock them. They also produce apricots, prunes, and other dried fruit that is great for on-the-go snacking or other recipes.

6 servings

Prepare pasta according to package directions. Drain and rinse pasta with cold water. Drain thoroughly and set aside. Combine mozzarella, salami, artichoke hearts, olives, and tomatoes in a medium serving bowl. Add garlic, olive oil, vinegar, and herbs, adjusting to taste. Season with salt and pepper. Add pasta and mix well. Serve at room temperature.

Note: Whole artichokes are a better quality than quartered artichokes. Avoid marinated artichokes.

French New Potato Salad with Summer Herb Coulis

Chef Lynne Vea - Seattle, Washington

Lynne has graciously contributed many recipes throughout this book!

ingredients:

2 pounds new potatoes, washed

1 cup loosely packed basil leaves

½ cup flat leaf parsley, stems removed

1 sprig tarragon, leaves only

3-4 garlic cloves

½ cup white or sherry wine vinegar

¼ cup hazelnuts, toasted and
   skins removed*

¼ cup dry white wine,
   (a Washington Sauvignon Blanc is good)

¾ cup extra virgin olive oil

Summer greens (sorrel, arugula,
   butter lettuce, frisée, etc.)

Accompaniments listed in recipe

chef's comment:

My favorite summer crop by far is the lowly potato. I can hardly wait each year as the moment arrives to begin digging in the warm ground for the first little treasures. Silky and moist, a tiny new potato is indeed a gift from the earth. Our local farmer's markets offer a dazzling variety as the summer progresses. This recipe, in the French fashion, dresses them lightly and with respect!

4 servings

Cut potatoes in half or into bite sized pieces. Simmer gently in salted water for 20 minutes, or until tender. Drain. (If you plan to dress the potatoes later in the day, toss potatoes with about ⅛ cup olive oil and season with salt and pepper immediately after cooking and draining. Refrigerate.)

While potatoes are cooking, combine basil, parsley, tarragon, garlic, vinegar, hazelnuts, and wine in a food processor. Process until well blended. Add olive oil gradually while blending. Process until relatively smooth. Pour over warm potatoes and toss gently.

Arrange summer greens around the perimeter of each plate. Place a mound of potato salad in the center of each plate and arrange any combination of the following accompaniments around the plate:
   Smoked oysters or smoked trout; Nicoise, Picholine, and/or Moroccan olives; Roasted red peppers;
   Sugar peas in the shell, lightly blanched; Thin slices of sweet Walla Walla or Vidalia onions;
   Goat cheese; Fresh mozzarella cheese.

wine suggestion: Washington Sauvignon Blanc

Notes: *If you can find the thin-skinned Duchilly, you can skip the step of removing the skin. To skin hazelnuts, spread on a baking sheet in an even layer. Roast at 350°F. for 10-15 minutes, or until skins begin to flake. Place a handful of hazelnuts in a dish towel and rub together until most of the skin is removed. Repeat with remaining hazelnuts.

Seasonal Greens and Garden Cucumbers

ingredients:

1 small garlic clove

½ teaspoon salt

1 head butter lettuce, rinsed, dried, and
    torn into bite-sized pieces

1 large garden fresh cucumber, sliced

4 tablespoons olive oil

1½ tablespoons brown rice vinegar

4 servings

Place salt and garlic clove in a wooden salad bowl. Rub the salt and clove into the bowl to season.

Toss lettuce, cucumber, oil, and vinegar together. Season with salt and pepper.

Cole Slaw

The illustrator of this book (my mother-in-law) kindly donated the watercolors and this recipe!

ingredients:

½ head green cabbage, chopped

¼ head red cabbage, chopped

2 carrots, grated

8 ounce can crushed pineapple, drained

1 cup raisins or currants

2 scallions, finely chopped

⅓ cup gluten-free mayonnaise

4 servings

Combine cabbage, carrots, raisins, scallions, and mayonnaise in a medium bowl. Season with salt and pepper.

Spicy Winter Tomato Salad

Chef Lynne Vea – Seattle, Washington

Lynne has graciously contributed many recipes throughout this book!

ingredients:

1½ cups chopped vine-ripened
winter tomatoes
2 tablespoons extra virgin olive oil
2 teaspoons balsamic vinegar or
1 teaspoon sherry vinegar
1 teaspoon sugar or maple syrup
Dash each cinnamon, cloves, and coriander
¼ teaspoon chipotle powder
¼ cup thinly sliced green onions
Pecorino cheese for garnish
A drizzle of Truffle Oil with Capers (optional)

Truffle Oil with Capers:

⅓ cup Spanish or Italian salted capers,
soaked in water for 10 minutes
and rinsed several times
3-5 large basil leaves
½ cup truffle-infused olive oil
Juice from ½ lemon

comment:

The key to this salad is to have the tomatoes chopped and ready to go for quick assembly and heating.

4 servings

Mix all ingredients except the onion together in a medium bowl. Season with salt and freshly ground white pepper. In a medium skillet over high heat, sauté the onion in a bit of olive oil for one minute. Add other salad ingredients, heating through for one minute more. Remove immediately from skillet and serve.

Truffle Oil with Capers: makes 1/2 cup

This oil adds an interesting dash of flavor that you must try at least once. Check Sources (page 228) on how to find the capers and truffle oil.

Place capers and basil leaves on cutting board. Cover with 1 tablespoon truffle-infused olive oil and finely chop. In a small bowl, combine lemon juice and remaining truffle oil. Add capers and basil and mix well. Set aside until ready to serve.

Black Bean Salad

ingredients:

2 cans (15 ounces each) black beans,
    rinsed and drained

4 scallions, finely chopped

1 cup chopped red and green peppers

1 cup frozen corn kernels

4 tablespoons finely chopped fresh cilantro

1-2 jalapeño or serrano chiles, finely minced

Juice of two limes

2 avocados, diced

4 servings

Combine beans, scallions, sweet peppers, corn, cilantro, jalapeños, and lime juice. Season with salt and pepper. Gently toss avocado into the salad and serve.

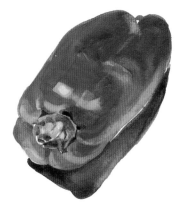

Tomato Bread Salad

This recipe works well with the recommended bread. If you have found a good gluten-free Italian bread, you may use it instead.
Recipe provided by talented home cook, Amy Bogino Eernissee.

ingredients:

4-5 fresh, ripe tomatoes
    (try different varieties)
1-2 medium sweet onions, sliced
    (Vidalia, Oso, Rio, or Walla Walla)
1 cup fresh basil leaves, lightly packed
¾ cup olive oil or more to taste
¼ cup balsamic or red wine vinegar
½ loaf stale, gluten-free Brown Rice Bread
    or Quinoa Bread (pages 163-64)
3 garlic cloves

6 servings

Cut tomatoes into wedges and combine in a large salad bowl with onions, basil, ½ cup of olive oil, and vinegar. Season with salt and pepper. Cover tightly and refrigerate overnight to let the flavors marry.

Two hours before you plan to serve salad, remove from refrigerator to bring to room temperature. Slice bread 1-inch thick, brush with remaining olive oil, and toast under broiler. Remove bread from oven and rub one side of each slice with garlic cloves. Dice bread into 1-inch cubes and combine with tomato mixture. Taste, adding more oil, vinegar, or seasoning as needed. Serve at room temperature.

Spinach Salad with Dried Cranberries and Roasted Pumpkin Seeds

This recipe lends itself to substitution. Dried cherries can stand in for the cranberries, and both are available year round. Toasted pine nuts, walnuts, or pecans work well if you have no pumpkin seeds on hand.

ingredients:

1 bunch of spinach (about 10 ounces)
   washed and trimmed of coarse stems
½ cup dried cranberries or
   dried sour cherries
¼ cup roasted pumpkin seeds
   (see page 28)
4 tablespoons olive oil
1 tablespoon brown rice vinegar

4 servings

Toss all ingredients together in a salad bowl and serve.

Warm Beet Salad with Walnuts

Serve with a winter holiday meal such as prime rib.

ingredients:

½ head of red leaf lettuce, washed and dried

½ head of butter lettuce, washed and dried

3 ounces blue cheese or feta, crumbled

½ cup chopped walnuts, toasted

2-3 medium beets, cooked and still warm

4 tablespoons walnut or olive oil

1½ tablespoons brown rice vinegar

4 servings

Tear lettuce into bite size pieces and place in a large salad bowl. Add crumbled cheese and walnuts.

Just before serving the meal, toss warm beets with walnut oil and vinegar. Season with salt and pepper. Toss beets with salad and serve.

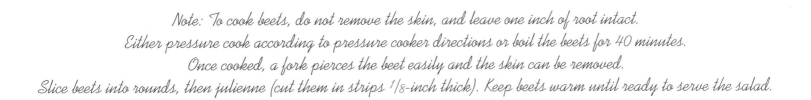

Note: To cook beets, do not remove the skin, and leave one inch of root intact.
Either pressure cook according to pressure cooker directions or boil the beets for 40 minutes.
Once cooked, a fork pierces the beet easily and the skin can be removed.
Slice beets into rounds, then julienne (cut them in strips ⅛-inch thick). Keep beets warm until ready to serve the salad.

Jicama Slaw

Chef Bob Kinkead, Kinkead's - Washington D.C.

In 1983, *Food & Wine* magazine named Bob Kinkead one of the nations' most promising culinary talents. He has lived up to that title over the years with multiple nominations and awards from the James Beard Foundation. Countless magazines, from *Esquire* to *Gourmet*, have featured Chef Kinkead. He has served as executive chef and partner at 21 Federal in Nantucket and Twenty-One Federal in Washington D.C. He now owns Kinkead's, where he continues to work his magic.

ingredients:

2 large jicama, peeled and julienned

12 radishes, julienned

6 scallions, finely chopped

3 oranges, sectioned

1 cup cilantro leaves, loosely packed

¼ cup lime juice

2 teaspoons red wine vinegar

1 teaspoon sugar

2 poblano chiles (optional), roasted,
     peeled, and julienned

1 medium red onion, julienned

makes 1 quart, plus extra

Toss everything together in a stainless steel bowl, season with salt and pepper, and serve.

Banana-Pineapple Sauté

A sweet complement to many Mexican dishes.

ingredients:

2-3 bananas, peeled and sliced

½ fresh pineapple, cut in chunks, or 1 can
    (16-ounces) chunk pineapple, drained

2 tablespoons butter

2 teaspoons cinnamon

4 servings

Melt butter in a medium skillet. Add bananas and pineapple.
Sauté briefly, then add cinnamon. Cook for 5-10 minutes,
until softened and lightly browned.

Apple Sauté

This is an all time favorite at our house. We use it as a side dish with eggs, pork, or sausages.
If you like, you may add a dash of brandy or sherry while cooking the apples.

ingredients:

3-4 Golden Delicious apples, peeled,
    cored and sliced

2-3 tablespoons butter

1-2 tablespoons sugar

1-2 teaspoons cinnamon

4 servings

Melt butter in large skillet. Add apples, sugar, and cinnamon.
Cook for 15 minutes, or until apples are tender and golden brown.

Grilled Garlic-Studded Portobello Mushrooms with Roasted Tomato-Basil Sauce

Chef Erol Tugrul, Café Margaux — Cocoa, Florida

Café Margaux is a recommended restaurant that is frequented by Gluten Intolerance Group members when attending conferences in Florida. Zagat consistently awards Café Margaux with "Top Restaurant" status as well. This dish would make a nice quick meal paired with a salad, provided you are able to marinate the mushrooms early in the day.

ingredients:

1 cup olive oil (scant)
4 large portobello mushrooms
¼ cup balsamic vinegar
¼ cup chopped shallots
5 sprigs fresh rosemary
2 sprigs fresh thyme
8 garlic cloves, peeled

Tomato Basil Sauce:

8 ripe Italian plum tomatoes
1 medium onion, quartered
1 teaspoon garlic, chopped
1 teaspoon shallots, chopped
2 tablespoons olive oil
½ cup fresh basil, chopped
¼ cup heavy cream

4 servings

Rub 4 tablespoons (1 tablespoon per mushroom) olive oil into mushrooms until absorbed. Combine ½ cup olive oil, vinegar, shallots, rosemary, and thyme. Pour marinade over mushrooms and marinate for eight hours.

Preheat oven to 300°F. Cover the bottom of a small roasting pan with 3 tablespoons olive oil, add garlic cloves, and roast for 20 minutes, or until tender. Turn garlic cloves in pan occasionally to make sure they do not burn. When done, cut garlic into small slivers and set aside.

Preheat an outdoor grill. Grill mushrooms for 3-4 minutes per side. Cut a few slits in the top of each mushroom and insert garlic slivers into the slits. Serve immediately with Tomato Basil Sauce.

Tomato Basil Sauce: Preheat oven to 400°F.

Roast whole tomatoes, onion, garlic, and shallots in oil in a shallow roasting pan for 15 minutes, or until tomatoes are soft and "saucy." Puree mixture in a blender, then pour into a saucepan. Set saucepan over low heat. Add fresh basil and cream. Heat through. Season with salt and pepper.

To serve, pour basil sauce onto four warm serving plates.
Top with grilled garlic-studded mushrooms.

Roasted Asparagus

This is an unusual preparation method for many home cooks but is easy and heightens the vegetable's flavor.
Roasted asparagus is best served immediately, as it tends to soften after cooking.

ingredients:

1 bunch asparagus
Olive oil

4 servings

Heat oven to 400°F.

Wash and dry asparagus. Holding a stalk of asparagus, bend until it snaps in two, discarding the lower portion. Repeat with remaining stalks. Place asparagus in one layer on the baking sheet, spray (or brush) lightly with olive oil, and season with salt and pepper. Roll stalks to coat with oil and seasoning on all sides. Bake for 10-15 minutes, then serve right away.

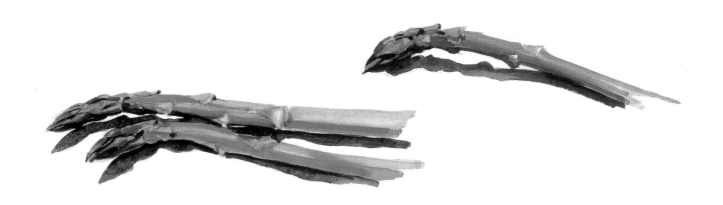

Fresh Artichokes

In the spring, artichokes are at their peak, and are delicious when treated with simplicity. They take awhile to boil but are otherwise effortless. Most people eat fresh artichokes as an appetizer, but we like to serve them as part of the entrée. Look for dark green artichokes with tight, unblemished leaves. If you own one of the new pressure cookers your cooking time will be cut in half. Follow pressure cooker directions for amount of water and cooking time.

ingredients:

4 globe artichokes

4 quarts water

4 tablespoons melted butter or
    gluten-free mayonnaise

4 servings

Bring a large pot of water to boil and add salt. While waiting for the water to boil, prepare artichokes by slicing 1-inch off the pointed end and about ¼-inch off the stem end. Using kitchen scissors, snip the prickly end of each leaf off with a straight cut. You may also want to strip a few of the large, coarse leaves from the stem. Place artichokes into the boiling water, and cook for 30-40 minutes. When a leaf pulls off easily, the artichoke is ready; you may also want to try piercing the stem and bottom with a fork to test for tenderness. Remove artichokes from water and drain upside down. Serve with butter or mayonnaise.

tip for eating
an artichoke:

Remove a leaf and dip the wide meaty end into butter or mayonnaise. Scrape the leaf with your teeth to get the soft, succulent part. Once you finish the leaves, the cone shaped prickly "choke" remains; it is inedible. At the bottom of the choke is the tender artichoke bottom or "heart", recognizable by its cup shape once separated from the choke. Cut the bottom off, discard the choke, and savor the meaty heart. You may wish to save the stem to dice and add to a salad.

Oven Roasted Red Potatoes

ingredients:

2 pounds baby red potatoes, quartered
Olive oil

4 servings

Preheat oven to 400°F. Brush a baking sheet with olive oil and arrange potatoes on sheet. Season with salt and pepper. Bake for 30 minutes, stirring occasionally, or until crisp and lightly browned.

Fried Sage Green Beans

The process of frying sage is quick and adds a new dimension to green beans, potatoes, asparagus, etc.

ingredients:

¼ cup vegetable oil
1 ounce large sage leaves
¾ pound green beans, trimmed

4 servings

Heat oil over medium heat in a small skillet. Add sage leaves. Cook for about 10 seconds (leaves should be lightly crisped). Remove with a slotted spoon and drain on paper toweling.

Cook green beans quickly in boiling salted water until crisp tender. Drain well. Toss with butter and season with salt and pepper. Top with fried sage leaves immediately before serving.

Garlic Mashed Potatoes

I don't bother with a potato ricer, as we like our mashed potatoes with a rougher texture, and often use unpeeled organic potatoes.

ingredients:

4 medium potatoes, peeled and quartered

4 tablespoons butter

2 garlic cloves, finely chopped or
    passed through a garlic press

¼ cup heavy cream, warmed

Fresh chives, cut into 1-inch pieces

4 servings

Place potatoes in a large pot of water and bring to a boil. When potatoes are easily pierced with a fork (about 20 minutes cooking time), turn off the heat. Place cooked potatoes, butter, and garlic in the bowl of a heavy-duty stand mixer. Using the paddle attachment, mix for a minute or two. Add cream and blend until smooth. Season with salt and pepper. Serve with chives as garnish.

Oven Roasted Butternut Squash

ingredients:

1 large butternut squash

½ tablespoon olive oil

1 tablespoon unsalted butter

4 teaspoons brown sugar

4 servings

Heat oven to 400°F. Cut butternut squash in half lengthwise and scrape seeds out with a spoon. Brush flesh of each squash half with olive oil and place cut side down on a roasting pan. Bake for 15 minutes. Turn and season with salt and pepper. Fill each cavity with a piece of butter and 2 teaspoons of brown sugar. Bake for about 45 minutes, brushing with butter-sugar mixture in the squash cavities every 15 minutes, until flesh is golden brown and tests done with a fork. Cut each squash in half again to make four pieces and serve.

Turnip Timbale Soufflé

Chef Hans Bergmann, Cacharel – Arlington, Texas

Cacharel is a great restaurant situated between Dallas and Fort Worth.
The restaurant has received top restaurant status in *Zagat Restaurant Survey* as well as in *Condé Nast* and *Gourmet* magazines.

ingredients:

1 pound turnips

2 eggs

1 egg yolk

½ cup whipping cream

Nutmeg

2 tablespoons butter, softened

makes 6 timbales (2 ½ ounces each)

Peel and cook turnips in boiling water (or pressure cook) until easily pierced with a fork. Once cooked, drain and place a weight on the turnips to remove excess water. Preheat oven to 300°F.

Weigh ½ pound of cooked turnips and place in a blender. Add eggs, egg yolk, and cream. Season with salt, pepper, and nutmeg. Blend until smooth. Brush timbale forms or soufflé ramekins with soft butter and fill the timbales with the mixture.

Fill a shallow roasting pan with an inch or so of water and place the timbales or ramekins in the water. (The French call this a water bath, or bain-marie, and it allows the timbales to cook in gentle heat without breaking or curdling them.) Place water bath in the oven and bake for 45 minutes to an hour (they will be firm but still springy, not hard). Unmold and serve.

variation:

Instead of turnips you can use red beets. For a great color contrast, fill the timbales with half turnip and half red beet mixture.

Turnips: Turnips are white-fleshed, with a white skin and purplish top. When shopping, look for a small size and a relatively heavy weight, as these younger specimens will have a delicate, slightly sweet flavor. Store turnips at 55°F. in a well-ventilated area. They should be washed, trimmed and peeled before using. Peak season is October-February.

Beets: Beets range in color from the familiar garnet red to white, and are available year round. The green, leafy tops are also edible and very nutritious. Be sure to cut them off before storing, as they leach moisture from the bulb. Choose beets that are firm and have smooth skin. Be careful not to puncture the thin skin, which can cause nutrient and color loss, and always leave about 1-inch of stem to prevent the same during cooking. Peel beets after they have cooked. An easy way to peel cooked beets is by holding the beet in a paper towel, using the paper towel to rub off the skin.

Sweet Sautéed Yams

ingredients:

3 medium yams
2 tablespoons olive oil
2 tablespoons butter

4 servings

Peel the yams and cut into ¼-inch round slices. In a large, heavy bottomed pan, heat the oil and butter over a medium-high flame. Add the sliced yams. Cook for a few minutes, stirring frequently, then lower heat to medium low. Season with salt and pepper. Cook, covered, for 10-15 minutes, stirring occasionally, until yams are tender.

Roasted Beets

ingredients:

4 medium beets

4 servings

Preheat oven to 425°F. Wash beets, but do not peel. Leave an inch or two of the stem intact, which will help to retain the nutrients while cooking. In a shallow baking dish, place beets and ½ cup water. Cover dish and bake until fork tender (about 30-60 minutes, depending on number and size of beets). Remove from oven and cool, uncovered. Remove skin and stem. Cut into ¼-inch slices. Refrigerate until ready to use.

(Note: You may also use a pressure cooker, which will cut the time in half.)

Sugar Peas

ingredients:

¾ pound sugar peas, stringed

4 servings

Just before the rest of the meal is served, bring a medium pot of water to boil. Drop peas into the boiling water. Cook for a minute or two until color brightens. Drain thoroughly. Add salt and pepper to taste, toss, and serve immediately.

Curry Roasted Vegetables

Chef Tom Douglas, Dahlia Lounge, Etta's Seafood, and Palace Kitchen — Seattle, Washington

Tom Douglas is a winner of the James Beard Award, considered the Academy Award of the culinary world!
He is known for his wonderful restaurants and his Rub with Love meat rubs that add great flavor to salmon, pork, and chicken.

ingredients:

2 carrots, peeled and
   cut on an angle into ¼-inch thick slices
½ small acorn squash,
   seeded and cut into ¼-inch thick
   "half moon" slices (leave skin on)
1 medium potato, peeled and
   cut into ¼-inch thick slices
½ small head cauliflower,
   broken into clumps about 1½-inches wide
2 tablespoons olive oil
2 teaspoons curry powder

4 servings

Preheat oven to 425°F. Put all vegetables in a bowl and toss with olive oil, curry powder, salt, and pepper. Spread vegetables on a baking sheet and roast in oven for 20 minutes, turning once with a spatula. When vegetables are tender and slightly browned around the edges, remove from oven and serve.

Potato Pancakes

A crunchy, soul-satisfying side dish. Potato pancakes are great with lox and cream cheese, topped with gluten-free capers or chives, for a Sunday brunch.

ingredients:

⅓ cup gluten-free flour mix

⅛ teaspoon salt

1 large egg

½ cup milk

2 medium potatoes, peeled and grated

⅓ cup vegetable oil

4 servings, 2 pancakes per person

In a small bowl combine the flour and salt. Using a wire whisk or fork, beat in the egg and milk until almost smooth. Set batter aside. In a skillet over medium heat, heat 2 teaspoons oil. Add ¼ cup grated potato. Spread grated potato in a very thin layer and cook until golden brown on one side. Pour 1 tablespoon of batter over the cooked potato, trying to keep batter within the confines of the cooked potato. Cook 2 minutes until top is set and bottom is browned, then turn over and cook the other side. Longer cooking time results in crispier potato pancakes. Repeat steps to make seven more pancakes. Keep warm until ready to serve.

Caramelized Ginger Carrots

ingredients:

6 medium carrots, peeled and sliced

2½ tablespoons butter

¼ cup loosely packed brown sugar

1 teaspoon minced ginger or ginger juice

4 servings

Place carrots, butter, and brown sugar in a medium saucepan. Pour in just enough water to cover the carrots. Cook over medium-high heat, covered, for about 30 minutes. When all water is absorbed and carrots are caramelized to a golden brown color, remove from heat and serve.

Green Beans with Pecan Paste

Chef Lynne Vea – Seattle, Washington

Lynne is a talented rising star in the culinary world. Her years as a chef on the Pacific Coast have given her the opportunity to explore and celebrate the diversity of the culinary world. Lynne's creations are a taste sensation, and I always look forward to attending her cooking classes in the Seattle area.

She is also working with Chef John Sarich (of Chateau Ste. Michelle winery fame) as his production assistant for the television show, *Best of Taste.*

ingredients:

¼ cup toasted pecans, finely chopped

2 tablespoons finely chopped Italian parsley

1 clove garlic, finely minced

Splash Tabasco

Squeeze lemon juice

½ cup freshly grated
Parmigiano Reggiano cheese

Extra virgin olive oil to hold it together
and form a paste

¾ pound green beans, trimmed

chef's comment:

The paste can be made the day before and refrigerated.

4 servings

Blend together all ingredients up to and including Parmigiano Reggiano. Add just enough olive oil to hold the mixture together and form a paste.

Quickly cook green beans in a pot of boiling salted water. Drain well, toss with pecan paste, and serve right away.

Alternative pecan paste preparation:

Once ingredients are combined, roll mixture into a log wrapped in plastic wrap. Refrigerate until firm, then cut into medallions. Serve as a garnish on top of vegetables, grilled fish, etc.

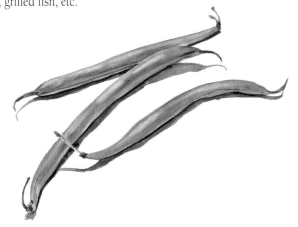

Mushroom Mélange

A quick, earthy side dish that complements an entrée such as Apricot Pecan Chicken (page 105).

ingredients:

4 tablespoons butter

2 tablespoons olive oil

1 shallot, chopped

3 cups of sliced shiitake, oyster,
   and cremini mushrooms

4 servings

Melt butter and oil together in skillet over medium heat. Add shallot and cook for a minute. Add mushrooms and cover skillet while turning heat to low. Cook for about 10 minutes. Mushrooms will release their moisture and become tender. Remove to a warm covered dish until ready to serve.

Spinach Sautéed with Garlic and Lemon

This has become a favorite at our house. One would never believe that this recipe would appeal to children, but ours now prefer spinach prepared this way, and request it often.

ingredients:

4 tablespoons butter

4 tablespoons olive oil

2 cloves garlic, finely chopped

10-12 ounces spinach, coarse stems removed

1 tablespoon lemon juice

4 servings

Melt butter with the oil. Cook garlic, stirring frequently, for one minute. (Do not allow it to brown.) Add spinach and cook until it wilts (a minute or two). Add lemon juice, mix well, and serve.

This dish cooks up quickly. Prepare it a few minutes before you sit down to eat, in order to prevent it from cooling while waiting for the other items.

Braised Winter Greens with Garlic

Chef Lynne Vea – Seattle, Washington

Lynne has graciously contributed many recipes throughout this book!

ingredients:

4-5 cups loosely packed young winter
    braising greens (chard, kale, spinach,
    or broccoli rabe)

1-2 teaspoons sesame oil

3 cloves garlic, peeled and minced

Splash of sherry vinegar

4 servings

Wash and dry the greens, leaving a bit of moisture still clinging to the greens.
Chop coarsely.

Heat oil in a heavy pan over medium-high heat. Add garlic. Stir briefly and add the greens.
Stir again to coat greens with oil and cover pan. Cook for 3-5 minutes, stirring occasionally, until the leaves have wilted and turned darker green. Season with sherry vinegar, salt, and pepper. Serve immediately.

Note: If you have access to a specialty import shop, look for fig-infused balsamic vinegar
as a substitute for the sherry vinegar; it is a real treat.

Corn on the Cob

ingredients:

4-8 ears fresh corn, shucked and trimmed

4 servings

In a large pot of boiling water, cook corn for 3-5 minutes. Serve immediately, buttered and seasoned with salt and pepper.

To grill corn, place shucked and trimmed corn directly on a hot grill. Turn each cob to cook evenly on all sides. Total cooking time is 3-4 minutes.

Creamy Polenta

This method is a convenient way to make polenta, as only 15 minutes is spent stirring over the flame and the remaining cooking time is in the oven. The process of combining the cornmeal with some of the cold water or stock is better than pouring the cornmeal directly into the boiling water or stock, as it will prevent lumps from forming.

ingredients:

2 tablespoons butter
¼ cup finely chopped onions
4 cups water (salted), vegetable stock,
   or chicken stock
1 cup cornmeal
2 ounces mozzarella cheese, grated
2 ounces Reggiano Parmesan cheese, grated

4 servings

Preheat oven to 350°F. Melt butter in a large heavy saucepan. Add onion and cook, stirring frequently, until translucent. Add 3 cups water or stock and bring to a boil. Combine cornmeal and 1 cup of cold water or stock. Gradually stir into boiling liquid. Reduce heat to low and stir constantly with a wooden spoon for 15 minutes, or until thickened.

In a buttered 1½-2 quart baking dish, alternate half the thickened cornmeal mixture with half the grated mozzarella and Parmesan cheese, spreading in even layers. Repeat with remaining cornmeal mixture and cheese. Bake for 35 minutes until top is browned. Let stand for 10 minutes, then serve right away while piping hot.

Homemade Fries

ingredients:

2-3 medium russet potatoes,
4 tablespoons olive oil
1 teaspoon dried basil
1 teaspoon dried oregano

4 servings

Preheat oven to 400°F. Slice potatoes into strips about 3 inches long and ¼ to ½-inch thick. Place potatoes in a large bowl. Add olive oil and herbs, tossing until well coated. Arrange potatoes in one layer on a baking sheet. Bake for 30 minutes, or until crisp and nicely browned.

Roasted Vegetables

An easy and elegant way to serve vegetables.

ingredients:

1 bunch asparagus

3 medium leeks

2 medium crookneck yellow squash

1 large red bell pepper

Olive oil

4 servings

Preheat oven to 400°F. Wash and dry asparagus. Holding a stalk of asparagus, bend until it snaps in two, discarding the lower portion. Repeat with remaining stalks. Wash leeks thoroughly and remove root end and dull green tops. Slice leeks in half lengthwise and cut crosswise into 4-inch pieces. Slice squash into several lengthwise 4-inch pieces. Cut pepper in half lengthwise and remove stem, membrane, and seeds. Slice pepper into ½-inch strips.

Place vegetables in a large bowl and drizzle with a few tablespoons of olive oil to lightly coat vegetables. Season with salt. Arrange vegetables on one or two large baking sheets in an even layer. Bake for about 20 minutes, stirring occasionally, or until crisp-tender.

Note: Thin asparagus and leeks cook more quickly (in about 10 minutes); you may want to put them on a separate baking sheet.

Roasted Mushrooms

Chef Charlie Trotter, Charlie Trotter's — Chicago, Illinois

Charlie Trotter's offers highly personal cuisine combining impeccable products, French techniques, and Asian influences.
Charlie's restaurant and cookbooks are well known across the country. The restaurant's list of awards ranges from Relais Gourmand to the *Wine Spectator*,
the James Beard Foundation, AAA—the list goes on and on. Recipe with permission from *Charlie Trotter's Seafood*, (Ten Speed Press, 1997).

ingredients:

2½ cups cleaned and stemmed mushrooms

2 sprigs thyme or rosemary

½ cup chopped onion

1 tablespoon olive oil

⅓ cup water

chef's comment:

The juices that come out of the mushrooms make a great sauce with a little bit of butter.

makes 1 ½ cups

Preheat oven to 325°F.

Place all ingredients in an ovenproof pan and season to taste with salt and pepper. Cover and roast for 30-40 minutes, or until tender. Cool in the juices and refrigerate for up to 4 days.

Master Recipe for Long Grain White Rice

(Modified Stovetop Method)

Chef Christopher Kimball

Founder, editor, and publisher of *Cook's Illustrated* magazine – Author of *The Cook's Bible* and *The Yellow Farmhouse Cookbook*

ingredients:

2 cups long grain white rice

2 cups water or gluten-free chicken stock

4 teaspoons olive oil

1 teaspoon kosher salt

   (or ⅔ teaspoon regular salt)

chef's comments:

For years, I used the basic stovetop recipe found on the back of the box, but when testing recipes for cooking kasha, I became interested in the notion of sautéing rice with a bit of oil and then cooking with less water. This recipe only uses 1 cup of water to 1 cup of rice, half the amount of water usually called for, and it makes great rice. Also note the rice has to sit for at least 10 minutes after cooking. This time is needed to finish the cooking and to let the grains "set" so they do not become sticky. If you are using commercial chicken stock, you will not need to add salt. Be sure to use a low-sodium brand.

4 servings

Heat oil over medium heat in a medium saucepan and add rice. Stir for 1 minute. Add water and bring to a boil. Reduce heat to low, cover, and simmer for 10 minutes. Check after 3 or 4 minutes to make sure that the water is at a slow simmer, not at a rapid boil. Remove from heat and let stand covered for 15 minutes, fluff with a fork and serve.

Brown Rice with Pine Nuts and Currants

Chef Tom Douglas, Dahlia Lounge, Etta's Seafood, and Palace Kitchen — Seattle, Washington

Tom Douglas is a winner of the James Beard Award, considered the Academy Award of the culinary world! He is known for his wonderful restaurants and his Rub with Love meat rubs that add great flavor to salmon, pork, and chicken.

ingredients:

1 cup long grain brown rice

2 cups water

½ teaspoon salt

1 tablespoon olive oil

¼ cup pine nuts, toasted

¼ cup currants, steeped in hot water
    and drained

2 tablespoons chopped fresh cilantro

4 servings

Place brown rice, water, salt, and olive oil in a heavy bottomed saucepan with a tight fitting lid. Bring to a boil over high heat, then cover and reduce heat to low. Cook for 45 minutes, or until rice is tender and all the water is absorbed. Remove from heat and fluff with a fork. Gently stir in pine nuts, currants, and cilantro.

Edamame

Pronounced ed-a-ma-me, these green soybeans are sold in many grocery stores in the frozen food aisle, either shelled or in the fuzzy green pod. If you can't find them at your local grocery, try an Asian market. Edamame has a wonderful nutty flavor and is a great way to add the benefits of soy to your diet. Many Japanese restaurants serve edamame as an appetizer.

I like to use edamame in the pod. Prepare according to package directions (which is generally boiling the beans for 5 minutes, then draining in a colander). Place beans in a serving dish, salt, and serve. To eat, pop the beans out of the shell and into your mouth. Some of the salt on the outside of the pod will be consumed as well.

Homemade Refried Beans

There are a variety of methods for soaking and preparing beans. The traditional overnight method is used here. Beans are soaked to replenish moisture, reduce cooking time, and remove the complex sugars that cause flatulence. While canned refried beans are my standard, due to the convenience factor, I like to make refried beans from scratch every now and then. If you own one of the new, safer pressure cookers, you can dramatically reduce the cooking time. Double the recipe and freeze in meal size servings.

ingredients:

1 pound pinto beans or black beans
7 cups water
1 inch strip of kombu (optional)
2 tablespoons plus ¼ cup vegetable oil
3 garlic cloves, peeled
½ medium onion, chopped
2 teaspoons salt

6 servings

Cover beans with water and soak overnight (4 cups of cold water for every cup of beans). The next day, drain and rinse beans, discarding water.

In a large pot, place 7 cups of water, soaked beans, 2 tablespoons oil, and kombu. Bring water to a brief boil, then let beans simmer for 1-1½ hours. If necessary, add more boiling water during cooking time. Add salt to beans when they have started to soften, but before they are tender. To test for doneness, remove a few beans and blow on them; if the skin breaks, they are done. Remove kombu and discard.

Puree half the beans in a food processor, or mash them well by hand. With the side of a large chef's knife, flatten garlic cloves. Heat ¼ cup oil in a large skillet and add garlic. Brown garlic lightly, stirring frequently, then discard. Add onion and cook until translucent and lightly browned. Add mashed beans, cooked whole beans, and salt. Cook until beans thicken and serve.

Note: Kombu is a sea vegetable sold in most stores with sushi ingredients.
It naturally tenderizes the beans and makes them more digestible (reduces flatulence).
Kombu will also reduce the cooking time by 15 minutes and enhance the flavor of the beans.
Cut kombu in one-inch strips, and it will melt away into the bean mixture.

Recipe requires an hour or more preparation/cooking time.

Macaroni and Cheese

This takes just a few more minutes to assemble than the boxed stuff, but it is so much better! For a quick meal, serve with organic frozen peas.

ingredients:

8 ounces gluten-free macaroni or penne
   (see Sources)
8 ounces cheddar cheese, sliced
½ cup half and half

4 servings

Butter an 8 x 8-inch glass baking dish. Preheat oven to 350°F.

Cook macaroni for a little less time than package directions indicate so that it stays slightly undercooked. Drain and rinse macaroni in cold water. Spread half the macaroni evenly in the baking dish and top with half the cheese. Layer remaining macaroni, then remaining cheese, on top. Pour in half and half. Bake, uncovered, for 15 minutes, or until heated through.

variation:

Try substituting Monterey Jack cheese for all or part of the cheddar cheese.

Chicken Stock 156

Chicken Noodle Soup 156

Nine Bean Soup 157

Smoky Chipotle Chili with Roasted Red Peppers 158

Split Pea Soup 160

(Quick soups are found in seasonal sections.)

LONG SIMMERING SOUP, CHILI, and STOCK

Chicken Stock

It is hard to find the time to make this, but the price of chicken stock is high and many are not gluten-free.
The quality of the soup you make from homemade stock is far superior to that of soup with a base of canned stock.
Start a collection of roasted poultry carcasses, necks, and leftover bones in the freezer, and make up a big pot of stock when you have accumulated enough.
Trimmings and leftovers from onions, celery, carrots, leeks, parsley, and mushrooms should be saved as well; all but the onions and leeks can be frozen.

ingredients:

2 pounds of chicken bones
  (Note: If you have whole carcasses,
  break them into smaller pieces)
10 cups cold water
1 onion, peeled and quartered
2-3 carrots, trimmed and cut in thirds
3 stalks of celery with leaves, cut in thirds
1 bay leaf
2-3 large cloves of garlic, cut into pieces
1-2 teaspoons freshly ground pepper
1 teaspoon each of dried basil and thyme
1 cup fresh flat leaf parsley

makes 5-6 cups

Wash the chicken parts if raw (omit this step if cooked) and put them in a large stockpot. Add water, vegetables, seasonings and additional water necessary to cover chicken pieces and vegetables. Bring to a boil, reduce heat to medium low, and simmer. Skim off any film or impurities that might appear on the surface; do this regularly to prevent emulsification with the stock. Simmer partially covered for 4-5 hours. Strain through a colander. Cool, uncovered, in an ice bath, stirring frequently. You may also cool the stock in a flat pan in the refrigerator. Do not cover while still warm, or it may turn sour.

Tip: A basic stock should not be salted until it is used as an ingredient in another recipe.

Notes: Do not remove the layer of fat on top of the stock until you are ready to use it, as this will act as a preservative seal.

Chicken Noodle Soup

Save a few cups of chicken stock and add chopped up pieces of the cooked chicken pieces, carrots, celery, and onions used for making the stock. Add salt and pepper to taste and some cooked gluten-free noodles. It is so nice to have this on hand, especially if you are sick and need some comfort food!

Nine Bean Soup

A great soup for a cold winter evening. Serve with Cornbread (page 166).

ingredients:

2 cups of mixed beans (see list below)

1 medium ham hock (about 1½ pounds)
with lots of meat

1 large onion, chopped

1 can (28 ounces) crushed tomatoes
(including liquid)

1 teaspoon chili powder

Juice of two fresh lemons

10-12 servings

Wash beans and place in a large bowl. Cover beans with water (4 cups of cold water for every cup of beans) and let sit overnight. (Add more water if necessary to keep beans covered.)

The next day, drain and rinse beans, discard soaking water. Place beans in a soup pot with the ham hock and 2 quarts of water. Bring to a boil, then simmer for one hour, stirring occasionally.

Remove ham hock and cool for a few minutes on a plate. Once cool, remove tasty ham pieces from the fat and bones. Set aside the ham pieces, discarding fat and bones. Continue to simmer soup.

Add ham pieces, onion, tomatoes, chili powder, and lemon juice to the soup pot. Season with salt and pepper and simmer for 30 minutes more or longer if desired, stirring occasionally.

wine suggestion: Côtes-du-Rhône

beans: Buy a bag of each kind of bean at the store, then mix them all together in a large container. An airtight glass canister is a nice display case for the bright array of colors. Buy your beans in a store with high volume and quick turnover to get the best quality beans for your soup.

Pinto beans	*Split green peas*
Navy beans or Great Northern beans	*Lentils*
Small red beans	*Kidney beans*
Black-eyed peas	*Black turtle beans*
Split yellow peas	

Smoky Chipotle Chili with Roasted Red Peppers

Lorna Sass has several books dedicated to pressure cooking. This recipe is adapted from her book, *The Pressured Cook* (William Morrow, 1999). Smoky chipotle chilies, roasted red peppers, lime juice, and cilantro make this chili exceptional.
If you don't own one of the new, safe pressure cookers, instructions are also included for regular stockpot cooking.

ingredients:

Cilantro-Lime Cream

1 cup sour cream
½ cup tightly packed chopped fresh cilantro
1 tablespoon freshly squeezed lime juice
¼ teaspoon salt, or more to taste

1 cup red kidney beans, picked over,
    rinsed, and soaked overnight
2 tablespoons olive oil, or more if needed
2 pounds well-trimmed boneless beef chuck,
    cut into ½-inch pieces
2 cups coarsely chopped onions
2 teaspoons whole cumin seeds
2 tablespoons mild chili powder,
    or more to taste
2 cups beef or chicken broth
1 large green bell pepper, seeded and diced
¼ teaspoon ground cinnamon
2 dried chipotle chiles, stemmed, seeded,
    and finely chopped
    (or substitute ⅛ teaspoon cayenne)
3 tablespoons tomato paste
2 large cloves garlic, finely chopped or
    passed through a garlic press
1 teaspoon dried oregano leaves
2 large red bell peppers, roasted (page 34),
    seeded and cut into ½-inch squares
1 tablespoon freshly squeezed lime juice,
    or more to taste

4-6 servings

Make cilantro-lime cream by combining sour cream, cilantro, lime juice, and salt in a nonreactive bowl. Keep refrigerated until ready to use.

Drain and rinse soaked beans. Set aside.

Heat a tablespoon of oil in the pressure cooker over medium-high heat. Brown beef in small batches, adding more oil if needed. Set the beef aside on a plate. Heat another tablespoon of oil. Add onions and cumin and cook for 1 minute, stirring frequently. Return beef to the pot. Add chili powder, stir to completely coat beef, and cook for an additional minute. Add broth and stir well, scraping up any browned bits stuck to the bottom of the pot. Stir in beans, green pepper, cinnamon, and chipotle chiles.

Pressure cooker instructions: Lock lid of pressure cooker in place. Bring to high pressure over high heat. Lower heat while maintaining high pressure and cook for 15 minutes. Allow pressure to come down naturally; if short on time, use the quick-release method. Unlock the lid, lifting up and tilting away from you to allow any excess steam to escape. If the meat and/or beans are not fork tender, simmer over medium heat until done, or return to high pressure for 5 minutes more.

continued:

Smoky Chipotle Chili with Roasted Red Peppers

Regular stockpot cooking instructions: Bring to a boil, then turn down heat. Cook covered at a gentle simmer until meat is tender, about 1-1½ hours. If chili becomes dry as the stew cooks, stir in a bit more broth.

Blend tomato paste into chili. Add the garlic and oregano. Season with salt and pepper. Taste for seasoning, stirring in more chili powder if needed. Simmer for a few minutes more over medium heat until flavors mingle and garlic loses its raw taste. If the chili is too soupy, add about ½ cup of mashed beans and stir in.

Minutes before serving, stir in the roasted red peppers and cook for another minute. Stir in lime juice to enhance the flavors. Top each portion with a generous spoonful of Cilantro-Lime Cream.

wine suggestion: California Syrah

Split Pea Soup

When we brought our first child home from the hospital, my mother-in-law brought over a big pot of this soup.
I did not think I liked split pea soup, but it was the perfect meal on a cold November day for two very sleep deprived parents. Now our children ask for it all winter long.
Although it is not necessary to sauté the onion, carrots, oregano, and garlic, the end result will be a more flavorful soup. Serve with cornbread.

ingredients:

2 tablespoons butter

1 medium onion, chopped

3-4 medium carrots, sliced

1 teaspoon dried oregano

2 cloves garlic, finely chopped or
　　passed through a garlic press

3 quarts of water

1 package (16 ounces)
　　split green peas, rinsed

1 medium ham hock
　　(about 1½-2 pounds) with lots of meat

1 bay leaf

6 servings (1 ½ cup serving size)

In a large soup pot, sauté onion, carrots, and oregano in butter for a few minutes until onion appears translucent. Add garlic and sauté for one minute more. Add water, peas, ham hock, and bay leaf. Bring to a boil, then turn heat down to low. Simmer for at least one hour, preferably 2 hours. Stir occasionally. After one hour of cooking, remove ham hock and remove all meat from the bones. Discard bones, cut meat into bite size pieces, and return meat to the soup pot. Continue cooking for another hour to marry flavors further, or serve as is.

wine suggestion:　California Chardonnay

Note: This recipe freezes well; you may want to make a double batch,
freezing the extra for another meal.

Bread Making 162

Sandwich Bread and Buns
    Brown Rice Bread 163
    Quinoa Bread 164
    Amaranth Bread 164
    Buckwheat Bread 164
    Hamburger Buns 164

Basics
    Breadsticks 165
    Cornbread 166
    Homemade Flour Tortillas 167
    Italian Bread Crumbs 168
    Workable Wonder Dough 169
    Buttermilk Biscuits 170
    Thick Pizza Crust 171

Sweet Breads & Muffins
    Chocolate Zucchini Bread 172
    Pumpkin Bread 173
    Carrot Bread 174
    Blueberry Muffins 175
    Banana Bread 176
    Hazelnut Zucchini Bread 177

BREAD

Bread Making

BAKING GLUTEN-FREE BREAD CAN BE CHALLENGING. This section offers high quality recipes for the basic necessities.

A common problem exists in gluten-free bread making. A perfect loaf of bread emerges from the oven, only to collapse while cooling. I have found two elements to cause this unfortunate experience: a) too much liquid in the recipe during periods of high humidity, or b) the type of flour.

I have tested many bread recipes, and have had my greatest success with those provided here; they turn out perfect loaves every time, and are favorites in my cooking classes. They also possess versatility; for instance, the sandwich bread recipe can be used to make hamburger buns as well.

The texture of brown rice flour, teff flour, amaranth flour, buckwheat flour, or quinoa flour actually seems to prevent the bread from collapsing. You will want to reduce the liquid of all gluten-free bread recipes by ⅛–¼ cup until you learn how to recognize when the batter is the right texture and when it is too wet.

A stand mixer is essential for gluten-free bread making, as it aerates the batter, producing lighter bread with a fine crumb and more height. It is a far better choice than a bread machine, as only a few brands can produce satisfactory gluten-free bread. If you absolutely have your heart set on a bread machine, call Red Star Yeast for recommended models (see Sources).

The variety of flours used in gluten-free baking is tremendous. Read Gluten-Free Flours (page 231) to learn more about each type. This knowledge will help as you venture forth with your own recipes.

If you are lactose intolerant, dairy-free substitutions can be found in the Appendix.

SWEET BREADS, FLOUR TORTILLAS, AND BISCUITS ARE EXCELLENT WITH TEFF, QUINOA, AMARANTH, OR BUCKWHEAT FLOUR SUBSTITUTED FOR UP TO ONE HALF OF THE FLOUR IN A RECIPE.

Brown Rice Bread

So far, this is the best gluten-free bread we have tried, and it makes a good hamburger bun as well. Recipe adapted from Barbara Emch's, a fellow celiac.

ingredients:

3 large eggs

¼ cup vegetable oil

1 teaspoon lemon juice

1¼ cups warm water (105º-115ºF.)

4 tablespoons sugar, divided

1½ tablespoons active dry yeast

2 cups tapioca starch flour

2 cups fine brown rice flour

⅔ cup instant non-fat dry milk powder

2 teaspoons xanthan gum

1 teaspoon salt

2 tablespoons ground flax seed (optional)

comment:

Quinoa flour is a great source of protein, calcium, and phosphorus, and can be substituted for some of the brown rice flour (see variation on next page).

makes one loaf

Bring all refrigerated ingredients to room temperature. Grease a 5 x 9-inch loaf pan.

In the bowl of a stand mixer, combine eggs, oil, and lemon juice. In a large measuring cup, combine water, 1 tablespoon sugar, and yeast; let stand for 5 minutes, or until foamy. In a medium bowl, combine tapioca starch flour, brown rice flour, dry milk powder, xanthan gum, salt, flax seed, and 3 tablespoons sugar. Add yeast mixture to the egg mixture, then slowly add dry ingredients a little at a time until completely incorporated. Mix batter on high speed for 3½ minutes, then pour into prepared pan.

Cover bread with foil and place in a cold oven. Set a pan of hot water on a lower shelf underneath the bread. Leave for 10 minutes with oven door closed. (This will cause the bread to rise quickly.) Remove bread from oven (do not uncover) and place in a warm place in the kitchen. Preheat oven to 400ºF. Bread will continue to rise as oven preheats.

Uncover bread and bake for 10 minutes to brown the top. Cover bread with foil and continue to bake bread for 30 minutes. Turn bread out onto a cooling rack. When completely cooled, wrap tightly to maintain freshness for as long as possible.

Tips: If humidity is high, reduce the amount of water in the recipe to avoid overrising. Many gluten-free bakers experience the frustrating situation in which a beautiful loaf of bread deflates once removed from the oven. You will need to experiment a little to get just the right amount of water in your bread depending on the humidity in the air. If in question, use less water than the recipe calls for.

You may use rapid rise yeast instead of regular yeast. If doing so, eliminate the cold oven rise method with a pan of hot water, follow yeast package directions instead for rise time. *(continued on page 164) continued from page 163:*

Variations: Teff Bread, Quinoa Bread, Amaranth Bread, or Buckwheat Bread

Using the Brown Rice Bread recipe, substitute the following combination of flours for straight brown rice flour and tapioca flour:

1½ cups tapioca starch flour

1½ cups brown rice flour

1 cup teff flour, quinoa flour, amaranth flour, or buckwheat flour

Be certain you are using flour that is considered completely gluten-free (meaning that it is grown in dedicated fields and processed on dedicated equipment). See Sources.

Hamburger Buns

Pour batter into English muffin rings, follow directions above. Bake for just 15 minutes.

Once completely cooled these buns freeze well. Always serve buns warmed, otherwise they will be crumbly.

Note: Each of these alternative grains are complex carbohydrates and they provide necessary nutrition for the gluten intolerant. Buckwheat is a great source of B vitamins and high-quality protein. Buckwheat appears to help lower cholesterol as well. Teff provides B vitamins, calcium, iron, and protein. Amaranth is high in protein and contains more calcium, vitamin A, and vitamin C than most grains.

Breadsticks

Wendy Wark's recipe for breadsticks is the best gluten-free version I have ever had. Once you make them a few times, it becomes quite easy to do them quickly and well. These breadsticks are quite versatile, as you can mix in garlic salt, herbs, Parmesan cheese, or cinnamon sugar (2 tablespoons sugar with 2 teaspoons cinnamon), creating a wide range of variety from a single recipe. Recipe from *Living Healthy with Celiac Disease* (AnAffect, 1998).

ingredients:

2 teaspoons unflavored dry gelatin

2¼ teaspoons active dry yeast

⅔ cup warm water (105°-115°F.)

2 tablespoons sugar

2½ cups Wendy Wark's gluten-free
   flour mix (page 181)

2½ teaspoons xanthan gum

¼ cup instant non-fat dry milk powder

½ teaspoon salt

2 eggs

3 tablespoons olive oil

Seasoning additions (see ideas above)

Melted butter to taste

makes 24

Preheat oven to 400°F.

Combine gelatin, yeast, water, and sugar in a large measuring cup. Let stand 5 minutes. In the bowl of a stand mixer, combine flour, xanthan gum, milk powder, salt, and the seasoning additions of choice. Add eggs and oil to dry mixture, then beat in yeast mixture.

On a floured surface (tapioca flour works well), roll out dough into a large rectangle 5 x 18 inches. Cut into strips 5 inches long and ¾-inch wide. Twist each strip a couple times and place on a lightly oiled baking sheet, pressing ends down onto the baking sheet. Brush generously with melted butter. Bake 7-8 minutes until lightly golden.

Cornbread

This is my grandmothers' cornbread recipe. (She always served it with butter and honey.)
Until I tried this recipe with Wendy Wark's flour mix, my gluten-free version did not taste right.
Her mix makes this taste just like the wheat flour cornbread my grandmother made.
The original recipe calls for shortening, though I prefer butter. Using buttermilk instead of milk creates a moister cornbread.

ingredients:

½ cup sugar

1 teaspoon baking soda

½ teaspoon salt

¼ teaspoon xanthan gum

½ cup Wendy Wark's gluten-free
   flour mix (page 181)

1 cup corn meal

2 tablespoons butter or
   organic shortening, melted

1 large egg

1 cup buttermilk or milk

16 servings

Preheat oven to 400°F. Butter an 8-inch baking dish.

Combine sugar, baking soda, salt, xanthan gum, flour mix, and corn meal in a medium bowl. Combine butter, egg, and buttermilk in a small bowl. Slowly add the egg mixture to the flour mixture until blended. Pour batter into prepared baking dish. Bake for 20-25 minutes, or until toothpick tests clean.

Homemade Flour Tortillas

This is the best gluten-free flour tortilla we have tasted. Recipe adapted from Wendy Wark's, *Living Healthy with Celiac Disease* (AnAffect, 1998).

ingredients:

2 cups Wendy Wark's
   gluten-free flour mix (page 181)
¾ teaspoon salt
1½ teaspoons xanthan gum
1½ teaspoons baking powder
2½ tablespoons vegetable oil
¾ cup water

makes eight, 8-inch tortillas

Mix dry ingredients together, then add oil and water. (This works well in a Kitchenaid stand mixer, using the paddle attachment instead of the dough hook) Mix on high speed for a few minutes until dough is well blended and forms a smooth ball. Let dough rest for 10 minutes, then divide into 8 equal sized balls. Flatten each portion slightly and roll out on a floured work surface (tapioca flour works nicely). Heat an ungreased griddle until very hot. Using a large spatula, place rolled-out tortilla on griddle, and cook for a minute or so on each side.

Tip: Depending on the weather, you may want to vary the amount of water until you get the right consistency. Try holding back ⅛ to ¼ cup water in the beginning. Flour tends to absorb moisture from the air during periods of high humidity, while on dryer days you may need to add another tablespoon or so of water.

Makes great communion wafers.

*Note: Wendy suggests keeping the cooked tortillas covered with a warm, damp towel;
you can also wrap the tortillas in foil and keep warm in a 200°F. oven.
(Tortillas can be frozen and reheated on a griddle.
Quickly steaming each side is another good trick to "bring them back to life.")*

Italian Bread Crumbs

You may substitute dried herbs in this recipe. Remember that 1 tablespoon of finely chopped fresh herbs equals 1 teaspoon of dried herbs.

ingredients:

2 slices stale gluten-free bread

¾ tablespoon finely chopped fresh rosemary

½ tablespoon finely chopped fresh oregano

¾ tablespoon finely chopped fresh thyme

1 tablespoon finely chopped fresh basil

makes 1 cup

Place bread in a small food processor and process into fine crumbs. Transfer crumbs to a bowl. Add herbs and toss until well combined.

Workable Wonder Dough

You will probably find many uses for this good, user-friendly dough. Recipe from Wendy Wark's *Living Healthy with Celiac Disease* (AnAffect, 1998). Wendy uses this for pretzels, breadsticks, cinnamon rolls, and pizza crust. Use it as a substitute for wheat flour dough in your favorite recipes.

ingredients:

2 teaspoons unflavored dry gelatin

2¼ teaspoons active dry yeast

⅔ cup warm water (105°-115°F.)

2 tablespoons sugar

2½ cups Wendy Wark's gluten-free
flour mix (page 181)

2½ teaspoons xanthan gum

¼ cup instant non-fat dry milk powder

½ teaspoon salt

3 tablespoons vegetable oil

2 eggs

makes 1 ½ pounds dough

Combine gelatin, yeast, water, and sugar together in a 2-cup glass measure. Let stand for 5 minutes, or until foamy. In the bowl of a stand mixer, add flour mix, xanthan gum, milk powder, and salt. Mix briefly, then add oil and eggs, followed by yeast mixture. Beat on high speed for 2 minutes, using the paddle attachment until a soft dough forms. Use dough in your favorite recipe.

Buttermilk Biscuits

Try these today and celebrate the return of a quick, scrumptious bread to your evening meal!

ingredients:

1 cup Wendy Wark's gluten-free
   flour mix (page 181)

¾ cup teff flour

½ teaspoon xanthan gum

½ teaspoon salt

1 teaspoon baking powder

⅛ teaspoon baking soda

½ cup (1 stick) cold butter, unsalted

¾ cup buttermilk

comment:

Teff flour provides B vitamins, calcium, iron, and protein. The addition of teff flour to this recipe make the biscuits more of a complex carbohydrate as well.

makes 6 biscuits

Preheat oven to 500°F. Combine flours, xanthan gum, salt, baking powder, and baking soda in a medium bowl. Cut in cold butter with a pastry blender until butter pieces are the size of peas. Add buttermilk, folding gently with a rubber spatula to make a soft dough.

Roll out dough between two sheets of wax paper into a 4 x 5-inch rectangle of about ¾-inch thickness. Peel wax paper away from dough several times to prevent sticking. Fold dough like a letter into thirds, give the dough a quarter turn, and roll out again to same dimensions. Repeat, folding once more. Wrap dough in the wax paper and refrigerate for 20 minutes.

Divide dough into six equal pieces and hand shape biscuits.
Place biscuits on a baking sheet lined with parchment.

Bake for 4 minutes at 500°F., then lower temperature to 375°F. Continue baking until golden brown, about 20 to 25 minutes. (Cover biscuits with foil if they brown too quickly before they are done in the center.)
Serve warm.

Note: You may omit the teff flour and use a total 1³/4 cups of Wendy's flour mix instead.

Thick Pizza Crust

This recipe is adapted from Bette Hagman's first book, *The Gluten-Free Gourmet* (Henry Holt, 1990).
The tricks I have learned over the years to produce a perfect crust are part of the recipe.
You may use all brown rice flour if you can't find the amaranth or quinoa flour, although the health benefits of these latter two make them well worth the search.

ingredients:

1½ cups brown rice flour

½ cup amaranth or quinoa flour

2 cups tapioca flour

⅔ cup instant non-fat dry milk powder

3 teaspoons xanthan gum

1 teaspoon salt

1 cup water (105°-115°F.)

2 tablespoons active dry yeast

1 tablespoon sugar

½ cup warm water

3 tablespoons olive oil

4 egg whites at room temperature

Olive oil for spreading pizza dough

makes two 13-inch pizzas

Grease two 13-inch pizza pans, using organic shortening.

In the bowl of a stand mixer, combine the flours, milk powder, xanthan gum, and salt. In a large measuring cup, combine the 1 cup water, yeast, and sugar. Let stand until yeast proofs (becomes foamy). In another measuring cup, combine the ½ cup water and 3 tablespoons olive oil. Add olive oil-water mixture to dry ingredients, then egg whites, mixing well after each addition. Finally add yeast mixture and beat on high speed for 4 minutes.

Divide dough into two equal portions. Place each portion on a prepared pizza pan. Cover your hand with a clean plastic bag. Drizzle about a tablespoon of olive oil over your hand and one portion of dough. Spread the dough out evenly over the pizza pan, forming a ridge around the edge to contain the pizza toppings. Repeat process for second portion of dough. Let dough rise for about 20 minutes. Preheat oven to 400°F. Bake pizza crusts for 7 minutes (until lightly golden) and remove from oven. At this point you can either cool the crusts, wrapping and freezing them for future use, or you can spread tomato sauce on the crust and top with your favorite toppings (see Scratch Pizza Sauce and topping suggestions, page 69).

Chocolate Zucchini Bread

Here is a quick recipe for a goodie to keep on hand in the freezer. It's especially convenient to take along to the office, or to pack with your child's lunch.
You might want to prepare the dry ingredients in advance for a quick mix to use later. (Be sure to refrigerate any prepared dry mixes.)
Recipe adapted from *Breakfast in Bed*, Carol Frieberg (Sasquatch Books, 1990).

ingredients:

3 eggs plus 1 egg white

1 cup vegetable oil (or ½ cup applesauce
    and ½ cup oil)

2 teaspoons vanilla extract

2 cups sugar

3 cups grated zucchini

2⅓ cups Wendy Wark's gluten-free
    flour mix (page 181)

½ teaspoon xanthan gum

½ cup unsweetened cocoa

2 teaspoons baking soda

1 teaspoon cinnamon

1 teaspoon salt

¼ teaspoon baking powder

¾ cup chocolate chips

makes 2 loaves

Preheat oven to 350°F. Butter two 5 x 9-inch loaf pans.

Combine eggs, oil, vanilla, and sugar in a large bowl. Add zucchini, mixing well. In a medium bowl, sift flour, xanthan gum, cocoa, baking soda, cinnamon, salt, and baking powder. Slowly add sifted mix to the zucchini mixture. Blend well and stir in chocolate chips.

Divide mixture between the two prepared loaf pans and bake for 50-55 minutes, until a toothpick inserted near the center comes out clean with a few crumbs clinging to it. Remove bread from pans and cool completely on a wire rack.

Notes: Slices of bread freeze well wrapped individually.
If using a standard gluten-free flour blend, add ½ teaspoon xanthan gum to the dry ingredients.

Pumpkin Bread

One day I was trying to use up my remaining supply of a standard gluten-free flour blend, and wanted to add some quinoa flour to the mix.
This recipe is the result. Although the glaze is a great way to gild the lily, it is perfectly good on its own.
If you prefer, you can substitute Wendy's gluten-free flour mix for all of the flour in this recipe while reducing the xanthan gum by half.

ingredients:

¾ cup vegetable oil

4 eggs

One can (15-ounces) pumpkin puree

1¾ cups sugar

¼ cup orange juice

½ cup quinoa flour

2 cups standard gluten-free flour blend
    (page 181)

¾ cup sweet rice flour

¼ cup cornstarch

1¾ teaspoons xanthan gum

2 teaspoons baking powder

2 teaspoons baking soda

¾ teaspoon salt

½ teaspoon ground cloves

1 teaspoon cinnamon

1 teaspoon nutmeg

1 cup chopped pecans

Glaze

1 cup confectioners' sugar

¼ teaspoon nutmeg

¼ teaspoon cinnamon

⅓ cup orange juice

makes 2 loaves

Preheat oven to 350°F. Butter two 5 x 9-inch loaf pans.

Blend oil, eggs, and pumpkin puree together in a large bowl. Gradually add sugar, mixing well. Stir in orange juice.

Sift together flours, cornstarch, xanthan gum, baking powder, baking soda, salt, cloves, cinnamon, and nutmeg in a medium bowl. Slowly add sifted ingredients to the pumpkin mixture until well combined. Stir in pecans.

Pour batter into prepared pans and bake for 55 minutes, or until a toothpick inserted near the center comes out clean with a few crumbs clinging to it. Remove bread from pans. If you want to glaze the bread, whisk sugar, nutmeg, cinnamon, and orange juice together in a small bowl. Pour glaze over each loaf of warm pumpkin bread and allow it to soak in for a minute. Cool loaves completely on a wire rack.

Note: The addition of sweet rice flour and cornstarch provides a smooth texture to the otherwise gritty standard gluten-free flour blend.

Carrot Bread

A tasty, hearty sweet bread, so good that you will never miss the wheat! Make muffins from this recipe for a quick on-the-go snack.
You can substitute amaranth or quinoa flour for up to half of the flour mix.
Recipe adapted from *Breakfast in Bed*, Carol Frieberg (Sasquatch Books, 1990).

ingredients:

3 eggs plus 1 egg white

½ cup vegetable oil

½ cup unsweetened applesauce

2 teaspoons vanilla extract

2 cups finely grated carrots

2 cups grated unsweetened coconut*

1 cup raisins or currants

1 cup chopped walnuts

2 cups Wendy Wark's gluten-free
　flour mix (page 181)

¾ teaspoon xanthan gum

1 cup sugar

1 teaspoon baking powder

1 teaspoon baking soda

1 teaspoon ground cinnamon

½ teaspoon salt

Ask the folks at Ener-G Foods about their coconut. It is not on the price list, but they sometimes sell it in bulk. Their coconut is more finely grated than the brands in the local grocery store, and it is guaranteed gluten-free.

makes one loaf or 18 muffins

Preheat oven to 350°F. Butter a 5 x 9-inch loaf pan or 18 muffin cups.

In a large bowl, beat eggs until yolks and whites are well combined. Add oil, applesauce, and vanilla, mixing well. Stir in carrots, coconut, raisins, and walnuts.

Sift flour, xanthan gum, sugar, baking powder, baking soda, cinnamon, and salt in a medium bowl. Add sifted mix to carrot mixture gradually until thoroughly combined.

Pour batter into prepared pan or muffin tin. Bake loaf for 1 hour, muffins for 30 minutes. (A toothpick inserted near the center should come out clean with a few crumbs clinging to it.) Remove bread from pan and cool completely on a wire rack.

Note: If using a standard gluten-free flour blend, add 1/2 teaspoon xanthan gum to the dry ingredients.

Blueberry Muffins

These muffins are easy to make fresh in the morning. They take about 10 minutes to mix and about 20 minutes to bake.
To make a healthier muffin, try substituting at least ½ cup of amaranth or quinoa flour for the flour mix.

ingredients:

1½ cups Wendy Wark's gluten-free
    flour mix (page 181).

½ teaspoon xanthan gum

¾ cups sugar

2 teaspoons baking powder

1 teaspoon cinnamon

¼ teaspoon salt

1½ teaspoons lemon zest
    (grated lemon peel)

½ cup milk

½ cup vegetable oil

1 large egg

1 cup fresh or frozen blueberries

makes 12 muffins

Preheat oven to 350°F. Use a non-stick muffin tin if available; if not, butter 12 standard muffin cups.

In a medium mixing bowl, combine flour, xanthan gum, sugar, baking powder, cinnamon, and salt. Make a well in the center of the flour mix and add lemon zest, milk, vegetable oil, and egg. Blend thoroughly with a fork until smooth, then fold in the berries. (Be very careful not to over mix.) Divide batter into prepared muffin cups.

Bake for 20-25 minutes, or until a toothpick inserted near the center comes out clean with a few crumbs clinging to it. Cool muffins in the tin for a few minutes. Remove muffins and serve warm, or cool completely on wire rack and keep on hand for breakfast on the run.

Note: If using a standard gluten-free flour blend, add ¼ teaspoon xanthan gum to the dry ingredients.

Banana Bread

If you do not have time to make the bread right away, freeze your ripe bananas for later use in this recipe.

ingredients:

½ cup unsalted butter, softened

1 cup sugar

1 teaspoon vanilla extract

2 eggs

4 medium, ripe bananas, peeled and mashed

1 teaspoon milk

2 cups Wendy Wark's flour mix (page 181)

½ teaspoon xanthan gum

1 teaspoon baking soda

¼ teaspoon salt

makes one loaf

Preheat oven to 350°F. Butter a 5 x 9-inch loaf pan.

Cream butter, sugar, and vanilla on high speed until pale in color and light in texture. Beat in eggs one at a time until well blended. With a fork, mix bananas and milk in a small bowl and set aside. In another small bowl, combine the flour, xanthan gum, baking soda, and salt. Blend dry ingredients into the creamed mixture alternately with banana mixture.

Turn batter into prepared pan and bake for 1 hour, until a toothpick inserted near the center comes out clean with a few crumbs clinging to it. Remove from pan and cool completely on a wire rack.

Note: If using a standard gluten-free flour blend, add ¼ teaspoon xanthan gum to the dry ingredients.

Hazelnut Zucchini Bread

Each year our garden overflows with zucchini, thus the need for a variety of zucchini bread recipes in our home.
Hazelnuts add a wonderful flavor; if you can find the thin-skinned Duchilly variety, you can save yourself the trouble of roasting them and rubbing off the skin.

ingredients:

2 cups Wendy Wark's gluten-free
   flour mix (page 181)
¾ teaspoon xanthan gum
1 teaspoon baking soda
¾ teaspoon baking powder
¼ teaspoon salt
1¼ cups sugar
2 large eggs
½ cup vegetable oil
⅓ cup orange juice
2 teaspoons orange zest
2 teaspoons ginger juice or
   peeled grated ginger root
1 teaspoon vanilla extract
1½ cups grated zucchini
½ cup finely chopped hazelnuts,
   bitter skin removed*

*To remove the skin, spread hazelnuts on a baking sheet in an even layer. Roast at 350°F. for 10-15 minutes, or until skins begin to flake. Place a handful of hazelnuts into a dish towel and rub the nuts until most of the skin is removed. Repeat with remaining hazelnuts.

makes one loaf or 18 muffins

Preheat oven to 350°F. Butter a 5 x 9-inch loaf pan or 18 muffin cups.

Sift flour, xanthan gum, baking soda, baking powder, salt, and sugar into a large bowl. Whisk eggs, oil, orange juice, zest, ginger, and vanilla together in a small bowl. Stir the egg mixture into the flour mixture until combined. Gently stir in zucchini and hazelnuts.

Pour batter into prepared pan or muffin tin. Bake for 45-50 minutes (20-25 minutes for muffins), or until a toothpick inserted near the center comes out clean with a few crumbs clinging to it. Cool in the pan for 10 minutes, then turn out onto a wire rack to cool completely.

Note: If using a standard gluten-free flour blend, add 1/4 teaspoon xanthan gum to the dry ingredients.

Introduction to Sweets 180

Recommended Flours 181

Cookies

Almond Quinoa Cookies 182

Macaroons 183

Chocolate Chip Cookies 184

Molasses Cookies 185

Cut-out Cookies with Royal Icing 186

Gingersnap Cookies 187

Mexican Wedding Cakes 188

Chocolate Confections

Rocky Road 189

Java Chocolate Truffles 190

Cakes

Chewy Brownies
with Raspberry Sauce 191

Yellow Butter Cake
with Chocolate Frosting 192

Sour Cream Coffee Cake 193

Lemon Cake 194

Pound Cake 195

Chocolate Cashew Cake 196

Chocolate Cake with
Chocolate Glaze 198

Carrot Cake 200

Orange Cheesecake 201

Pies and Tarts

Pie Crust Dough 202

Pumpkin Pie 203

Apple Pie 204

Apple Tart 205

Elegant Fruit Desserts

Grand Marnier Semifreddo
with Bittersweet Chocolate Sauce
and Local Blackberries 206
Chef Todd Gray

Baked Pears 207

Cranberry Soufflé 208
Chef Hans Bergmann

Local Berries with Crème Fraîche 209

Panna Cotta
with Dried Fruit Compote 210
Chef Suzanne Goin

Floating Islands
with Caramel Blood Oranges 212
Chef Gerry Hayden

SWEETS

Sweets

This chapter is the home of decadent treats. If you take the time to bake for yourself, you will no longer feel deprived. Whether you believe it or not, you have the ability to make delicious, tempting baked goods. There is no need to eat dry, tasteless gluten-free duds. If you are going to eat something fattening, it should taste fabulous. (Make it worth the indulgence!). If you freeze your baked goods, you will always have something on hand when time is short. Keep in mind that children find it very important to have terrific gluten-free goodies on hand.

Home baking allows you to control the ingredients for the healthiest possible baked goods. You can both exclude saturated fats and include nutritious flours such as teff, quinoa, amaranth, and buckwheat. Try using unrefined sugar as much as possible. See Sources in the Appendix for sugar substitutes and the new organic shortening available in many natural food markets.

TEFF, QUINOA, AMARANTH, AND BUCKWHEAT FLOURS ARE GREAT IN SWEET BREADS, PANCAKES, CARROT CAKES, AND SOME COOKIES. WHEN USING THESE FLOURS SUBSTITUTE THEM FOR UP TO ONE HALF OF THE FLOUR IN A RECIPE.

Substitutions for the lactose intolerant are found on page 217.

Don't be concerned if a recipe seems to have a lot of ingredients. Mixing the many dry ingredients takes just five minutes longer than opening up a prepackaged mix, and your results will be far superior in taste, quality, and healthfulness.

Be sure to keep gluten-free flours in airtight containers, as the flour will absorb moisture from the air, affecting the outcome of your baked goods.

Many of the recipes suggest using parchment lined baking sheets. You may grease your baking sheets with organic shortening instead, but parchment provides for much easier cleanup.

Recommended Flours

This mix makes the best gluten-free baked goods. It produces a tender, moist end product that I have not found with any other formula. Triple the measurements to have a large supply on hand for all your baking. It should be refrigerated in an airtight container to keep the brown rice flour fresh.

Wendy Wark's Gluten-Free Flour Mix

Flour mix recipe from Wendy Wark's book, *Living Healthy with Celiac Disease* (AnAffect, 1998). This book is full of recipes and resources. Wendy has graciously allowed me to include several of her recipes in my book. To order her book, see the Appendix.

1 cup brown rice flour
1¼ cup white rice flour*
¼ cup potato starch flour
⅔ cup tapioca starch flour
¾ cup sweet rice flour
⅓ cup cornstarch
2 teaspoons xanthan or guar gum

* I like to omit the white rice flour and use all brown rice flour (2¼ cups).

Authentic Foods provides this flour mix under the name Multi Blend Gluten-Free Flour. You may purchase this flour blend at www.authenticfoods.com or 1.800.806.4737. The blend is also available in natural food markets nationwide.

Healthy Alternative Flour Guideline

For healthier baked goods, use an alternative flour such as teff, quinoa, amaranth, or buckweat for ½ the flour in a recipe and use Wendy's mix for the other ½ of the flour in a recipe.

Optional Flour Base
(Standard Gluten-Free Flour Blend)

Though I never use it, this blend is available from several gluten-free mail order sources. Recipes in this book show a xanthan gum addition (at the bottom of each page) for readers who choose to use this standard gluten-free flour blend.

2 parts rice flour (use brown rice flour for healthier results)
⅔ part potato starch flour
⅓ part tapioca starch flour

Xanthan Gum

You can revise your favorite recipes by using this guideline for adding xanthan gum. Xanthan gum replaces gluten and acts as a binding agent. It must be an ingredient in all baked goods based on gluten-free flour. When using Wendy Wark's flour, use this guideline but reduce the xanthan gum by ¼ teaspoon or so, since her mix already includes some.

Bread   *1 teaspoon per cup of flour mix*
Cakes   *½ teaspoon per cup of flour mix*
Cookies   *¼ teaspoon per cup of flour mix*

Almond Quinoa Cookies

We have really missed the flavor, texture, and nutrition of oatmeal cookies. After some experimentation, I have recreated an "oatmeal cookie" with quinoa flakes and ground almonds. The cookies are fabulous! Guittard chocolate chips are optional; any gluten-free chocolate chip will work, but in taste testing conducted at our home and at *Cook's Illustrated* magazine, Guittard chocolate chips were the number one choice. I use Ancient Harvest quinoa flakes (see Sources).

ingredients:

1 cup unsalted butter, softened

1 cup granulated sugar

1 cup packed brown sugar

2 eggs plus one egg white

1 teaspoon vanilla extract

2 cups Wendy Wark's gluten-free
    flour mix (page 181)

½ teaspoon xanthan gum

1½ cups almonds or pecans, finely ground

1⅛ cups quinoa flakes

7 ounces finely grated Guittard bulk
    chocolate

½ teaspoon salt

1 teaspoon baking powder

1 teaspoon baking soda

12 ounces Guittard chocolate chips or raisins

makes 5 dozen cookies

Preheat oven to 375°F. In a large bowl, cream butter and sugars on high speed until light in texture. Add eggs and vanilla, mixing well. Combine flour, xanthan gum, ground nuts, quinoa flakes, grated chocolate, salt, baking powder, and baking soda in a medium mixing bowl. Slowly add flour mixture to creamed butter, mixing until well incorporated. Add chocolate chips and mix well.

Drop by rounded teaspoonfuls on a cookie sheet lined with parchment and bake for 8–10 minutes. Remove to a cooling rack.

variation:

You may substitute quinoa flakes for the almonds and omit the grated chocolate. This version tastes a lot like oatmeal cookies and is less time consuming.

Notes: If using a standard gluten-free flour blend, add ¹/₂ teaspoon xanthan gum to the dry ingredients.
A rotary grater makes the task of grating chocolate much easier.
A Hershey bar may be substituted for the Guittard bulk chocolate.

Macaroons

This is a yummy sweet to add to your holiday cookie assortment. I have found that these are the ones that usually disappear first!
The texture of unsweetened coconut is preferred, though it can be difficult to find. If you use unsweetened coconut, triple the amount of sugar in the recipe.

ingredients:

½ cup sugar

4 cups sweetened coconut

3 large egg whites

Pinch of salt

2 tablespoons unsalted butter, melted

1 teaspoon vanilla extract

4 ounces semi-sweet chocolate

½ teaspoon organic shortening

makes 35 pyramid-shaped macaroons

Using your hands, mix together sugar, coconut, egg whites, and salt in a large bowl. Add butter and vanilla, mixing well. Refrigerate mixture for at least an hour.

Preheat oven to 350°F. Line two baking sheets with parchment paper. Run cool water over your hands, shaking off excess water, and shape coconut mixture by tablespoons into pyramid forms. Place macaroons on prepared baking sheets, spacing 1-inch apart. Bake for 15 minutes, or until edges are golden brown. Transfer baking sheet to a wire rack. Let macaroons cool completely before removing.

Melt chocolate and shortening in the top of a double boiler, stirring occasionally. Dip top of each macaroon in the melted chocolate to a depth of ½-inch. Let chocolate set until firm before serving. (Brief refrigeration will hasten the process.)

Chocolate Chip Cookies

This is the basic recipe on the back of most chocolate chip bags. You can use the standard gluten-free flour blend, though Wendy's flour mix will yield a better result.

ingredients:

2 sticks (1 cup) unsalted butter, softened

¾ cup granulated sugar

¾ cup packed brown sugar

2 eggs

1 teaspoon vanilla extract

2¼ cups Wendy Wark's gluten-free
   flour mix (page 181)

½ teaspoon xanthan gum

1 teaspoon baking soda

1 teaspoon salt

1 cup chopped walnuts

2 cups chocolate chips

makes 5 dozen cookies

Preheat oven to 375°F.

Cream butter and sugars on high speed until light in texture. Add eggs and vanilla, mixing well. Combine flour, xanthan gum, baking soda, and salt in a medium bowl. Add gradually to the creamed mixture until well incorporated. Add walnuts and chocolate chips, mixing well.

Drop mixture by rounded teaspoonful onto an ungreased baking sheet and bake for 8 minutes. Remove baking sheet from oven. Let stand for a few minutes before transferring cookies to a cooling rack.

Molasses Cookies

Every year during the holidays, my grandma made "from scratch" cookies and peanut brittle. The molasses cookies were always my favorite. Luckily for all of us, Grandma's recipe was handed down through the family. This recipe does not use eggs, has a higher proportion of spices than other molasses cookie recipes, and uses cold coffee for a big flavor punch. As the standard gluten-free flour blend is a bit too grainy for this recipe, I highly recommend using Wendy Wark's flour mix.

ingredients:

1½ cups granulated sugar

1 cup organic shortening

½ cup molasses

½ cup cold coffee

3¾ cups Wendy Wark's gluten-free
    flour mix (page 181)

½ teaspoon xanthan gum

2 teaspoons baking soda

1 teaspoon ground cloves

1 teaspoon ginger

1 teaspoon cinnamon

Granulated sugar

makes 6 dozen small cookies

Preheat oven to 375°F.

Cream sugar and shortening on high speed until pale in color and light in texture. Add molasses and coffee, mixing well. In a medium bowl, combine flour, xanthan gum, baking soda, cloves, ginger, and cinnamon. Slowly add flour mixture to molasses mixture until well incorporated. Chill dough for 20 minutes.

Roll cookie dough into balls the size of walnuts and dip one side into sugar. Place sugar side up on a parchment lined baking sheet. Bake for 7 minutes.

Notes: These cookies make a great cheesecake crust.
If using a standard gluten-free flour blend, add ½ teaspoon xanthan gum to the dry ingredients.

Cut-out Cookies with Royal Icing

Gluten intolerant children really enjoy having holiday cookies to roll, cut out, and decorate.
The recipe was adapted from Carol Fenster's version found in a back issue of *Living Without*. (See Sources for more information on this helpful magazine.)

ingredients:

¼ cup unsalted butter, softened

2 tablespoons honey

½ cup sugar

1 tablespoon vanilla

2 teaspoons grated lemon peel

1½ cups Wendy Wark's gluten-free
   flour mix (page 181)

½ teaspoon salt

1 teaspoon baking powder

½ teaspoon baking soda

2-3 tablespoons water

Royal Icing

½ cup organic shortening

4 cups confectioners' sugar

¼ cup water

Food coloring

makes thirty 3-inch cookies

Cream butter, honey, and sugar on high speed until pale in color and light in texture; scrape the bowl periodically while creaming. Add vanilla and grated lemon peel, combining thoroughly. Sift flour, salt, baking powder, and baking soda. Gradually add flour mixture to creamed mixture. Once combined, add water as needed to form a soft dough. Gather dough into a ball, wrap tightly in plastic wrap, and chill in the refrigerator for 30 minutes.

Preheat oven to 325°F. Line two baking sheets with parchment paper.

Remove half of the dough from the refrigerator. Roll out dough to ¼-inch thickness between two sheets of wax paper. Cut out cookies with a cookie cutter, then lift cookies off wax paper with a spatula and transfer to prepared baking sheet. Place baking sheet in the refrigerator while rolling out the second half of the dough.

Bake for 10-12 minutes. Cool on baking sheet for a few minutes, then turn out onto a wire rack to cool completely before frosting.

Royal Icing:

In a small bowl, combine shortening and sugar with a fork. Add water gradually to a spreading consistency. Mix in food coloring to desired tint. Fill a pastry decorating bag with icing (or use a sandwich size plastic bag with one corner snipped off). Squeeze icing out in a decorative pattern.

Gingersnap Cookies

When you roll out these cookies, the dough will seem terribly crumbly, and you may wonder if you have gone wrong somewhere. Don't worry; they will hold together beautifully and make a delicious, crispy ginger snap. This recipe makes good "gingerbread people."

ingredients:

6 tablespoons unsalted butter

½ cup sugar

2 tablespoons light corn syrup

1½ cups Wendy Wark's gluten-free
   flour mix (page 181)

¼ teaspoon xanthan gum

2 teaspoons ground ginger

½ teaspoon baking soda

Icing

½ cup confectioners' sugar

2 teaspoons water

makes 8 large cookies (using 6-inch cookie cutters)

Preheat oven to 350°F. Grease two cookie sheets or line them with parchment paper.

Melt butter, sugar, and corn syrup in a heavy-bottomed saucepan, stirring occasionally. Remove from heat when butter is melted and ingredients are well combined. Let cool while mixing dry ingredients.

Sift flour, xanthan gum, ginger, and baking soda in a medium bowl. Make a well in the center of the flour mixture. Pour melted butter mixture into well and mix thoroughly with a wooden spoon.

Using your hands, form the dough into a ball. Roll out dough on a lightly floured surface to ¼-inch thickness. Cut out cookies with cookie cutter. Carefully lift each cookie with a spatula and transfer to prepared cookie sheet.

Bake for 10-12 minutes. Cool cookies on baking sheet for a few minutes before transferring to a wire rack. Let cool 5 minutes longer.

Icing: While cookies are cooling, sift confectioners' sugar into a small bowl. Add water and beat until smooth. Spoon icing into a pastry bag with a small decorating tip (or spoon into a clean plastic bag with one corner snipped off). Decorate cookies and let icing set for one hour, or until hardened.

Note: If using a standard gluten-free flour blend, add ⅛ teaspoon xanthan gum to the dry ingredients.

Mexican Wedding Cakes

My sister-in-law has made these cookies a Christmas tradition.
Present them on a beautiful platter with other assorted holiday cookies such as macaroons, cut-out cookies decorated with icing, shortbread, or any of your family favorites.
The secret of converting the original recipe to a gluten-free version is the substitution of either sour cream or cream cheese for some or all of the butter.

ingredients:

¾ cup unsalted butter, softened

¼ cup gluten-free sour cream or
  cream cheese, room temperature

½ cup confectioners' sugar

1 teaspoon vanilla extract

2 cups Wendy Wark's gluten-free
  flour mix (page 181)

Scant ½ teaspoon xanthan gum

¼ teaspoon salt

¼ cup jam, raspberry or boysenberry

makes four dozen 1 1/2-inch cookies

Preheat oven to 400°F.

Cream butter, sour cream, and sugar together on high speed until light and airy in texture. Add vanilla and mix well. Sift flour, xanthan gum, and salt into a small bowl. Gradually add flour mixture to creamed butter, mixing well. (Dough will look like a coarse meal.) Continue to beat on high speed long enough for the butter to soften and the dough to form a soft mass.

Shape the dough by tablespoons into balls. Place onto an ungreased baking sheet. Make a thumbprint impression in each ball and fill with a bit of jam. Refrigerate cookies for 15 minutes prior to baking. Bake cookies for 11-12 minutes, or until lightly browned. Remove to a wire rack to cool completely, then sprinkle lightly with confectioners' sugar.

Rocky Road

Another holiday favorite that is especially easy for children learning how to cook.
If you have gluten intolerant children, introduce them to the kitchen early in life to develop a love of cooking.

ingredients:

8 ounces semi-sweet chocolate

1 cup gluten-free miniature marshmallows

½ cup chopped walnuts

makes 35 bite-sized pieces

Microwave chocolate in a glass bowl on high heat for 20 seconds. Stir with a rubber spatula. Repeat heating in 10-20 second increments, stirring each time, until chocolate is melted. (The repeated stirring will prevent burning.) Stir in marshmallows and nuts until thoroughly coated.

Spread mixture evenly onto a baking sheet. Cover and refrigerate to harden (about 30 minutes). Bring candy to room temperature, then cut into bite-size pieces.

Java Chocolate Truffles

Prior to writing this cookbook, I was known within the Gluten Intolerance Group as the gluten-free chocolate truffle lady.
The truffles are so fresh they rival those purchased at the fancy chocolate shops. This is a quick home version that anyone can handle.
If you would like to hand dip your truffles, rent a Sinsation tempering machine to simplify that process. Fine European chocolate is recommended for the best results.
Recipe provided by Bill Fredericks, The Chocolate Man, purveyor of fine chocolates and truffle-making supplies (see Sources).

ingredients:

8 ounces milk chocolate

¼ cup mocha coffee beans

⅔ cup cream

1 cup cocoa for coating

makes 3 dozen

Place chocolate in a glass bowl. Heat in a microwave oven for 30 seconds. Remove and stir until smooth. If some bits of chocolate remain, microwave in 10-20 second increments until completely melted.

Grind coffee coarsely, then pass through a sieve to remove fine particles. (This will prevent a gritty texture in the truffle mixture.)

Mix cream and ground coffee together in a small saucepan. Bring to a simmer and remove from heat. For a stronger coffee flavor, simmer for a few minutes.

Pour cream into a small bowl through a sieve to catch the coffee grounds. When chocolate and cream have cooled to lukewarm, combine and whisk together thoroughly. This mixture is called ganache. Once ganache has cooled, cover with plastic wrap and chill to set.

Scoop ganache into balls, using a 1-inch scoop with a release lever. (You may also form a 1-inch piece with a spoon and roll into a ball with your fingers). Drop each ganache ball into a shallow bowl of cocoa and roll about until thoroughly coated. Shake off excess and arrange on a serving plate.

Notes: Oils can be used to flavor the ganache, as opposed to the liqueurs commonly used.
Since it is difficult to determine the gluten-free status of liqueurs, flavored oils are a better choice (see Sources).
For the dark chocolate lover, try substituting 4 ounces of bittersweet and
4 ounces of semi-sweet chocolate for the milk chocolate.

Chewy Brownies with Raspberry Sauce

There are many ways to make brownies, but we prefer the kind that are chewy, crackled on top, and intensely chocolate. This recipe is an improved version of the brownie recipe in the first edition of the book; it was adapted from *Cook's Illustrated* (May & June 2000). Raspberry sauce and a scoop of vanilla ice cream can transform a brownie into an elegant dessert. The contrasting flavors work very well together.

ingredients:

½ cup (1 stick) unsalted butter

5 ounces semisweet chocolate

2 ounces unsweetened chocolate

3 tablespoons cocoa powder

3 large eggs

1¼ cups sugar

2 teaspoons vanilla extract

½ teaspoon salt

1 cup Wendy Wark's gluten-free
   flour mix (page 181)

½ teaspoon xanthan gum

¾ semisweet chocolate chips (optional)

Raspberry Sauce

2 cups raspberries

½ cup sugar

½ cup water

1 teaspoon lemon juice

makes 16 brownies (2-inches square)

Preheat oven to 350°F. Butter an 8-inch square glass baking dish. Line the bottom with parchment and then butter the parchment.

Melt butter and chocolate in the top of a double boiler, stirring occasionally until smooth. Remove from heat, whisk in cocoa powder, and let cool slightly.

In a medium bowl, whisk together eggs, sugar, vanilla, and salt until thoroughly blended. Whisk in warm chocolate mixture then stir in flour and xanthan gum until just combined. Pour ½ of the batter into the prepared baking dish and sprinkle chocolate chips evenly over the top. Pour the last ½ of the batter over the top of the chips, covering completely and scraping the bowl well.

Bake for 35-40 minutes, or until a toothpick comes out clean with a few crumbs clinging to it. Set the dish on a wire rack until cool enough to handle. Run a knife between the walls of the dish and the baked brownie mixture and invert onto a flat surface to release. Peel off the parchment and place brownie sheet on the rack to cool completely.

When completely cool, place brownie sheet on a cutting board. Using a thin, sharp knife, cut into 16 squares, wiping the knife between cuts to ensure smooth, clean edges. Brownies can be frozen in individual serving sizes; wrap each tightly in plastic wrap, then seal in a large freezer bag.

Raspberry Sauce:
Bring raspberries, sugar, and water to a boil in a nonreactive saucepan, stirring occasionally. Remove from heat. Stir in lemon juice. Puree in a blender. Strain through a sieve, pushing on the solids and discarding the seeds. Adjust quantity of sugar or lemon juice if necessary.

Note: If using a standard gluten-free flour blend, add ¹/₂ teaspoon xanthan gum to the dry ingredients.

Yellow Butter Cake with Chocolate Frosting

This simple cake with chocolate frosting is a birthday classic. As with all cakes made with Wendy's flour mix, this cake will stay moist for several days — if it lasts that long!

ingredients:

8 tablespoons (1 stick) unsalted butter,
    softened

1 cup sugar

4 eggs, separated, plus one egg white

½ cup cold water

1 teaspoon vanilla extract

2 cups Wendy Wark's gluten-free
    flour mix (page 181)

½ teaspoon xanthan gum

½ teaspoon salt

4 teaspoons baking powder

Chocolate Frosting

2 ounces unsweetened chocolate

1 tablespoon butter

⅓ cup milk

2 cups confectioner's sugar, sifted

1 teaspoon vanilla extract

comment:

The Chocolate Frosting recipe makes enough for an 8-inch or 9-inch two-layer cake. This is a smooth, spreadable frosting. If you like a thick layer of frosting, you will want to double the recipe.

makes two, 8-inch rounds or 18 cupcakes

Preheat oven to 350°F. Butter and lightly flour two 8-inch round cake pans.

In a large bowl, beat the butter and sugar until pale in color and light in texture. Add egg yolks and cold water, mixing well. Add vanilla and blend. In a medium bowl, combine flour, xanthan gum, salt, and baking powder. Add to the butter mixture. In a small bowl, using an electric mixer, beat the egg whites until stiff but not dry. Carefully fold egg whites into the cake batter. Pour batter into prepared pans. Bake for 20-25 minutes, until a toothpick inserted near the center comes out clean with a few crumbs clinging to it. Let cake rest in pans for 5-10 minutes, then turn out onto a cooling rack. Cool completely before frosting.

If making cupcakes, use a non-stick muffin tin or butter 18 muffin cups. Divide batter into muffin cups and bake for 12-13 minutes, until the toothpick test shows them to be done. Allow cupcakes to cool for 5 minutes in the tin before turning out onto a cooling rack.

Chocolate Frosting: In a double boiler, melt chocolate, butter, and milk together. Remove from heat and cool to lukewarm. Add sugar and vanilla. Beat with an electric mixer to a spreading consistency.

Note: If using a standard gluten-free flour blend, add ½ teaspoon xanthan gum to the dry ingredients.

Sour Cream Coffee Cake

This is an old family recipe that we make throughout the year. It is also part of our Christmas morning breakfast each year.
My husband is from a family of accomplished cooks, and they could not believe I made the cake with gluten-free ingredients. It is fantastic!

ingredients:

½ cup organic shortening

¾ cup sugar

1 teaspoon vanilla extract

3 eggs

2 cups Wendy Wark's gluten-free
   flour mix (page 181)

½ teaspoon xanthan gum

1 teaspoon baking powder

1 teaspoon baking soda

1¼ cups gluten-free sour cream

6 tablespoons unsalted butter, softened

1 cup brown sugar

2 teaspoons cinnamon

1 cup chopped nuts (walnuts or pecans)

makes one 10-inch cake

Preheat oven to 350°F. Butter a 10-inch tube pan, then line with parchment cut to cover the bottom and sides. Butter inner surface of parchment.

In a large bowl, beat shortening and sugar until pale in color and light in texture. Add vanilla, then add eggs one at a time, beating well after each addition.

Sift flour, xanthan gum, baking powder, and baking soda in a medium bowl. Add sifted mix to creamed mixture alternately with sour cream, blending after each addition. Spread half the batter in prepared tube pan. Using a pastry blender or a fork, combine butter, brown sugar, cinnamon, and nuts in a medium bowl. Sprinkle half of the nut mixture over the batter, then cover nut mixture with remaining batter. Sprinkle remaining nut mixture on top.

Bake for 50-55 minutes, until a toothpick inserted near the center comes out clean with a few crumbs clinging to it. Allow cake to cool in the pan for 15 minutes. Invert cake and place on a cooling rack. Let cake cool completely before slicing.

Notes: If using a standard gluten-free flour blend, add ¹/₂ teaspoon xanthan gum to the dry ingredients.
You may substitute regular shortening for organic shortening,
although the latter is strongly recommended as it is much healthier.

Lemon Cake

Many lemon cakes are too sweet and heavily glazed. This version has a nice lemon flavor and a light glaze. It is an excellent and easy-to-make recipe.
Recipe adapted from *The Silver Palate Cookbook*, Rosso and Lukins (Workman Publishing, 1982).

ingredients:

½ pound (2 sticks) unsalted butter,
   room temperature
2 cups sugar
3 large eggs plus 1 egg white
3 cups Wendy Wark's gluten-free
   flour mix (page 181)
1 teaspoon xanthan gum
½ teaspoon baking soda
½ teaspoon salt
1 cup buttermilk
1 tablespoon grated lemon peel
2 tablespoons fresh lemon juice

Lemon Glaze

1 cup confectioners' sugar
6 tablespoons unsalted butter,
   room temperature
1 tablespoon grated lemon peel
¼ cup fresh lemon juice

makes one 10-inch cake

Preheat oven to 325°F. Butter and flour a 10-inch tube pan or a 12-cup Bundt pan.

In a large bowl, beat butter and sugar on medium-high speed until pale in color and a light texture. Add eggs one at a time, mixing well after each addition.

Sift together flour mix, xanthan gum, baking soda, and salt in a medium bowl. Add flour mixture to egg mixture a little at a time, alternating with buttermilk, until all is well incorporated. Add grated lemon peel and juice.

Pour batter into prepared pan and bake for 1 hour and 5 minutes, or until a toothpick inserted near the center comes out clean with a few crumbs clinging to it. Cool for 12 minutes in the pan before turning out onto a wire rack. Prepare Lemon Glaze.

Lemon Glaze: In a small mixing bowl, beat butter and sugar on medium-high speed until light and creamy. Add grated lemon peel and juice, mixing well. Spread glaze over the top of warm cake. (The icing will soak in a little, and it will crystallize at room temperature.)

Note: If using a standard gluten-free flour blend, add ¹/₄ teaspoon xanthan gum to the dry ingredients.

Pound Cake

Known affectionately in the Robertson family as a sandtorte, this cake has gone through much testing to get the gluten-free version right. Our daughter Carmen has begun to cook and has further refined this recipe to excellence! Serve with fresh, local strawberries and vanilla ice cream for a fantastic dessert!

ingredients:

1 cup unsalted butter, room temperature

3 cups sugar

6 eggs

3 cups Wendy Wark's gluten-free
   flour mix (page 181) **

½ teaspoon xanthan gum

¼ teaspoon baking powder

¾ cup gluten-free sour cream

1½ teaspoons vanilla extract

Confectioners' sugar for dusting top of cake

** this dense cake requires that you make the Wendy Wark's flour mix yourself with a fine brown rice flour from Ener-G Foods. Be sure to use white rice flour in the mix too.

makes one 10-inch cake

Preheat oven to 350°F. Butter and flour a 10-inch tube pan or a 12-cup Bundt pan.

Cream butter and sugar in a medium bowl on high speed until pale colored and light in texture. Add eggs one at a time, blending well after each addition.

Sift flour, xanthan gum, and baking powder in a small bowl. Add flour mixture to creamed mixture, alternating with sour cream. Add vanilla and mix well.

Bake for 1 hour and 30 minutes, or until a toothpick inserted near the center comes out clean with a few crumbs clinging to it. Let cake stand for 10-15 minutes in the pan before turning out onto a cooling rack.

When cake is completely cool, sprinkle with a light dusting of confectioners' sugar, using a fine mesh sieve.

Note: If using a standard gluten-free flour blend, add 1/2 teaspoon xanthan gum to the dry ingredients.

Chocolate Cashew Cake

This cake is absolutely decadent. Although it takes a bit of time, it is well worth the effort.
My sister-in-law introduced this cake to our family. Since then, every birthday cake request has become one for cashew cake! (Thank you, Heather!)
To fit the preparation time into your busy schedule, make the filling and frosting one day then make the cake the following day.

ingredients:

Cake

½ cup unsweetened cocoa

½ cup boiling water

½ cup unsalted butter, softened

2 cups sugar

2 eggs plus 1 egg white

1 teaspoon vanilla extract

1¾ cups Wendy Wark's gluten-free
   flour mix (page 181)

½ teaspoon xanthan gum

1 teaspoon baking powder

1 teaspoon baking soda

1⅓ cups buttermilk

1½ cups finely chopped cashews

frosting:

Six 1-ounce squares semi-sweet
   chocolate

¼ cup Wendy Wark's gluten-free
   flour mix (page 181)

⅔ cup sugar

¾ cup milk

1½ teaspoons vanilla extract

1 cup cold unsalted butter,
   cut into tablespoons

filling:

¾ cup whipping cream

2 teaspoons vanilla extract

1 tablespoon sugar

makes three 8-inch rounds

Preheat oven to 350°F. Butter and lightly flour three 8-inch round cake pans.

In a small heatproof bowl, stir cocoa into boiling water. Set aside to cool.

In a large bowl, cream butter and sugar until pale in color and light in texture. Add eggs and vanilla, mixing well. Sift flour, xanthan gum, baking powder, and baking soda in a medium bowl.

Add flour mixture slowly to butter mixture, blending until combined. Add buttermilk and mix thoroughly.

In a small bowl, mix 1⅓ cups of cake batter with cashews. Pour into one of the prepared cake pans.

Add the cooled cocoa mixture to the remaining batter, mixing well. Divide chocolate batter between two remaining cake pans.

Bake for 30-35 minutes, or until a toothpick inserted near the center comes out clean with a few crumbs clinging to it. Let cake layers stand for five minutes before removing from pans. Cool completely on a wire rack before frosting.

continued:

Chocolate Cashew Cake

Frosting: Melt semi-sweet chocolate in the top of a double boiler and cool to room temperature. (Chocolate can also be microwaved in 20 second increments. Stir frequently to avoid burning).

In a small heavy saucepan, combine flour and sugar over medium heat. Add milk and stir until thick and smooth. Cool to room temperature. Add vanilla and butter (3-4 tablespoons at a time) and beat until smooth with an electric mixer. Add chocolate and mix well. Set aside.

Filling: In a small bowl, combine whipping cream, vanilla, and sugar. Using an electric mixer, whip on high speed until thick.

Once cake layers have completely cooled, assemble cake in the following order on a serving plate: chocolate cake round, half of the filling, cashew cake round, remaining filling, chocolate cake round. Frost the cake.

Note: If using a standard gluten-free flour blend, add 1/4 teaspoon xanthan gum to the dry ingredients.

Chocolate Cake with Chocolate Glaze

This recipe is adapted from Christopher Kimball's master recipe in *The Cook's Bible* (Little Brown, 1996).
The cake provides complete satisfaction for the true chocolate lover. All ingredients should be at room temperature.

ingredients:

1½ cups Wendy Wark's gluten-free
    flour mix (page 181)

½ teaspoon xanthan gum

½ cup unsweetened Dutch process cocoa

¼ teaspoon baking powder

½ teaspoon baking soda

¼ heaping teaspoon salt

12 tablespoons (1½ sticks) unsalted butter,
    room temperature

1¼ cups sugar

2 whole eggs

2 egg whites

1½ teaspoons vanilla extract

½ cup espresso

½ cup buttermilk

Chocolate Glaze

8 ounces semisweet chocolate

1 cup heavy cream

¼ cup light corn syrup

½ teaspoon vanilla extract

comment:

Chocolate Glaze recipe makes enough for a 12-cup Bundt cake or two 8-inch rounds.

makes two 8-inch rounds

Preheat oven to 350°F. Prepare two 8-inch round cake pans or one 12-cup Bundt pan by buttering, lightly coating with cocoa, and tapping out excess cocoa.

Sift flour mix, xanthan gum, cocoa, baking powder, baking soda, and salt into a medium bowl and set aside. Using an electric mixer, beat butter on high speed until pale colored. Add sugar gradually and beat until light and airy in texture (about 3 minutes), scraping the bowl often. On low speed, add eggs and whites one at a time, mixing after each addition. Add vanilla and mix briefly. Then add espresso and buttermilk, alternating with the flour mixture until all is added. Blend well but don't overbeat.

Pour batter into prepared cake pans and bake for 25-30 minutes (10 minutes longer if using a Bundt pan), or until a toothpick inserted near the center comes out clean with a few crumbs clinging to it. Let stand for 10 minutes in the pan before turning out onto a wire rack. Cool completely before frosting.

Note: If using a standard gluten-free flour blend, add 1/4 teaspoon xanthan gum to the dry ingredients.

continued:

Chocolate Cake
with Chocolate Glaze

Chocolate Glaze:

Microwave chocolate in a glass bowl on medium heat for 20 seconds. Remove from oven and stir with a rubber spatula. Repeat heating in 10-20 second increments, stirring each time you heat to prevent burning, until chocolate is melted. (Chocolate tends to hold its shape even when partially melted; stirring will tell you whether it is actually melted or not.)

Combine cream and corn syrup in a heavy saucepan and heat to a simmer. Remove from heat, cool slightly, and slowly add to melted chocolate. Whisk until well blended and smooth. Add vanilla. Allow glaze to cool. (In a 70°F kitchen this can take a few hours). Lift some glaze up with a spoon and allow it to drizzle back into the bowl; when glaze forms a small mound it is ready to use.

For a Bundt cake, simply pour glaze over cake and allow it to drip down the sides. For a 2-layer cake, pour half the glaze over the bottom cake layer, spreading glaze along cake edges with a knife. Allow glaze to set for 5 minutes, then put top cake layer in place. Pour remaining glaze on top layer, spreading evenly over the cake and down the sides.

To make a thick frosting, add confectioners' sugar and beat until desired consistency is reached.

Carrot Cake

This cake uses a carrot puree, which is actually less labor intensive than grating raw carrots. You can cook and puree the carrots the day before.
Recipe adapted from *The Silver Palate Cookbook,* Rosso and Lukins (Workman Publishing, 1982).

ingredients:

3 cups Wendy Wark's gluten-free
   flour mix (page 181)
1 teaspoon xanthan gum
3 cups sugar
1 teaspoon salt
1 tablespoon baking soda
1 tablespoon ground cinnamon
1½ cups vegetable oil
4 large eggs plus 1 egg white, lightly beaten
1 tablespoon vanilla extract
1½ cups walnuts, chopped (optional)
1½ cups unsweetened flaked coconut
1⅓ cups pureed cooked carrots
   (about 5 medium carrots)
¾ cup drained crushed pineapple

Cream Cheese Frosting

16 ounces cream cheese, softened
   (don't use the new spreadable style)
1½ sticks (12 tablespoons) unsalted butter,
   softened
4 cups confectioners' sugar, sifted
2 teaspoons vanilla extract
Juice of one lemon

comment:

Cream Cheese Frosting recipe makes enough for a two 9-inch rounds. This recipe yields a generous amount of frosting. If you prefer a thinner layer on your cake, you can cut the recipe in half and still have enough.

makes two 9-inch rounds

Preheat oven to 350°F. Butter two 9-inch round cake pans and line with parchment. Butter inner surface of parchment as well.

Sift flour mix, xanthan gum, sugar, salt, baking soda, and cinnamon into a medium bowl. In a large bowl whisk oil, eggs, and vanilla. Slowly add flour mixture to egg mixture, mixing thoroughly but lightly. Fold in nuts, coconut, carrots, and pineapple.

Pour batter into prepared pans and bake for 50-55 minutes, or until edges pull away from the pan. (A toothpick inserted near the center should come out clean with a few crumbs clinging to it.) Remove pans from oven and let stand for five minutes before turning out onto wire racks. Cool cakes completely (about 3 hours) before frosting.

Cream Cheese Frosting: In a medium bowl, beat together cream cheese and butter until smooth. Slowly add confectioners' sugar until well blended and free of lumps. Add vanilla and lemon juice and mix until smooth.

*Note: If using a standard gluten-free flour blend, add
1/2 teaspoon xanthan gum to the dry ingredients.
Use a half recipe of Royal Icing (page 186) to add some
carrot decoration to the top of the cake.*

Orange Cheesecake

Several different cheesecake recipes were used to develop this version.
You can change the flavor by using cherry brandy or flavored oils (those used in chocolate truffle making - see Sources). Many cheesecake recipes use liqueurs for flavoring; however, as it is difficult to determine their gluten-free status, flavored oils are a better choice. Have some fun and come up with your own creations!

ingredients:

2 cups gluten-free cookie crumbs
   (molasses cookies work well)

½ teaspoon cinnamon

5 tablespoons unsalted butter, melted

16 ounces cream cheese, softened

1½ cups sugar

4 eggs

2 cups sour cream

2 tablespoons gluten-free flour mix
   (page 181)

1 teaspoon vanilla

1 tablespoon orange zest

2 tablespoons orange juice concentrate

makes 12-20 servings

Preheat oven to 350°F. Combine cookie crumbs, cinnamon, and melted butter in a small bowl. Press mixture evenly into the bottom of a 9½-inch springform pan. Bake for 5 minutes. Cool completely before filling.

Reduce oven temperature to 300°F. Beat cream cheese and sugar together until smooth and well blended, scraping down bowl several times. Add eggs one at a time, incorporating lightly after each addition. (Be careful not to overbeat.) Blend in sour cream, flour mix, vanilla, orange zest, and orange juice concentrate. Pour into prepared crust. Bake for 60-75 minutes. (Cake should be slightly risen, with a golden top and a custard-like consistency in the center.) Allow cheesecake to cool completely. Refrigerate for at least 8 hours before serving.

Note: Bake cheesecake in a hot water bath to avoid cracking on top.

Pie Crust Dough

Recipe adapted from *Great Gluten Free Goodies* by Rebecca Reilly (Rebecca's Kitchen, 1997)

ingredients:

1¾ cups (scant) Wendy Wark's
   gluten-free flour mix (page 181)

½ teaspoon salt

1 tablespoon sugar (omit if using crust for a
   savory recipe such as a quiche)

9 tablespoons cold unsalted butter,
   cut into pieces

1 jumbo egg plus one egg yolk, lightly beaten

1½ tablespoons gluten-free
   sour cream or cider vinegar

makes enough dough for two 9-inch pie shells or a 2-crust pie

Combine flour, salt, and sugar. Using a pastry blender or a fork, work the butter in until small bits the size of peas are distributed throughout the flour mix. Make a well in the mixture and add the egg and sour cream, mixing thoroughly with a fork. If the mixture is crumbly, knead very lightly until the dough just holds together.

Gather half of the dough into a ball and shape it into a 5-inch disk. Repeat with remaining dough. Wrap both disks tightly in plastic wrap and refrigerate for 30 minutes. Follow directions for individual pie or tart recipes.

Notes: A marble surface provides the ideal cool work surface; however, if you don't have one, place ice or gel ice packs on your countertop prior to rolling out the dough. Once a crust is blind baked, you can freeze it for future use.

Pumpkin Pie

This pie stands out from all the rest, with its intensely full, spice-perfumed pumpkin flavor.
I tried many recipes to see if I could find a top-notch pumpkin pie, but nothing beats this one from my grandma and Aunt Judy.

ingredients:

Pie Crust Dough (page 202)

One 29-ounce can pumpkin

4 eggs, slightly beaten

2 tablespoons of any gluten-free flour mix

1 teaspoon salt

1 teaspoon ground cinnamon

¼ teaspoon ground cloves

½ teaspoon allspice

1 teaspoon ginger

2 cups sugar

1 teaspoon vanilla extract

2½ cups evaporated milk

makes two 9-inch pies

to bake the crust:

On a cool countertop, between two sheets of wax paper or plastic wrap, roll half the Pie Crust Dough into an 11-inch circle. Remove wax paper from one side. Pick up the crust with your hand on the wax paper side. Place crust into a 9-inch pie plate and remove wax paper. Make a fluted pie edge by tucking the overhanging dough under to make a double edge and pressing the two layers together. Pinch a V shape every ½-inch around the edge of the pie crust. Repeat steps with remaining dough and place in another 9-inch pie plate.

Cover crust-lined pie plates with foil and heap dried beans or pie weights inside. Place pie plates in the refrigerator for 15 minutes while preheating oven to 400°F. Bake crust for 20 minutes, or until edges turn golden. Allow crust to cool for 5 minutes, then remove foil and weights. Return crust to oven for 5 more minutes if a crisp, golden crust is desired. Allow crust to cool for 10 minutes before filling.

to make the filling:

Reduce oven temperature to 325°F. Blend pumpkin and eggs together in a large bowl. Mix together flour, salt, cinnamon, cloves, allspice, and ginger in a medium bowl. Slowly add the spice mixture to the pumpkin blend. Add sugar and vanilla, mixing well. Add evaporated milk in a slow stream, mixing thoroughly. Pour mixture into prepared pie crusts and bake pies for one hour. Test for doneness by inserting a knife into each pie; it should come out clean.

Note: A cool countertop is essential to help the dough stay chilled; otherwise, it will stick to the wax paper.

Apple Pie

My father made most of the apple pies of my childhood using his mothers' recipe. Their pies are known far and wide (to friends and family) as the best apple pie!

ingredients:

6 Granny Smith apples

1 teaspoon lemon juice

Pie Crust Dough (page 202)

2-3 tablespoons of any gluten-free flour mix

1-2 teaspoons cinnamon

½ -¾ cups sugar (depending on
    acidity of apples)

1 tablespoon unsalted butter

1 egg yolk

1 teaspoon milk

Notes: Other apple varieties that work well in pies include Golden Delicious, Jonagold, Newtown Pippin, and Rome.

A cool countertop is essential to help the dough stay chilled; otherwise, it will stick to the wax paper.

makes one 9-inch pie

Peel, core, and slice apples into bite-sized pieces. Fill a large bowl with water. Add lemon juice and apples.

to bake the crust:

On a cool countertop, between two sheets of wax paper or plastic wrap, roll half the Pie Crust Dough into an 11-inch circle. Remove wax paper from one side. Pick up the crust with your hand on the wax paper side. Place crust into a 9-inch pie plate and remove wax paper. Make a fluted pie edge by tucking the overhanging dough under to make a double edge and pressing the two layers together. Pinch a V shape every ½-inch around the edge of the pie crust.

Cover crust-lined pie plate with foil and heap dried beans or pie weights inside. Place pie plate in the refrigerator for 15 minutes while preheating oven to 400°F. Bake crust for 20 minutes, or until edges turn golden. Allow crust to cool for 5 minutes, then remove foil and weights. Return crust to oven for 5 more minutes if a crisp, golden crust is desired. Allow crust to cool for 10 minutes before filling.

to make the filling:

Meanwhile, drain apples in a colander (they should be as free of excess moisture as possible before baking).

Reduce oven temperature to 350°F. Sprinkle a little flour, cinnamon, and sugar on the bottom pie crust. Cover with one third of the apple slices. Sprinkle another layer of flour, cinnamon, and sugar over the apples, and dot with small pieces of butter. Cover with half the remaining apples, followed by another layer of flour, cinnamon, sugar, and butter. Top with remaining apples, flour, cinnamon, sugar, and butter.

Roll out the second crust and place on top of apples (you will have a high mound of apples, but it will settle down). Press edges of top and bottom crust together. Cut slits in top crust to allow steam to escape. Whisk egg yolk and milk together to make an egg wash. Brush liberally over top crust.

Place pie in center of oven and bake for one hour or until apples are tender.

Apple Tart

This recipe could be short and sweet, but I added a lot of explanation to help the first-time tart maker. I have eaten many pies and tarts with a wheat flour crust that are not nearly as good as this one made with a gluten-free crust. There is no gluten to overwork! Wonderful alone or with a scoop of vanilla ice cream.

ingredients:

Pie Crust Dough (page 202)

4 pounds Granny Smith apples,
    peeled, cored, and quartered

3 tablespoons plus 1 teaspoon lemon juice

3 tablespoons plus 1 teaspoon brandy

3 tablespoons sugar

2-3 Granny Smith apples, peeled,
    cored, and sliced very thin

3 tablespoons unsalted butter, melted

½ cup apricot jam

makes 10-12 servings

to bake the crust:

Roll dough into a 12-inch circle on a cool countertop between two sheets of wax paper. (The cool countertop is essential to help the dough stay chilled; otherwise, it will stick to the wax paper.) Remove one piece of wax paper, pick up the crust, and place it into an 11-inch tart pan. Remove top piece of wax paper. Make a double edge by tucking the overhanging dough under and pressing the layers together into the fluted sides of the tart pan.

Let crust rest in the refrigerator for 15 minutes while preheating oven to 400°F. Cover crust with foil and mound dry beans or pie weights on top of foil to keep crust from puffing up. Bake for 20 minutes, or until edges turn golden. Allow crust to cool for 5 minutes, then remove foil and weights. This process is known as blind baking the crust; although it is not an absolutely necessary step, it makes for a crisper crust.

to make the filling:

Toss quartered apples with 3 tablespoons each of lemon juice and brandy and sprinkle with 1 tablespoon sugar. Spread apples out in a single layer on a roasting pan. Bake at 250°F for 2 hours, stirring occasionally. Let apples cool slightly, then chop into smaller pieces and puree in a food processor. Spread puree evenly over baked crust. Arrange the thinly sliced apples in a circular pattern in the tart pan. Brush apples with melted butter and sprinkle with remaining sugar.

Bake at 350°F for 25 minutes, then place under broiler (watching carefully) for up to 10 minutes.

While tart is baking, heat apricot jam, remaining lemon juice, and brandy in a small saucepan, stirring occasionally with a wire whisk, until heated through and smoothly combined. Brush warm tart with this mixture. Serve tart warm or at room temperature.

Grand Marnier Semifreddo with Bittersweet Chocolate Sauce and Local Blackberries

Chef Todd Gray, Equinox – Washington D.C.

Equinox is one of this city's premier fine dining establishments, offering sophisticated, pure American cuisine.
Chef Gray uses fresh, local organic ingredients whenever possible. He is a James Beard Award Nominee for Chef of the Year, Mid-Atlantic, in 2001.
The gluten-free version of this terrific dessert calls for a substitution for the Grand Marnier, unless you are able to determine that Grand Marnier is absolutely gluten-free.
An intense orange flavor can be derived from orange zest or orange extract.

ingredients:

1½ cups egg yolks (about 18 yolks)
1 cup sugar
½ cup PS Moscato
    (an Italian sparkling wine)
½ cup Grand Marnier or orange juice
    combined with 2 teaspoons of
    orange extract or orange zest
2 gelatin sheets or 2 tablespoons granulated
    gelatin dissolved in ¼ cup of water
2 cups heavy cream, whipped
4-5 cups local blackberries

Bittersweet Chocolate Sauce

9 ounces bittersweet chocolate
4½ ounces fresh-squeezed orange juice
3 tablespoons butter
1 cup plus 2 tablespoons heavy cream
1 teaspoon vanilla extract

chef's comment:

Try using fresh, organic eggs from cage-free hens.

makes 6-8 servings

Combine yolks, sugar, sparkling wine, and orange juice with zest in a stainless steel bowl. Beat over a double boiler, whisking vigorously, until mix is thick, pale, and has doubled in volume. (It will fall in a ribbon when the whisk is lifted from the bowl.)

Remove bowl from heat. Add dissolved gelatin, mix well, and cool. When mixture thickens to the consistency of egg whites, but is not yet firm, fold in whipped cream. Pour into a film-lined terrine mold or jelly roll pan. Cover and freeze overnight.

Bittersweet Chocolate Sauce: Combine chocolate, orange juice, and butter in a large glass bowl. Heat in microwave oven for 30-60 seconds. Whisk mixture to combine thoroughly. (If chocolate has not completely melted, microwave for 30 seconds longer.) Add cream and microwave for about 10 seconds longer, or until slightly warmed. Add vanilla extract and whisk mixture until smooth once again. If sauce is too thick, whisk in additional orange juice and/or cream until desired consistency is reached.

To serve, cut in slices with a knife dipped in hot water. Top with bittersweet chocolate sauce and local blackberries.

Baked Pears

Such a simple delicacy!

ingredients:

1 tablespoon sugar

3 Bosc pears, halved and seeded

1 tablespoon unsalted butter

⅔ cup heavy cream

4 servings

Preheat oven to 400ºF. Butter an 8-inch baking dish and sprinkle with ½ tablespoon sugar. Place pears, cut side down, in dish. Dot pears with butter and sprinkle with remaining sugar. Bake for 10 minutes, then add cream and bake for another 15 minutes. Serve warm.

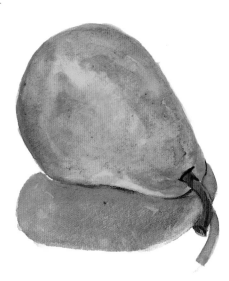

Cranberry Soufflé

Chef Hans Bergmann, Cacharel — Arlington, Texas

Cacharel is a great restaurant situated between Dallas and Fort Worth.
The restaurant has received top restaurant status in the *Zagat Restaurant Survey* as well as in *Condé Nast* and *Gourmet* magazines.

ingredients:

6 ounces fresh cranberries

7 ounces granulated sugar

2½ ounces butter, softened

¼ cup water

6 ounces egg whites

Dash of salt

Confectioners' sugar

4 ounces whipped cream

makes 6 soufflés (8 ounces each)

Preheat oven to 450°F.

Place cranberries and 3 ounces granulated sugar in a saucepan. Bring slowly to a boil, then simmer until mixture becomes almost dry. Set aside to cool.

Brush inside of soufflé dishes with soft butter.

In a heavy bottomed saucepan bring water and 4 ounces granulated sugar to boil. Cook until mixture reaches 240°F. (This is the soft-ball stage; when you drop a bit of the hot sugar syrup in cold water you can form a soft ball that will flatten on its own.)

Whip egg whites with a dash of salt and the hot sugar syrup to the soft peak stage. Add cranberry reduction and fold in gently.

Using a spoon, fill the prepared soufflé dishes with the mixture up to the rim and bake in a convection oven for 10-12 minutes until the soufflés rise to double their original size and are cooked in the middle. (If you do not have a convection oven, cooking the time may be longer. Be careful not to overbake, or the edges will burn and the soufflés will fall upon being removed from the oven.)

Sprinkle with confectioners' sugar and serve immediately, with whipped cream on the side.

Note: If there aren't any fresh cranberries available, substitute frozen.
Cranberries are one of the few types of fruit you can freeze without loss of quality.

Local Berries with Crème Fraîche

This is a very elegant way to serve local berries. Serve over any fresh in-season berry.
I find this more interesting than ice cream when fruit is at its peak, since the sweetness of the fruit is the focus.

ingredients:

1 cup whipping cream

2 tablespoons buttermilk

2 cups local strawberries, raspberries,
   or blackberries

4 servings

Crème fraîche: Combine whipping cream and buttermilk in a glass measuring cup. Stir well and let sit at 70ºF for 8-24 hours, or until mixture thickens. Stir, cover, and refrigerate. (It will keep for about 10 days.)

Divide berries between four bowls and spoon ¼ cup of crème fraîche over each bowl. Garnish with a fresh mint sprig.

Panna Cotta with Dried Fruit Compote

Chef Suzanne Goin, Lucques — West Hollywood, California

Panna cotta is Italian for "cooked cream," a light, silky egg custard served with fruit or chocolate sauce. This version is accented by a dried fruit compote flavored with ginger, citrus, and spices. Suzanne was featured in *Food & Wine* magazine as one of America's Best New Chefs in 1999.

ingredients:

4 teaspoons unflavored gelatin

2 cups whole milk

1 cup confectioners' sugar

2 cups heavy cream

1 vanilla bean, split down the middle lengthwise

1 teaspoon vanilla extract

Dried Fruit Compote

1 teaspoon black peppercorns

2 cloves

1 teaspoon coriander seeds

4 bay leaves

1 pinch grated nutmeg

1 pinch cinnamon

1 cinnamon stick

3 cups red wine

3 cups port

½ cup sugar

Juice of 2 lemons

Juice of 1 orange

2 pounds high quality dried fruit
  (which may include pears, peaches, plums, prunes, figs, and flame raisins)

Hot water

1 tablespoon freshly grated ginger

Zest of one orange and one lemon

12 servings

Butter 12 small ramekins and place on a sheet tray.

In a small bowl, sprinkle the gelatin over ¼ cup of the milk and stir to blend. Set aside until the gelatin completely absorbs the milk, 2-3 minutes.

In a large saucepan, combine the remaining 1¾ cups milk, sugar, and cream. Using a small knife, scrape the beans from the vanilla pod and add them to the liquid. Add the scraped pod as well. Bring to a boil over moderate heat and whisk to dissolve the sugar.

As soon as the liquid comes to a boil, remove the pot from the heat and add the softened gelatin-milk mixture and the vanilla extract. Whisk to completely dissolve the gelatin. Strain the mixture through a fine mesh sieve into a container.

Pour the mixture into the ramekins. Cover with plastic wrap and refrigerate until set, about 4 hours.

Tie all spices together in a square of cheesecloth to form a pouch. In a stainless steel saucepan, place spice pouch, red wine, port, sugar, and juice of lemons and orange. Bring to a boil and set aside. This will be the poaching liquid for the dried fruit.

continued:

Panna Cotta with Dried Fruit Compote

Cut fruit into slightly bigger than bite-sized pieces. Place fruit in a bowl and cover with hot water. Let fruit plump for 30 minutes.

Drain fruit and place it in the pot of poaching liquid. Simmer fruit for 20-30 minutes, until tender and well flavored by the aromatics in the poaching liquid.

Remove fruit from poaching liquid. Add ginger and zest of orange and lemon to the pot and reduce the liquid down to make a sauce.

Keep the fruit in the sauce, refrigerated, until ready to serve.

To serve, run a sharp knife along the inside of each ramekin to help loosen the cream. Dip the bottom of each ramekin in a bowl of hot water, shaking to completely loosen the cream. Invert onto chilled dessert plates. Spoon the fruit compote around the panna cotta and serve.

wine suggestion: a dessert wine such as Vin Santo or Sauternes

Notes: Panna cotta is also good served with fresh berries marinated in a little sugar and mint.
Sometimes in the manufacturing process, dried fruit is dusted with flour to prevent sticking; be sure your choices are gluten-free.
You may substitute yellow raisins or any other large raisin for the flame raisins.

Floating Islands with Caramel Blood Oranges

Chef Gerry Hayden, Aureole – New York, New York

Charlie Palmer's Aureole is revered as a paradigm of progressive American cuisine. It is one of New York's finest restaurants. Restaurant critic Bob Lape says of Aureole, "An elegant dining experience packed with punch … boldly flavored seasonal dishes … theatrically inspired three-dimensional desserts serve to delight all the senses." Chef de cuisine Gerry Hayden taps his experience from some of the finest kitchens in America: the critically acclaimed River Café, Marguery Grill, Tribeca Grill, and Aqua.

ingredients:

3 egg whites

1½ cups sugar, divided

½ cup water

2 blood oranges, sectioned, juice reserved

1 rosemary branch (optional)

comment:

This dessert complements Gerry's other contributions to this book, Caramelized Crimini Mushroom Soup with Fresh Rosemary (page 97) and Pan-Roasted Pork Tenderloin with Fennel, Radish, and Arugula Salad (page 98).

4 servings

Preheat oven to 250°F. Spray four 4-ounce aluminum cups with a non-stick gluten-free spray.

Combine egg whites and ½ cup sugar in a metal mixing bowl. (If you have a stand mixer, use its bowl attachment.) Set bowl atop a saucepan of simmering water. The bowl should fit snugly on the pot without touching the water.

Whisk the sugar mixture gently until the whites are warm and the sugar is completely dissolved. Remove the bowl from heat and lock in stand mixer. Using the whip attachment, whip until soft peaks form.

Fill a pastry bag, fitted with a large plain tip, with the beaten egg whites and pipe into the center of the aluminum tins. Allow the filling to move outwards from the center. Smooth tops with a spatula, set in a water bath, and cover loosely with foil sprayed with non-stick spray. Bake for 20-30 minutes, until the meringue is firm but still moist. Remove from water bath and refrigerate.

Place remaining cup of sugar and just enough water to moisten a heavy-bottomed saucepan. Bring to a boil and continue to cook until the sugar turns amber. Pour in reserved blood orange juice, rosemary branch, and the remaining water. Bring caramel back to a boil and continue to cook for 2 minutes, then strain over blood orange sections. Cool.

Remove meringues from their molds and place on plates. Spoon blood orange sections and caramel sauce around the meringues.

Note: If you do not own pastry bags and tips, use a clean plastic bag with one corner snipped off.

The Gluten-Free Diet 214

Patient Support Organizations 216

Dairy-Free Substitutions 217

Recipe Conversion Ideas 217

Gluten Intolerant Children 218

Lunch and Snack Ideas 221

Outdoor Cooking 222

Pantry Basics 223

Utensils & Cookware 225

Chef Contributors 226

Sources 228

Measurement Conversion Chart 230

Gluten-Free Flour 231

Glossary of Cooking Terms 233

Index 236

APPENDIX

The Gluten-Free Diet

ANY OF THE GLUTEN INTOLERANT SUPPORT GROUPS can provide extensively researched dietary guidelines. I strongly suggest that you contact these groups and request their information (see page 216 for contact information). Shelley Case, Registered Dietitian, has published a highly recommended book called *Gluten-Free Diet: A Comprehensive Resource Guide* (Case Nutrition Consulting, 2002). Shelley has graciously allowed me to use material from her book to help you get started. Her book not only goes into great detail about the diet, it also features over 1600 gluten-free specialty foods, a directory of more than 130 American, Canadian, and international companies, the nutrient composition of gluten-free flours, grains, legumes, nuts, and seeds, and many other resources for the gluten intolerant individual (see Sources).

Every attempt was made to alert the user of *Cooking Gluten-Free!* to ingredients that might include gluten. Questionable ingredients in a recipe are generally preceded with the words gluten-free (i.e. gluten-free sour cream). It is imperative that the user of this book read all product ingredient labels and research the gluten content of any product used in a recipe.

Flours from the following sources are allowed on the gluten-free diet: Rice (white, brown, or sweet), corn, soy, tapioca, potato, quinoa, buckwheat, amaranth, sorghum, arrowroot, teff, nut, millet, and bean.

Both growing and manufacturing should take place in a gluten-free environment.

Many prepared foods contain gluten. Until you become proficient at reading labels, beware of "hidden gluten" in:

Broth	Sauces
Imitation bacon and seafood	Self-basting poultry
Marinades	Soup
Processed meats	Soy sauce
Salad dressings	Thickeners

These foods often contain gluten, but are sometimes overlooked by the uninitiated:

Breading	Croutons	Roux
Coating mixes	Pasta	Stuffing
Communion wafers		

Read all labels carefully. If any uncertainty exists about a particular ingredient, call the manufacturer for clarification.

In addition to Shelly's information on the following page, be aware that the following ingredients may contain gluten:

- Brown rice syrup (often made from barley)
- Caramel color (it is usually made from corn, but the FDA allows barley as well)
- Monoglycerides & diglycerides (in dry products only) - Check gluten status of carrier agent
- Vegetable gum - Generally not a problem, though the FDA allows it to be sourced from oat gum

Excerpt from *Gluten-Free Diet: A Comprehensive Resource Guide,*
Shelley Case, Registered Dietitian, (Case Nutrition Consulting, 2002).

GLUTEN IS THE GENERAL NAME for the storage proteins (prolamins) in
wheat, rye, and barley. These specific prolamins damage the small
intestine in people with celiac disease and dermatitis herpetiformis. The
actual names of the toxic prolamins are gliadin in wheat, secalin in rye,
and hordein in barley. Up until 1996, the avenin prolamin in oats was
considered to be toxic; however new research indicates that avenin in
oats is not harmful.*** Although corn contains the prolamin zein and
rice contains the prolamin orzenin, these prolamins do not have toxic
effect on the intestine of persons with celiac disease.

Gluten is the substance in flour responsible for forming the
structure of dough, holding products together, and leavening. While
the presence of gluten is evident in baked goods (e.g., breads, cookies,
and cakes) and pasta, it is often a "hidden ingredient" in many other
items such as sauces, seasonings, soups, salad dressings, and candy, as
well as some vitamins and pharmaceuticals. The challenge for individuals on a gluten-free diet is to avoid these hidden sources.

Gluten-Containing Ingredients To Be Avoided:

Barley	Graham flour	Rye
Bulgur	Kamut*	Semolina
Cereal binding	Malt**	Spelt (dinkel)*
Couscous	Malt extract**	Triticale
Durum*	Malt flavoring**	Wheat
Einkorn*	Malt syrup**	Wheat bran
Emmer*	Oat bran***	Wheat germ
Filler	Oat syrup***	Wheat starch
Farro*	Oats***	

*   *Types of wheat*
** *Derived from barley*
*** *Many recent studies have demonstrated that consumption of oats (25-60 g/
day) is safe for children and adults with celiac disease. However, further studies
are needed to determine the long-term safety of oat consumption. Also, the
issue of cross contamination of oats with wheat and/or barley remains a major
concern in North America, therefore, oats are NOT recommended by celiac
organizations in Canada and the USA.*

Ingredients To Question:

Hydrolyzed plant or vegetable protein (HPP/HVP)
Seasonings
Flavorings
Starch
Modified food starch
Dextrin

Specific labeling regulations in the USA and Canada for these ingredients
can be found in *Gluten-Free Diet: A Comprehensive Resource Guide,* Shelley
Case, Registered Dietitian, (Case Nutrition Consulting 2002).

Patient Support Organizations

Gluten Intolerance Group, GIG
15110 10th Ave. SW, Suite A
Seattle, WA 98166-1820
Phone: 206.246.6652
Fax: 206.246.6531
Email: info@gluten.net
Website: www.gluten.net
Executive Director: Cynthia Kupper

Celiac Disease Foundation, CDF
13251 Ventura Blvd., Suite 1
Studio City, CA 91604-1838
Phone: 818.990.2354
Fax: 818.990.2379
Email: cdf@celiac.org
Website: www.celiac.org
Executive Director: Elaine Monarch

Canadian Celiac Association, CCA
5170 Dixie Road, Suite 204
Mississauga, Ontario, L4W 1E3
Phone: 905.507.6208
Toll-free: 800.363.7296
Fax: 905.507.4673
Email: celiac@look.ca
Website: www.celiac.ca
Executive Director: Karen Logan

Celiac Sprue Association/USA, Inc., CSA/USA
P. O. Box 31700
Omaha, NE 68131-0700
Phone: 402.558.0600
Fax: 402.558.1347
Email: celiacs@csaceliacs.org
Website: www.csaceliacs.org
President and Acting Executive Director: Mary Schluckebier

Celiac Chat Group on-line http://forums.delphiforums.com/celiac/start

The Celiac Disease & Gluten-free Diet Support Page
www.celiac.com

Dairy-Free Substitutions

Foods to remove from your diet:

- All types of milk products, including yogurt, cream, buttermilk, evaporated milk, condensed milk, sheep's milk, and goat's milk
- Butter and most margarines
- All types of cheese (including cottage cheese and cream cheese)
- Milk proteins (as "hidden" ingredients on product labels): casein, caseinate, whey, lactalbumin, sodium caseinate, and lactoglobulin

Always start with high-quality recipes, such as those found in this book, to achieve a moist, delicious result, and to help ensure that the substitution of these dairy-free ingredients work successfully. Check with your physician before using the following substitutions.

Instead of:

Cow's milk — Use gluten-free rice milk or gluten-free soy milk. These types of milk are thinner than cow's milk, so you may need to use about 1 tablespoon less. Coconut milk makes a good non-dairy ice cream.

Dry milk powder — Use non-dairy milk powder. Always read product labels to be sure contents do not contain milk proteins. Finely ground nuts can also be substituted in equal proportions (by volume).

Buttermilk — Use gluten-free rice milk or gluten-free soy milk mixed with 1 tablespoon lemon juice or cider vinegar.

Yogurt — Use soy yogurt. Cookbook authors Knox and Lowman use soy yogurt in many of their recipes in *Lactose-Free* (Fireside, 2000).

Butter — Use organic shortening or vegetable oil. Nucoa margarine is an option for margarine lovers.

Sour cream — Use IMO or non-dairy versions (available at natural food markets).

Cream cheese — Use rice-based versions (available at natural food markets).

Look for gluten-free, tofu-based cheese, yogurt, milk, and margarine as well.

Carol Fenster's book, *Special Diet Solutions* (Savory Palate, Inc., 1997) has an appendix full of substitution ideas for wheat, gluten, dairy, eggs, yeast, or refined sugar.

Recipe Conversion Ideas

THE PROCESS OF CONVERTING A FAVORITE RECIPE to a gluten-free version is a relatively easy process. Once you learn how to make basics such as gluten-free pizza crusts, biscuits, and flour tortillas, the conversion of a dinner recipe is quite easy. Now that good gluten-free pasta is available (see Sources) you will not be obliged to make it yourself.

Guidelines for cooking:

- Choose recipes that don't involve French bread, Asian pastes (though many Thai Kitchen products are gluten-free), bouillon cubes, grain-based alcohol, or any other ingredient that is just too difficult to replace with a gluten-free version.

- Get creative. Since I have not found a gluten-free cannelloni shell, I use lasagna noodles and roll them around the filling.

- Thicken sauces with cornstarch, arrowroot, or sweet rice flour.

- You can generally find good gluten-free substitutions for questionable ingredients. Chef Tom Douglas demonstrates this in one of his contributed recipes, replacing the couscous in the original version with brown rice.

(continued on next page)

(continued from page 217)

Guidelines for baking:

- If you use Wendy Wark's gluten-free flour mix, you are on your way to great baked goods. This flour mix will greatly improve any gluten-free recipe you are now using.
- Follow the guidelines for adding xanthan gum on page 181.
- Add an extra egg white to light-textured cake recipes, but do not add any extra eggs or whites to heavy cakes such as pound cake or coffee cake. Sometimes sour cream cakes benefit from a little extra sour cream; try an extra ¼ cup if you need more moisture.
- In my quest to create a gluten-free "oatmeal" cookie, I replaced the oatmeal with half ground nuts and half quinoa flakes. The quinoa absorbs liquid, so I also added an extra egg white.
- Most cookie recipes require a simple flour replacement and a little xanthan gum.
- Some cookie recipes use a great deal of butter, rather than eggs, to impart moisture. This kind of recipe requires an additional adjustment: replace ¼ of the butter with either sour cream or cream cheese. I discovered this solution when converting the Mexican Wedding Cake recipe. Gluten-free flour doesn't behave like wheat flour does when mixed with some ingredients; this adjustment reduces the amount of spread caused by the butter.

Helping Children Enjoy Life on a Gluten-Free Diet

THIS IS A DIFFICULT CHAPTER TO WRITE, as children's eating habits can be a very touchy subject. The very essence of the gluten-free diet requires much time, thought, and patience from the parents. Attitude is everything!

At a gluten-free conference, a woman discussed her 13-year old daughter's refusal to adhere to her special diet. Both mother and daughter were understandably frustrated. Food can be such a difficult issue between parents and children; add to that the challenges of a special diet, and you have the makings of a constant struggle.

Every family adjusts to the gluten-free diet differently. In this chapter, I will show you what works for mine. My goal is to inspire parents to have compassion for their gluten intolerant children, and to make cooking a greater part of their daily lives.

It is hard to see the gluten-free diet as a blessing, but it is a healthy way to eat. The trick is to learn how to cook well so that the entire family can enjoy the same meal together. Gluten-free food can rank with that served in a first-class restaurant, and you can make simple versions easily at home!

Some key points to remember in helping your child with a gluten-free diet:

- Prepare good, tasty food (yes, it is possible for every meal!)
- Plan "away from home" lunches
- Have your child **try** each item served at dinner
- Be sure your child comes to the dinner table hungry
- Teach your child how to cook, and make it fun for both of you!
- Gather new information and become more involved
- Plan gluten-free evening meals for the whole family (work toward doing this daily)
- Have ingredients for three quick evening meals on hand
- Be sure your child is getting enough B vitamins and folic acid

This may sound overwhelming, so take it a step at a time. It may be a year before you feel as if you have everything under control, but the dividends for your efforts will be great.

Prepare good, tasty food:

Establish a feeling within your household that a gluten-free diet is delicious and healthy. Remember, your child will develop the same attitude you display. Your child will be more willing to stick to her special diet when you are not around to supervise if the food tastes good. The more you make a gluten-free diet a part of your life, the better off your child will be. Some parents do not fully embrace this diet, and treat the gluten intolerant child as an outsider without realizing it. Food preparation for the special diet is viewed as a huge hassle, and very little creativity is devoted to making meals more than a refueling stop.

To avoid this complication, concentrate on what you do best. For instance, as making a really good loaf of gluten-free bread is difficult, why not focus your efforts on cooking great meals that don't include bread? Some of the best meals are a simple combination of meat, a vegetable, and a starch. You should try going beyond your comfort zone by adding ingredients that you may not have thought of before. For example, add raisins to wild rice as it is cooking, then add toasted pine nuts just before serving for a twist on that "side of rice."

Change your definition of what you consider to be simple food. A dish composed of exotic-looking ingredients might actually be a quick, tasty addition to your household bill of fare! Your family will be pleased, and your efforts will seem like much less of a burden.

Plan "away from home" lunches:

Encourage your child to prepare a list of things he likes to eat for lunch, and try to keep those items on hand. Inquire at his school about the availability of a microwave, so that he can sometimes enjoy a hot lunch. In our school, office personnel will microwave a frozen entrée in the teachers' lounge. (If you are able to secure this privilege, asking for it once a week or so should be acceptable.) Make special treats and freeze individual portions; they can be packed frozen in a lunchbox, and will thaw by lunchtime. The gluten intolerant child has enough to contend with when he can't eat like the other kids; providing him with snacks that are both healthy and tasty will help make him forget that he is on a special diet. The other children will see your child not as an outcast, but as someone who eats both differently and very well!

Have your child try each item served at dinner:

If a child thinks she doesn't like something, don't make her eat a whole serving, but do persuade her to try it. As her palate becomes more developed, she will find that something she once hated is now great. It may take 15-20 tries before her taste buds make the adjustment to the new food, but it is worth the effort. Just be sure you handle it in a matter-of-fact way without becoming emotional yourself. When I started sautéing fresh spinach in olive oil, garlic, and lemon juice, my children (6 and 3 years old at the time) said "yuck!" But after several months of having to try it from time to time, they both decided they loved it, and it is now a favorite of theirs. If you do not expose your children to high quality, well-prepared food, they will have a limited range of tastes and preferences. On the occasion that the child refuses to eat a food you know she likes, waiting for the next mealtime is a better lesson than fixing something else that evening.

Be sure your child comes to the dinner table hungry:

Most kids eat three meals a day and two solid snacks. Some are hearty eaters, while others seem to just pick at their food. Over the course of a week, most kids get the nutrition they need if their parents offer food from the four basic groups. Be sure your children don't take in lots of empty calories from juice or other sugary drinks between meals. Fruit juice lacks the fiber of fresh fruit, and it fills up tummies, making kids "not hungry" when dinnertime rolls around.

While you may be tempted to buy gluten-free junk food and candy to "compensate" for what your child can't have, don't buy it very often. You will find that they end up eating plenty of junk elsewhere, especially once they start school, and candy seems to seep out of the woodwork. My child can easily find gluten-free goodies when he is away from home, as his friends' parents buy these treats especially for him (even though they know all they need to have on hand is fresh fruit). That said, we keep a container of candy in our child's classroom and frozen novelties in the freezer at school for last minute celebrations.

Teach your children how to cook:

Another important aspect of the gluten-free diet is for children to learn how to cook on their own. When the child is young she can help by dumping a pre-measured ingredient into a bowl and stirring it around. As the child becomes more capable she can contribute more, and by the time she is a teenager she will know how to cook. She will know how scrumptious gluten-free dishes can be, and thus have less desire to cheat. It is important to help the child develop this confidence so she will not feel inferior because of her special diet. The time spent teaching her will represent valuable quality time together, and will be both creative and fun!

Gather new information and become more involved:

If you don't normally shop at a natural food market, try it sometime. A whole new world of gluten-free products await you. Join patient support groups such as CDF, CSA/USA, CCA, and GIG (see Sources for contact information). Members receive a wealth of information through newsletters and by attending meetings. Every time I am in contact with one of these groups I learn something new.

Plan gluten-free evening meals for the whole family:

It sounds unrealistic, if not impossible, to those who have never tried cooking a gluten-free meal for the whole family, but the benefits are tremendous. Take it one step at a time and remember that many recipes can easily convert to gluten-free dishes. Reduce your reliance on bread, pasta, and pizza, and explore the recipes in this book. While it is difficult learning a week's worth of recipes in one fell swoop, adding one recipe each week will have your family converted to the gluten-free diet by the end of the year. It is essential to become comfortable with the new way of cooking, and to look upon new recipes and new ingredients as an adventure.

Once you and the rest of the family have converted to a gluten-free evening meal, your child will be a more willing participant. Everyone will benefit, as decreased gluten intake results in more energy and a more finely tuned digestive system. You may take advantage of breakfast, lunch, or snack time (when your child is not around) to indulge in any wheat items you crave.

Our family consumes only gluten-free condiments, jam, peanut butter, etc., which saves precious space in the pantry and refrigerator. A strict "no double dipping" rule is enforced. This means we don't dip a knife back into the jam once we have used it to spread the jam on wheat bread. If more jam is needed, a clean spoon or knife is used, thus avoiding cross-contamination. Additionally, all countertops, cooking utensils, and surfaces are cleaned thoroughly to avoid any stray wheat crumbs. We also have two separate toasters.

Have ingredients for three quick meals on hand:

Try to plan three meals in advance. It will take you about 10 minutes to put together the grocery list and about 30 minutes to shop. A little preparedness will go a long way. Always make double the recipe of soups and other freezable meals so as to have "fast food" on hand. Schedule your time wisely throughout the day so as to have more of it to invest in cooking.

Be sure your child is getting enough B vitamins and folic acid:

The importance of B vitamins and folic acid is a topic too infrequently addressed with regard to children and celiac disease. In our country, these vitamins are added to wheat bread, pasta, and cereal, but not to the gluten-free equivalents. B vitamins and folic acid are critical to growing bodies. Deficiency of these vitamins causes a host of problems with the nervous system, heart, brain, red blood cell production, and digestive system. A daily multiple vitamin for children is generally sufficient to provide the RDA. Your doctor can recommend the better brands; another good resource is William and Martha Sears' *The Family Nutrition Book* (Little, Brown, 1999). This volume covers all aspects of how food is responsible for the health of the human body. It is fascinating reading for all parents.

And finally, when my son was diagnosed with celiac disease, I became aware of all the chemicals and processed foods we had been eating. The knowledge I gained from reading labels made me glad we weren't eating all that junk anymore. Once you become a gluten-free expert, it is also important to think of the pesticides, hormones, and chemical fertilizers in the food we eat and water we drink. Organic foods, treated water, and hormone free meat make a lot of sense, especially for young growing bodies. By filtering out the impurities through careful buying, you prevent the body from becoming the filter.

Lunch and Snack Ideas

AT OUR HOME, bread and treats are often times gobbled up more quickly than I can make them. Therefore, it pays to have a variety of ideas for last minute lunches and snacks.

For lunches away from home, it helps to have an insulated lunch box, a small cold pack, and a high quality Thermos that will keep food hot for several hours.

Some ideas listed below require using items left over from a previous meal. For example, when you are steaming green beans, be sure to cook extra for later in the week. (Obviously, all items suggested are gluten-free.)

No Bread Days:

On the many days when you will not have bread available for sandwiches, try these ideas:

- Toaster waffles used as bread with peanut butter and jelly sandwiches.
- Crackers served with tuna, hummus, luncheon meat, or cheese. You can make a gluten-free version of the Oscar Mayer Lunchable that the other kids at school bring for lunch. Cut ham and cheese into squares, add crackers, a Capri Sun, and a little Snickers bar and you have a gluten-free "lunchable."
- Quesadillas or corn tortilla chips with black bean salsa (canned black beans, diced tomato, diced yellow pepper, cilantro, diced onion, and lime juice).
- Chicken salad made with leftover chicken (page 55).
- Homemade soup frozen in individual portions, heated, and placed in a warmed thermos. There are also some good gluten-free canned soups.
- Frozen entrées (if your child has access to a microwave) such as Amy's Cheese Enchiladas and Trader Joe's Chicken Taquitos (see Sources).
- Salads are great for older kids. Try lettuce with dried fruit and nuts/seeds, or a Caesar salad (page 41), or a salad with tomato and

cucumber slices. Keep all ingredients packed in separate containers to be assembled at lunchtime.
- Make Buttermilk Chicken (page 87), Sushi (page 88), or Pizza (page 69) for dinner and save some for lunches.
- Carrot sticks and sliced apple are great dipped in peanut butter, and are a favorite with kids.

Items to add to the lunch box or have for a snack:

- Dried fruit
- Sunflower seed kernels
- Pumpkin seeds
- Soy nuts
- Apple sauce
- Cheese slices
- Pudding
- Steamed green beans
- Slices of sweet red and yellow peppers
- Carrot sticks
- Granola bars (homemade or from Ener-G Foods)
- Yogurt
- Cottage cheese
- Fresh fruit (apples, satsumas, kiwi, bananas, pineapple chunks, strawberries, grapes, etc.)
- Frozen fruit and vegetables such as corn, peas, and raspberries
- Homemade trail mix with nuts, raisins, dried cranberries, and chocolate chips
- Trader Joe's gluten-free snacks (see in-store gluten-free list)
- Healthy homemade baked goods using quinoa, amaranth, and brown rice flours. Sweet breads with grated carrots, zucchini, pureed pumpkin, etc., are great guilt-free treats.

Two favorites that can't go in the lunch box but are good after school snacks:

- Smoothies (page 18). I will often make smoothies at home and take them to after-school pickup so the kids can have a snack in the car; this can fend off grouchiness before it has a chance to ruin a whole afternoon.
- Frozen novelties. Many of the ice cream bars and other frozen treats on the market are gluten-free.

Outdoor Cooking

COOKING OUTDOORS IS A GREAT WAY to avoid the heat in the kitchen. (There are also fewer pots and pans to wash afterwards!) We like to serve grilled meat, poultry, or fish with simple roasted vegetables to keep cooking time in the kitchen to a bare minimum. Another way to beat the heat is to cook ahead in the morning as much as possible.

Cooking outdoors takes a bit of know-how and skill. It pays to invest in a good grilling or barbecuing cookbook for the best results. Here are a few tips to get you started:

Grilling Versus Barbecue:

Most people use these words interchangeably but there is a difference. Grilling is quick cooking over high heat, and works best with tender foods such as fish, chicken, and certain cuts of meat. Barbecue is a slow process using indirect heat and smoke, and is ideal for tougher cuts of meat such as ribs, brisket, tri tip, etc. While gas grills are fine for grilling, a charcoal grill is needed to impart the characteristic smoky flavor of barbecue. Both grilled items and barbecue cooked on a charcoal grill can benefit by the addition of apple wood, cherry wood, mesquite, etc., to the charcoal fire.

Lighting the Fire for Grilling:

Preheat gas grill on high for 15 minutes to produce maximum heat. (A charcoal grill takes a little longer to get going, but we prefer the added flavor it imparts.) An electric starter is the easiest way to start a charcoal grill without the smell and hassle of lighter fluid. Remove the cooking grate and set the charcoal grate in the upper or middle position (depending on the desired degree of heat). Place the electric starter on the charcoal grating. Pile charcoal into a pyramid shape on top of the electric starter and plug the starter into an outlet. Be sure to use enough charcoal to cook the quantity of food you plan to make. Once coals have started, remove the electric starter and let coals heat until they are covered with a layer of gray ash. Spread out the charcoal in an even layer so that three-quarters of the grill is covered with charcoal. (The remaining cool space can be used for food that is cooking too quickly.) Place cooking grate over hot coals and allow the grate to heat up. Clean the grate with a wire brush to remove any dirt or particles of food. The grill is now ready. If you plan to barbecue, follow your recipe directions for setting up the grill.

Temperature:

If your grill does not come with a thermometer, be sure to place an oven thermometer on the cooking grate when barbecuing. For grilling, try this test (from *Cook's Illustrated* magazine July/August 2001) to determine when your gas grill or coals are ready: Hold your hand 5 inches above the cooking grate. If you can keep it there comfortably for 2 seconds or less, you have a hot fire. A medium-hot fire is a 3-4 second count. It is important to have a grill with a cover, which shortens cooking time and improves flavor.

Flavor:

Marinades, spice rubs, and wood chips can be used to add a unique flavor to meat, poultry, and fish. Rubs are the quickest and easiest, as very little advance preparation is needed; simply rub the spices into the meat and grill. Wood chips require a little more preparation. Soak chips in enough water to cover while the charcoal is heating. Drain chips and throw a handful onto the white coals. Let the wood burn for a few minutes before grilling.

Pantry Basics

IN THE GLUTEN-FREE KITCHEN, there are some basic elements you will want to have to make life easier. Don't rush out and buy everything on the list! Instead, buy what you need to make a specific recipe, and soon your pantry will be well stocked. Cooking will become less time-consuming, allowing latitude for last-minute baked goods, etc.

Baking Staples:
(Be sure they are manufactured in a gluten-free environment)

Brown rice flour (refrigerate)
White rice flour
Potato starch flour
Tapioca starch flour
Quinoa flour
Buckwheat flour
Amaranth flour
Sweet rice flour
Baking soda
Baking powder
Vanilla extract
Chocolate baking squares (sweetened and unsweetened)

Cocoa powder

Walnuts, pecans, almonds, soy nuts, pine nuts, cashews
(Note: Nuts should be frozen for maximum shelf life.)

Xanthan gum

Active dry yeast (refrigerate)

Cornstarch

Cornmeal

Unflavored gelatin

Honey

Sugar (white and brown)

Gluten-free chocolate chips

Flax seed (store in freezer)

Brown rice syrup (Lundberg's)

Molasses

Maple syrup

Instant non-fat dry milk powder

Cooking Staples:

Vinegars: red wine, rice wine, balsamic, sherry, apple cider vinegar, distilled white vinegar

Unprocessed Vegetable Oils: olive, canola, walnut, peanut, sesame, sunflower, safflower (buy small containers of oil and refrigerate to protect from rancidity)

Wines: Madeira, Sherry, Port, a bottle each of good inexpensive red and white wine

Seasonings: sea salt, fresh ground pepper, fresh herbs when possible

Fresh garlic cloves

Gluten-free chicken stock

Gluten-free ketchup, mustards, pickles, oil cured olives, capers, mayonnaise

Lemon juice (Frozen lemon juice is very handy; once defrosted, it keeps well in the refrigerator.)

Gluten-free tamari (Use to replace soy sauce; it is available most stores where soy sauce is sold.)

Gluten-free Dijon mustard

Finely ground cornmeal for polenta

Variety of your favorite beans

Kombu (Japanese seaweed)

Brown rice, wild rice, pearl or sushi rice, basmati rice, gluten-free buckwheat groats or kasha

Gluten-free pasta

Sun-dried tomatoes, dried prunes and apricots, raisins

Canned goods (refried beans, crushed tomatoes, whole tomatoes, tomato paste, etc.)

Slices of stale bread to make bread crumbs

Artichoke hearts, roasted red peppers (not marinated)

Dairy (refrigerate):

Butter (unsalted and salted)

Eggs

Cheeses (mozzarella, cheddar cheese, goat cheese, Swiss cheese, etc.)

Milk, whipping cream, half & half, gluten-free sour cream, gluten-free plain yogurt, gluten-free buttermilk

Frozen Foods:

Homemade gluten-free pasta sauces, pizza sauce, chicken stock, cookie crumbs for pie crust, granola bars, brownies, sweet breads, waffles, pizza crusts, pesto, pecan paste

Juice concentrate

Fruit for smoothies

Vegetables

Snacks:

There is no end to the number of packaged gluten-free snacks available for your pantry. Choose a few favorites to keep on hand.

Utensils & Cookware

SINCE YOU ARE GOING TO BE COOKING FOR A LONG TIME, you might as well make it more enjoyable by purchasing the best kitchen gear you can afford. The list is divided up into basics and good things to have. Over time you will discover which cookware works best for your needs. (Note: very few bread machines can make a good gluten-free loaf of bread; therefore, a bread machine is not included in the list.)

Basics:

Saucepans (1 quart, 2 quart, 3.5 quart)
Skillets (6-inch, 10-inch, 12-inch)
Dutch oven
Double boiler with steamer insert
   (usually comes with a 2 qt. saucepan)
8-quart (minimum) stock pot
12-inch iron skillet
KitchenAid mixer
   (very important for gluten-free cooking)
2 cutting boards — one dishwasher-safe
   plastic for meat cutting, one wood for
   vegetables
Knives — butcher, slicing, paring, bread,
   boning (German Solingen steel is
   recommended)
Pepper grinder
2 loaf pans and cooling racks
8-inch square glass baking dish
Tube cake pan
Three 8-inch round cake pans
Two 9-inch round cake pans
Colander

Measuring cups (both liquid and dry)
   and spoons
Cheese grater
Wooden spoons
Slotted spoon, spatula for flipping,
   rubber spatula for baking, soup ladle
Long-handled tongs
Toaster dedicated to gluten-free bread
Cookie sheets with edges
Wooden salad bowl with serving spoons
Salad spinner
9 x 13-inch oblong glass baking dish
Mixing bowls
Rolling pin
Garlic press (made of stainless steel,
   not plastic)
Vegetable peeler
Can opener
Meat thermometer
Pot holders
Dish towels
Egg white separator
Basting brush

Good things to have:

Wok
Rice cooker
Bundt pan
Mortar and pestle (great for grinding larger
   quantities of pepper and other spices)
Rotary grater (Zyliss has a good reputation for
   ease of use, cleaning, and durability)
2 large pizza pans
Upright poultry roasting column
Glass bowls of all sizes for mise en place
Hand held mixer
Food processor
Large heavy cutting board with moat
   (for meat carving)
Sieve
Zyliss nut chopper or mini-prep Cusinart
Potato ricer
Blender
Deep fryer
Espresso machine
Yogurt cheese strainer
Food mill

Chef Contributors (alphabetical by chef)

Hans Bergmann
Cacharel
2221 E. Lamar Blvd.
Arlington, Texas 76006-7429
Phone: 817.640.9981
Website: www.cacharel.net

Kathy Casey
Kathy Casey Food Studios®
5130 Ballard Ave. NW
Seattle, WA 98107
Phone: 206.784.7840
Website: www.kathycasey.com

Tom Douglas
Seattle area restaurants:
Dahlia Lounge, 206.682.4142
Etta's Seafood, 206.443.6000
Palace Kitchen, 206.448.2001
Website: www.tomdouglas.com

Barbara Figueroa
The Warwick Hotel
401 Lenora Street
Seattle, WA 98121
Phone: 206.443-4300, x256
Website: www.margauxseattle.com

Suzanne Goin
Lucques
8474 Melrose Ave.
West Hollywood, CA 90069
Phone: 323.655.6277
Website: www.lucques.com

Todd Gray
Equinox
818 Connecticut Ave. NW
Washington D.C. 20006
Phone: 202.331.8118
Website: www.equinoxrestaurant.com

Gerry Hayden
Charlie Palmer's Aureole
34 E. 61st St.
New York, New York 10021-8010
Phone: 212.319.1687
Website: www.aureolerestaurant.com

Christopher Kimball
Cook's Illustrated magazine
P.O. Box 7446
Red Oak, IA 51591-0446
Phone: 1.800.526.8442
Website: www.cooksillustrated.com

Bob Kinkead
Kinkead's
2000 Pennsylvania Ave. NW
Washington D.C. 20006
Phone: 202.296.7700
Website: www.kinkead.com

Michael Kornick
mk
868 N. Franklin
Chicago, IL 60610
Phone: 312.482.9179
Website: www.mkchicago.com

Dennis Leary
Larry Stone, sommelier
Rubicon
558 Sacramento St.
San Francisco, CA 94111
Phone: 415.434.4100
Website: www.myriadrestaurantgroup.com

Thoa Nguyen
Chinoise Café Sushi Bar and Asian Grill
Three Seattle area locations
Phone: 206.284.0958
Website: www.chinoisecafe.com

Marcella Rosene
Pasta & Co.
Five Seattle area locations
Phone: 1.800.943.6362
Website: www.pastaco.com
Email: pastaco@nwlink.com

Christian Svalesen
36° Restaurant and Net Result Fish Market
4140 Lemmon Ave. #134 and #132
Dallas, Texas 75216
Phone: 214.521.4488

Ludger Szmania
Szmania's
Two Seattle area locations
Phone: 206.284.7305
Website: www.szmanias.com

Charlie Trotter
Charlie Trotter's
816 West Armitage
Chicago, IL 60614
Phone: 773.248.6228
Website: www.charlietrotters.com

Erol Tugrul
Café Margaux
220 Brevard Ave.
Cocoa, Florida 32922-7907
Phone: 321.639.8343
Website: www.cafemargaux.com

Lynne Vea
Culinary Associate for television show
Best of Taste with John Sarich
Food Stylist
Cooking Instructor
Email: lvea@attbi.com

Linda Yamada
The Beach House
5022 Lawai Rd.
Koloa, Kauai, Hawaii 96756
Phone: 808.742.1097

Other Contributers

Shelley Case
Gluten-Free Diet: A Comprehensive Resource Guide
Case Nutrition Consulting
1940 Angley Court
Regina, Saskatchewan, Canada S4V 2V2
Phone/FAX: 306.751.1000
Email: scase@accesscomm.ca

Bill Fredericks
The Chocolate Man
Phone: 206.365.2025
Email: chocolate@chocolateman.net

Cynthia Lair
Feeding the Whole Family
Moon Smile Press
Phone: 800.561.3039
Website: www.feedingfamily.com

Dan McCarthy
McCarthy & Schiering Wine Merchants, Inc.
2401-B Queen Anne Ave. N.
Seattle, WA 98109
Phone: 206.282.8500
Email: msqa@sprynet.com

Joanne Van Roden
Wellspring Inc.
Phone: 1.800.533.3561 to find a store near you
    offering Wellspring products

Wendy Wark
Living Healthy with Celiac Disease
AnAffect Marketing
Phone: 610.524.1253
Email: anaffect@aol.com

Debra Daniels-Zeller
Nutritionally-oriented:
Cookbook author
    (vegetarian cookbook in process)
Free lance writer
Cooking instructor
Email: ddanzel@aol.com

Sources

Ancient Harvest Quinoa
  (flour and quinoa flakes)
Quinoa Corp.
P.O. Box 279
Gardena, CA 90248

Annie's Caesar Dressing
Annie's Naturals
792 Foster Hill Rd.
North Calais, Vermont 05650
Phone: 1.800.434.1234

Barbara's Brown Rice Crisps
Barbara's Bakery, Inc.
3900 Cypress Drive
Petaluma, CA 94954

Birkett Mills (buckwheat flour)
P.O. Box 440
Penn Yan, NY 14527
Phone: 315.536.3311
Website: www.thebirkettmills.com

Bob's Red Mill
Phone: 800.349.2173
Website: www.bobsredmill.com
  (allowed products have gluten-free logo)

Boyajian Toasted Sesame Oil
Boyajian, Inc.
349 Lenox St.
Norwood, MA 02062

Cascadian Farm (frozen organic fruits and
  vegetables, organic sauerkraut packed in water,
  and many other products)
Distributed by Small Planet Foods, Inc.
Sedro-Wooley, WA 98284
Website: www.cfarm.com

Chocolate Man
  (a great source for fine chocolate, vanilla
  beans, nut pastes, flavored oils, cocoa,
  chocolate making tools and supplies, tempering
  machine rentals, and truffle making classes)

Bill Fredericks
16580 35th Ave. NE
Lake Forest Park, WA 98155-6606
Phone: 206.365.2025
Website: www.chocolateman.net

DeLaurenti Specialty Food Market
  (offers a wide variety of hard-to-find items
  such as beans, channa dal, capers, oils,
  vinegars, and cheeses)
Phone: 206.622.0141 for mail order information.

Website: www.EthnicGrocer.com
I haven't tried this myself, but their website is full
of unique items from over 15 counties. It looks
like a great source for authentic imports.

Ginger Juice by The Ginger People
  (an easy way to add ginger to any recipe
  without peeling or grating)
Phone: 1.800.551.5284
Website: www.gingerpeople.com

Indian Harvest
  (the ultimate rice, grain, and bean catalog;
  some grains are not gluten-free)
Phone: 800.294.2433
Website: www.indianharvest.com

James Cook Cheese Company
  (offers a wide selection of specialty cheeses and
  a knowledgeable staff regarding cheese
  production — website features truffle oil,
  balsamic vinegar, olives, mustards, and
  chutneys as well)
Phone: 206.256.0510
Website: www.jamescookcheese.com
Email: cookscheese@yahoo.com

Living Without, a great magazine filled with
gluten-free product information and articles
P.O. Box 2126
Northbrook, IL 60065
Website: www.livingwithout.com

Lundberg Rice
  (a wide variety of wild rice blends, brown rice, etc.)
Website: www.lundberg.com

Mariani (dried fruit, sun-dried tomatoes)
Mariani Packing Co., Inc.
500 Crocker Drive
Vacaville, CA 95688
Phone: 1.800.774.2678

Maskal Teff
The Teff Co.
P.O. Box A
Caldwell, Idaho 83606
Phone: 208.455.0375

Muir Glen organic tomato products
(top-notch quality; also makes the best canned
pizza sauce)
Website: www.muirglen.com

Mystic Lake Dairy, Inc.
Mixed Fruit Concentrate Sweetener (use in place
of refined sugar, corn syrup, or honey)
24200 NE 14th St.
Redmond, WA 98053

Organic Shortening
Spectrum Organic Products, Inc.
Petaluma, CA 94954
Phone: 1.800.995.2705
Website: www.spectrumorganic.com

Papadini Orzo, Hi Protein Lentil Bean Pasta
(the only gluten-free orzo pasta I have found,
excellent in minestrone soup — other pasta
shapes available as well)
Adrienne's Gourmet Foods
849 Ward Drive
Santa Barbara, CA 93111
Phone 1.800.937.7010
Website: www.adriennes.com

Pasta & Co. offers a wide variety of specialty
items: Paradiso Italian-style tomatoes, olives,
oils, cheeses, quinoa pasta, etc. Visit their five
Seattle area locations or their website.
Phone 1.800.943.6362
Website: www.pastaco.com
Email: pastaco@nwlink.com

Red Star Yeast, Celiac Hotline
Phone: 1.800.423.5422

Rub with Love
(specialty rubs for salmon, pork, and chicken)
website: www.tomdouglas.com

San-J Int'l
Tamari (wheat-free soy sauce)
800.446.5500

Thai Kitchen (offers a wide variety of pastes,
coconut milk, and fish sauce)
Phone: 1.800.967.THAI
Website: www.thaikitchen.com
Email: info@thaikitchen.com

Tinkyada Pasta
(the best gluten-free pasta tested in our kitchen)
Food Directions, Inc.
150 Milner Ave., Units 21-23
Scarborough, Ontario, M1S 3R3 Canada
Website: www.tinkyada.com

Trader Joe's – under the direction of the Celiac
Disease Foundation, has put together a list of
their products that are gluten-free. Store
locations are found on their website.
Website: www.traderjoes.com/tj/locations

Wild Salmon Seafood Market ships fresh seafood
with ice packs in styrofoam shippers. I buy all my
fish here, and the staff are used to answering
questions about the method of flash-freezing at
sea. They do not dip shrimp and scallops in a
wheat slurry prior to freezing (as some do to
prevent the pieces from sticking together). Be sure
to ask questions to ensure gluten-free seafood.
Phone: 888.222.3474

Mail Order

THERE ARE MANY MAIL ORDER COMPANIES catering
to the gluten intolerant these days. Any of the
national support groups can provide you with
information about how to contact gluten-free
vendors. Shelley Case's book *Gluten-Free Diet*
(Case Nutrition Consulting, 2002) offers an
extensive list as well. A few companies are listed
here to get you started:

Authentic Foods
1850 W. 169th Street, Suite B
Gardena, CA 90247
Phone: 1.800.806.4737
Website: www.authenticfoods.com

(continued on next page)

(continued on from page 229)

Dietary Specialties
1248 Sussex Turnpike, Unit C-1
Randolph, NJ 07869
Phone: 1.888.640.2800
Website: www.dietspec.com
Email: info@dietspec.com

Ener-G Foods
5960 First Ave. South
P.O. Box 84487
Seattle, WA 98124-5787
Phone: 1.800.331.5222
Website: www.ener-g.com

Miss Roben's
P.O. Box 1149
Frederick, MD 21702
Phone: 1.800.891.0083
Website: www.missroben.com

The Gluten-Free Pantry
P.O. Box 840
Glastonbury, CT 06033
Phone: 1.800.291.8386
Email: pantry@glutenfree.com

Neither Celiac Publishing or Karen Robertson
received any payment for including these listings
as resources.

Measurement Conversion Chart

EQUIVALENTS ARE BASED on U.S. liquid measure. This volume standard actually applies to dry measure as well, and is used for not only liquids, but for flour, sugar, shortening, and so on (to name a few of many possible ingredients).

A pinch = a little less than ¼ teaspoon
A dash = a few drops
½ tablespoon = 1½ teaspoons
1 tablespoon = 3 teaspoons
2 tablespoons = 1 ounce = ⅛ cup
4 tablespoons = 2 ounces = ¼ cup
5⅓ tablespoons = 2⅔ ounces = ⅓ cup = 5 tablespoons + 1 teaspoon
8 tablespoons = 4 ounces = ½ cup
16 tablespoons = 8 ounces = 1 cup = ½ pint
2 cups = 16 ounces = 1 pint = ½ quart
4 cups = 32 ounces = 2 pints = 1 quart
16 cups = 128 ounces = 8 pints = 4 quarts = 1 gallon
1 tablespoon minced fresh herbs = 1 teaspoon dried leaf herbs =
    ½ teaspoon powdered herbs

Gluten-Free Flour

GLUTEN-FREE FLOURS ARE GENERALLY USED in combination with one another to make a flour mix. There is no single gluten-free flour that you can use alone for successful baked goods. The list below will help you understand the characteristics of the various flours.

Cross-contamination at the factory can cause diet compliance issues for the gluten intolerant. Call or write the manufacturers of your preferred flours to inquire about factory and field practices.

Arrowroot Flour can be used cup for cup in place of cornstarch if you are allergic to corn.

Bean Flour from Authentic Foods and Ener-G Foods is a light flour made from garbanzo and broad beans. When using this flour in your favorite recipes, replace the white sugar with brown or maple sugar (or combine with sorghum) to cut the bitter taste of the beans.

Brown Rice Flour is milled from unpolished brown rice, and has a higher nutrient value than white rice flour. Since this flour contains bran, it has a shorter shelf life and should be refrigerated. As with white rice flour, it is best to combine brown rice flour with several other flours to avoid the grainy texture.

Cornstarch is similar in use to sweet rice flour for thickening sauces. Best when used in combination with other flours.

Nut Flours are high in protein and, used in small portions, enhance the taste of homemade pasta, puddings, and cookies. They are somewhat expensive and difficult to find. Finely ground nuts added to a recipe increases the protein content and allows for a better rise.

Potato Starch Flour is used in combination with other flours; it is rarely used in its pure form. (Note: this is not potato flour.)

Sorghum Flour is a relatively new flour that is an excellent addition to bean flour mixes. (See Bean Flour)

Soy Flour has a nutty flavor, and is high in protein and fat. Best when used in small quantities in combination with other flours. Soy flour has a short shelf life.

Sweet Rice Flour is made from glutinous rice (which does not contain the gluten fraction that is prohibited to the gluten intolerant). Often used as a thickening agent. Sweet rice flour is becoming more common in gluten-free baking for tender pies and cakes.

Tapioca Starch Flour is a light, velvety flour made from the cassava root. It lightens gluten-free baked goods, and gives them a texture very much like those made with wheat flour. It is especially good in pizza crusts, where it is used in equal parts with either white rice flour or brown rice flour.

White Rice Flour is milled from polished white rice. It is best combined with several other flours to avoid the grainy texture rice flour alone imparts. Try to buy the finest texture possible.

Xanthan Gum is our substitute for gluten, as it has similar binding properties. See usage information on page 181.

(continued on next page)

(continued from page 231)

The following flours are fine for the gluten intolerant, providing you can find a pure source (grown in dedicated fields and processed on dedicated equipment). Contact GIG, CSA/USA, CCA, and CDF to research these flours further (see Sources for contact information).

Amaranth is a whole grain dating back to the time of the Aztecs. It is high in protein (15-18%), and contains more calcium, Vitamin A, and Vitamin C than most grains. The flavor is similar to that of graham crackers without the sweetness. To incorporate amaranth flour into a recipe, substitute amaranth flour for ¼ to ½ of the total flour; the remainder can include arrowroot flour or cornstarch (¼ of the total), with brown rice flour making up the remainder.

Buckwheat is the seed of a plant related to rhubarb. It is high in fiber, iron, and B vitamins.

Millet is a small round grain that is a major food source in Asia, North Africa, and India.

Quinoa (keen-wah), a staple food of the Incas, is a complete protein containing all 8 amino acids as well as a fair amount of calcium and iron. Ancient Harvest, distributed by the Quinoa Corporation in Torrance, CA, is a good source that also carries gluten-free pasta, flour, flakes, etc.

Teff is an ancient grain from Ethiopia, now grown in Idaho. It is always manufactured as a whole grain flour, since it is difficult to sift or separate.

GLOSSARY *of* COOKING TERMS

Selected terms are briefly defined in this glossary. Consult *Joy of Cooking,* Rombauer & Becker (Simon & Schuster, 1997) or *The New Food Lover's Companion,* Herbst (Barron's, 1995) for a more complete reference.

al dente — An Italian phrase that describes pasta cooked to the point where it offers some resistance when bitten into.

barbecuing — Slow-cooking larger cuts of meat, fish, or poultry on a covered grill for a long period of time. Hardwood or coals are used as the heat source, and low indirect heat (220°F.) is recommended.

baste — To periodically brush meat, fish, or poultry as it cooks with sauce, butter, or pan drippings. This process adds color and keeps the food from drying out.

blanch — To briefly boil fruits or vegetables and plunge them into cold water to stop the cooking. Blanching helps to easily remove the skin from such fruits as tomatoes and peaches.

blind baking — An English term for baking a pie crust before filling by covering the crust with foil, placing pie weights atop the foil, and baking the crust.

braising — A method of cooking in which meat, poultry, fish, or vegetables are browned, then simmered slowly in a pot with a small amount of liquid and a tight fitting lid. The slow cooking tenderizes and adds flavor.

browning — To cook meat briefly over high heat until the exterior caramelizes. This step adds flavor and color.

caramelizing — The browning of sugar that either occurs naturally in food or is added to the food. For example, when vegetables are roasted, their natural sugars are released, causing a nice browned exterior.

cream or beat — To combine ingredients on high speed until the mixture is light in color and smooth and creamy in texture.

cube — To cut an ingredient into a ½-inch cube shape.

deglazing — A cooking method that results in a simple sauce by adding wine or stock to the pan or pot used to cook meat, fish, or poultry. The liquid dissolves the browned bits stuck to the pan and develops into a flavorful sauce.

dice — To cut food into ⅛ -to ¼ -inch cubes.

Dutch oven — A large pot with a tight fitting lid used for braising and stewing.

ganache — A combination of chocolate and cream heated until the chocolate melts, then combined into a smooth mixture. Flavored oils, liqueurs, or coffee are often added. Ganache can be poured over a cake; it can also be cooled, rolled into balls, and dipped in chocolate to make truffles.

grilling — A method of cooking by which tender meat, fish, or poultry is quickly cooked uncovered over hot coals.

jelly roll pan — A large baking sheet or pan with shallow sides. Size is generally 17-inch x 13-inch x 1-inch.

julienne — To cut food into ⅛ -inch thin matchsticks.

kosher salt — A coarse grained salt that contains no additives.

mince — To cut food into extremely small cubes. This is a much finer cut than dicing, and is preferable to chopping in that the pieces are more uniform in size.

mise en place — A French term that means all ingredients are ready up to the point of cooking, thus avoiding last minute problems.

nonreactive — Cookware made of a material that does not have a chemical reaction with acidic ingredients such as tomatoes, lemon juice, buttermilk, etc. Glass or plastic is nonreactive. Aluminum and old copper pots are reactive.

poaching — A method of cooking food gently in liquid that completely covers the food and is just under the boiling point.

pressure cooking — A cooking method by which steam is trapped in a pot with a locked lid; the built-up pressure raises the temperature to cook food in ⅓ the regular cooking time. Old cookers such as the "jiggle top" are not as safe as the new cookers of today.

puree — To mash or process (in a food processor) cooked food to a smooth, sauce-like consistency.

reduce — To boil down a liquid (sometimes with other ingredients) until evaporation takes place and it achieves a thicker consistency. This process is used to make flavorful sauces.

roasting — Cooking uncovered without liquid, resulting in a nicely browned exterior and moist interior.

roulade — A French term for a thin slice of meat wrapped around vegetables or other fillings. The exterior is browned before baking or braising.

roux — Combining a fat with flour over low heat. Roux is used to thicken sauces or soups.

sauté — To cook food quickly in a skillet over medium-high heat with a bit of hot fat (generally a combination of butter and oil).

scant — A term used to describe a measurement that is almost as much as indicated.

sear — To cook meat, poultry, or fish quickly in a hot pan, browning all sides with the objective of sealing in the juices.

simmer — To cook food in liquid over a low heat. At a simmer, bubbles will rise and just barely break at the surface.

steam — The process of cooking food in a covered pan over boiling water. Steamed food retains most of its natural juices and nutrients.

stewing — A cooking method by which food is very slowly simmered with a small amount of liquid in a pan with a tight fitting lid. Stewing allows meat to tenderize and flavors to meld together.

stir-fry — To cook small pieces of food very quickly in a small amount of oil over high heat, stirring constantly. Either a skillet or a wok may be used.

sweat — To cook vegetables such as onions, celery, or garlic in a small amount of fat over low heat. Vegetables are covered directly with foil or parchment, and the pot is covered tightly. Sweating produces tender vegetables without browning.

timbale — A high sided mold that is slightly tapered at the bottom.

water bath or bain marie — A gentle cooking method whereby delicate food such as custards and soufflés are placed in a pan with very warm water and then baked. This helps to prevent cracking and curdling. It is beneficial to place a cooling rack or a dish towel in the bottom of the pan, and to not allow custard cups to touch one another or the walls of the pan.

whisk — To combine ingredients vigorously with a wire whip.

INDEX

al dente, 233
almond(s):
    Gnocchi Sautéed with Rosemary, Sage, and, 104
    Quinoa Cookies, 182
amaranth, 7, 11, 162, 180
    Bread, 164
    flour, 214, 232
    Pizza Crust, 171
Anaheim chile, about, 34
apple(s):
    Cider-Dijon Salmon, 64
    Granny Smith Chicken Salad, 55
    Pie, 204
    Sauté, 135
    Tart, 205
    varieties for pies, 204
    Warm Winter Scallop Salad with Shiitake Mushrooms
      and, 125
Apricot Pecan Chicken, 105
arrowroot, 214, 231
artichoke(s):
    canned, about, 126
    Fresh, 138
    Pesto, 27
    Savory Crustless Tart with Bacon and, 39
    tips for eating, 138

Arugula Salad, Pan-Roasted Pork Tenderloin with Fennel,
    Radish, and, 98
asparagus:
    Roasted, 137
    Roasted, Quesadillas with Cactus Salsa, 48
    White, Mustard Crusted Black Cod with Black
      Trumpet Mushrooms, Leek-Potato Puree, Seville
      Orange Vinaigrette, and, 72
Aureole Restaurant, Charlie Palmer's, 97, 98, 212, 226
Avocado, Yellow Tomato Soup with Red Onion, Mint, and, 63

baby lettuces:
    with Beets, Pumpkin Seeds, and Pesto, 123
    Cumin-Seared Tofu with Corn and, 109
Bacon, Savory Crustless Tart with Artichokes and, 39
baked:
    Cheese Wafers, 28
    Pears, 207
baking, tips, 180
banana:
    Bread, 176
    Pineapple Sauté, 135
barbecue(d):
    Baby Back Ribs, Slow, 74
    preparation, 222-23
    Tri Tip, 57
barbecuing, 233
basil:
    Oil Puree, 60
    Spinach, Kumquat Salad with Raspberry Vinaigrette, 124
    Spinach Salad, 121
    Tomato Sauce, Roasted, 136
    Tomato Soup, 84
baste, 233
Bathing Rama, 99
Beach House Restaurant, The, 66, 227

bean(s):
    Edamame, 152
    flour, 214, 231
    garbanzo, 24, 30, 86
    Green, Fried Sage, 139
    Green, with Pecan Paste, 145
    Nine, Soup, 157
    nutrition of, 30
    Refried, Homemade, 153
    Salad, Black Bean, 130
    Smoky Chipotle Chili with Roasted Red Peppers, 158
beef:
    Barbecued Tri Tip, 57
    Enchiladas Cazuela, 113
    Fajitas with Pico de Gallo, 111
    Hearty Spaghetti Sauce, 114
    Homemade Tacos, 80
    Kebabs, 61
    lasagna variation, 51
    marinades, 42, 65, 111
    Meatloaf, 101
    Pacific Rim Flank Steak, 42
    Smoky Chipotle Chili with Roasted Red Peppers, 158
    Sunday Slow-Cooked Roast Beef with Half a Bottle of
      Wine and a Cup of Garlic, 117
    Supper Nachos, 100
    Thyme-Marinated Flank Steaks, 65
beet(s):
    about, 141
    Baby Lettuces with Pumpkin Seeds, Pesto, and, 123
    boiling, 133
    Roasted, 142
    Salad, Warm, with Walnuts, 133
    Soufflé variation, 141
Bergmann, Hans, 107, 115, 141, 208, 226
Biscuits, Buttermilk, 170
Bittersweet Chocolate Sauce, 206

Black Bean Salad, 130

Blackberries, Local, Grand Marnier Semifreddo with
  Bittersweet Chocolate Sauce and, 206

Black Cod, Mustard Crusted, with White Asparagus,
  Black Trumpet Mushrooms, Leek- Potato Puree, and
  Seville Orange Vinaigrette, 72

Black Trumpet Mushrooms, Mustard Crusted Black Cod
  with White Asparagus, Leek-Potato Puree, Seville
  Orange Vinaigrette, and, 72

blanch, 233

blind baking, 233

Blueberry Muffins, 175

blue cheese, *see* gorgonzola

braised:

    Tuna with Ginger and Soy, 44

    Winter Greens with Garlic, 112, 147

braising, 233

bread:

    Amaranth, 164

    Biscuits, Buttermilk, 170

    Breadsticks, 165

    Brown Rice, 163

    Buckwheat, 164

    buns, 164

    Cinnamon Rolls, 21

    Cornbread, 166

    Crumbs, Italian, 168

    Donuts, Old Fashioned Cake, 22

    dough, 169

    French Toast, 21

    Hamburger Buns, 164

    and humidity, 163

    Pizza Crust, Thick, 171

    quick breads *see* sweet breads

    Quinoa, 164

    Sandwich, 163-64

    see sweet breads

    tips, 162

bread (*continued*):

    Tortillas, Flour, Homemade, 167

Bread Salad, Tomato, 131

Breadsticks, 165

Brownies, Chewy, with Raspberry Sauce, 191

browning, 233

brown rice:

    Bread, 163

    flour, 7, 11, 162, 181, 214, 231

    with Pine Nuts and Currants, 152

Brussels Sprouts, Pork Tenderloin with Pancetta and,
  in Madeira, 108

buckwheat, 7, 162, 180, 224, 228

    Bread, 164

    flour, 214, 232

buns, 163-64

Butter Cake, Yellow, with Chocolate Frosting, 192

Butterflied Leg of Lamb, 47

Butter Lettuce with Caramelized Nuts, 122

buttermilk:

    Biscuits, 170

    Chicken, 87

butternut squash:

    Oven Roasted, 140

    Soup with Roasted Chestnuts, 107

cabbage:

    Chicken Salad, 55

    Cole Slaw, 128

Cacharel Restaurant, 107, 115, 141, 208, 226

Caesar Salad, Dungeness Crab, 41

Café, Chinoise, 92, 227

Café Margaux, 79, 116, 136, 226

cake(s):

    Brownies, Chewy, with Raspberry Sauce, 191

    Carrot, 200

    Chocolate Cashew, 196

cakes (*continued*):

    Chocolate, with Chocolate Glaze, 198

    filling, vanilla, 196

    Lemon, 194

    Orange Cheesecake, 201

    Pound, 195

    Sandtorte, 195

    Sour Cream Coffee, 193

    Yellow Butter, with Chocolate Frosting, 192

Canadian Celiac Association, (CCA), 7, 9, 216

Cannelloni in Marinara Sauce, 106

Capers, Truffle Oil with, 129

Caramelized Ginger Carrots, 144

caramelizing, 233

carrot(s):

    Bread, 174

    Cake, 200

    Caramelized Ginger, 144

Case, Shelley, *Gluten-Free Diet*, 214-15, 227, 229

Casey, Kathy, 117, 226

cashew(s):

    Chocolate, Cake, 196

    Fried Rice with Snow Peas and, 36

Cazeula, Enchiladas, 113

celiac disease, 4-6, 9

    associated diseases to, 4, 9

    chat group on-line, 216

    medical tests for, 5

    research of, 4

Celiac Disease Foundation, (CDF), 7, 9, 216

Celiac Sprue Association, (CSA/USA), 7, 9, 216

Cereal, Granola, 16

Channa Dal Spread, 30

Chanterelle Mushrooms, Stuffed Quail with Spinach,
  Pine Nuts and, 102

Charlie Palmer's Aureole, 97, 98, 212, 226

Charlie Trotter's Restaurant, 70, 150, 227

cheese:
    Board, 26
    Dill Yogurt, 27
    and Macaroni, 154
    Wafers, Baked, 28
cheesecake:
    crumbs for crust, 185
    Orange, 201
chef contributors, 226-227
Chestnuts, Roasted, Butternut Squash Soup with, 107
chèvre (goat cheese):
    with Marinara Sauce, Spinach and Pasta, 37
    Medallions, 112
    Sautéed Lamb Chops on a Roasted Red Bell Pepper
       Sauce with Sun-Dried Tomatoes with, 115
chicken:
    a la Margaux, 116
    Apricot Pecan, 105
    Bathing Rama, 99
    Buttermilk, 87
    Coconut, 92
    Fajitas with Sweet Peppers, 43
    Fried Rice with Cashews and Snow Peas, 36
    Homemade Tacos, 80
    Jerk, with Cilantro Mango Salsa, 59
    Lopez Taquitos, 50
    marinades, 43, 92
    Noodle Soup, 156
    Northwest Paella, 40
    Pan-Fried, with Black Bean Salad, 67; with Leeks, 38;
      in Marsala, 85
    Roast, 49
    Salad, 55
    Stock, 156

chickpea(s):
    Channa Dal Spread, 30
    Hummus, 24
    Moroccan, Stew, 86
children and gluten intolerance, 218-22
chiles:
    about, 34
    Chipotle, Smoky, Chili with Roasted Red Peppers, 158
    Rellenos with Mango Salsa, 34
    roasting, 34
Chili, Smoky Chipotle, with Roasted Red Peppers, 158
Chinoise Café, 92, 227
chocolate:
    Bittersweet, Sauce, 206
    Brownies, Chewy, with Raspberry Sauce, 191
    Cake with Chocolate Glaze, 198
    Cashew Cake, 196
    Chip Cookies, 184
    Frosting, 192, 196
    Glaze, 198
    Java Truffles, 190
    Rocky Road, 189
    Zucchini Bread, 172
Chocolate Man, The, 227, 228
cilantro:
    Lime Cream, 158
    Mango Salsa, 59
    Oil, 46
Cinnamon Rolls, 21
clam(s):
    canned, about, 62
    fresh, cleaning, 62
    Mexican Green Soup, 68
    Northwest Paella, 40
    Sweet Butter, Pasta and Red Sauce with, 62

coconut:
    Chicken, 92
    Dipping Sauce, 92
    Macaroons, 183
    milk in dairy-free ice cream, 217
    unsweetened, purchasing, 174
coffee:
    Cake, Sour Cream, 193
    Java Chocolate Truffles, 190
Cole Slaw, 128
cookbooks, recommended, 14
cookie(s):
    Almond Quinoa, 182
    Chocolate Chip, 184
    Cut-out, with Royal Icing, 186
    Gingersnap, 187
    Macaroons, 183
    Mexican Wedding Cakes, 188
    Molasses, 185
Cook's Bible, The, 10, 44, 151, 198
Cook's Illustrated magazine, 14, 44, 151, 223, 226
cookware, 10, 11,
corn:
    Bread, 166
    chips, fried, 100
    on the Cob, 147
    Cumin-Seared Tofu with Baby Lettuces and, 109
    Polenta, Creamy, 148
    tortilla shells, fried, 80
cornstarch, 181, 231
crab(meat):
    Cakes, Pan-Fried, with Tomato Coulis and Cilantro
      Oil, 46
    Dungeness, Caesar Salad, 41
    Simple Sushi, 88

cranberry(ies):
    Dried, Spinach Salad with Roasted Pumpkin Seeds
      and, 132
    Essence, 66
    Soufflé, 208
cream, 233
Cream Cheese Frosting, 200
Crème Fraîche, Local Berries with, 209
Cremini Mushroom Soup, Caramelized,
  with Fresh Rosemary, 97
croutons, 41
crust:
    Pie, Dough, 202
    Thick Pizza, 171
cube, 233
Cucumbers, Seasonal Greens and Garden, 128
Cumin-Seared Tofu with Corn and Baby Lettuces, 109
Currants, Brown Rice with Pine Nuts and, 152
Curry Roasted Vegetables, 143
Cut-out Cookies with Royal Icing, 186

Dahlia Lounge, 86, 143, 152, 226
dairy-free substitutions, 217
deglazing, 233
dermatitis herpetiformis, 4, 6
dice, 234
Dijon-Apple Cider Salmon, 64
Dill Yogurt Cheese, 27
dining out, 14
dips, *see* salsas and spreads
Donuts, Old Fashioned Cake, 22
Douglas, Tom, 86, 143, 152, 226, 229
Dried Fruit Compote, 210
Dungeness Crab Caesar Salad, 41
Dutch oven, 234

Edamame, 152
egg(s):
    hard-boiled, 123
    Omelets, 90
    Savory Crustless Tart with Artichokes and Bacon, 39
Eggplant, Tapenade, Grilled, with Basil Oil and
  Grilled Swordfish Steak, 60
Enchiladas Cazuela, 113
Equinox Restaurant, 63, 82, 206, 226

fajitas:
    Beef, with Pico de Gallo, 111
    Chicken, with Sweet Peppers, 43
Fennel Salad, Pan-Roasted Pork Tenderloin with Radish,
  Arugula and, 98
Figueroa, Barbara, 40, 226
fish, *see* specific fish
flank steak (beef):
    Pacific Rim, 42
    Thyme-Marinated, 65
flax seed, nutrition of, 17
Flour Tortillas, Homemade, 167
Fredericks, Bill, 227, 228
French:
    New Potato Salad with Summer Herb Coulis, 127
    Toast, 21
fried:
    Rice with Cashews and Snow Peas, 36
    Sage Green Beans, 139
Fries, Homemade, 148
frosting:
    Chocolate, 192, 196, 199
    Cream Cheese, 200
fruit dessert(s):
    Apple, Pie, 204; Sauté, 135; Tart, 205
    Baked Pears, 207
    Banana-Pineapple Sauté, 135

fruit dessert(s) (*continued*):
    Chewy Brownies with Raspberry Sauce, 191
    Cranberry Soufflé, 208
    Crème Fraîche with Local Berries, 209
    Floating Islands with Caramel Blood Oranges, 212
    Grand Marnier Semifreddo with Bittersweet
      Chocolate Sauce and Local Blackberries, 206
    Panna Cotta with Dried Fruit Compote, 210
fruit in salads:
    Gorgonzola-Pear Salad, 121
    Seared Sea Scallop-Green Papaya Salad with
      Cranberry Essence, 66
    Spinach Basil Kumquat Salad with Raspberry
      Vinaigrette, 124
    Spinach Salad with Dried Cranberries and Roasted
      Pumpkin Seeds, 132
    Warm Winter Scallop Salad with Shiitake Mushrooms
      and Apples, 125
fruit salsas:
    Mango, 34, 59
    Peach, 31
Fruit Smoothies, 18

ganache, 190, 234
garbanzo beans *see* chickpeas or beans
Garlic Mashed Potatoes, 140
ginger:
    Braised Tuna with Soy and, 44
    Caramelized, Carrots, 144
Gingersnap Cookies, 187
glaze(s) for baked goods:
    Chocolate, 198
    Lemon, 194
    for Pumpkin Bread, 173
glossary of cooking terms, 233-35
gluten, 215
gluten-free diet, 4-9, 214-15

Gluten-Free Diet: A Comprehensive Resource Guide, 214-15, 227, 229
Gluten-Free Flour Mixes, 181
gluten-free flours, 231-32
gluten intolerance, 6
Gluten Intolerance Group, (GIG), 7, 9, 216
gluten intolerant children, 218-22
gnocchi:
    "Groovy", basic recipe for, 93
    Sautéed with Rosemary, Sage, and Almonds, 104
goat cheese *see* chèvre
Goin, Suzanne, 210, 226
gorgonzola (blue cheese):
    Cheese Board, 26
    Pear Salad, 121
Grand Marnier Semifreddo with Bittersweet Chocolate
  Sauce and Local Blackberries, 206
Granny Smith Chicken Salad, 55
granola:
    Bars, 17
    Cereal, 16
Gray, Todd, 63, 82, 206, 226
green beans:
    Fried Sage, 139
    with Pecan Paste, 145
greens:
    Braised Winter, with Garlic, 147
    Seasonal, and Garden Cucumbers, 128
grilled:
    Eggplant Tapenade with Basil Oil, 60
    Garlic-Studded Portobello Mushrooms with Roasted
      Tomato-Basil Sauce, 136
    Mahi-Mahi with Tomatillo Sauce, 56
    Swordfish Steak over Grilled Eggplant Tapenade with
      Basil Oil, 60
grilling, 12, 222-23, 234

Grits, Caramelized Onion-Strewn, Sautéed Salmon with,
    and Portobello Mushroom-Red Wine Sauce, 70

halibut:
    and Chips, 58
    Mexican Green Soup, 68
    Northwest Paella, 40
Hamburger Buns, 164
Hayden, Gerry, 97, 98, 212, 226
hazelnut(s):
    Duchilly, 127, 177
    to skin, 127, 177
    Zucchini Bread, 177
Herb Coulis, French New Potato Salad with Summer, 127
herbes de Provence, 28
homemade:
    Flour Tortillas, 167
    Fries, 148
    Pesto, 69
    Refried Beans, 153
    Taco Seasoning, 80
Honey Mustard Glaze, 64
Hummus, 24

icing:
    for cookies, 187
    Royal, 186
Italian Bread Crumbs, 168

Java Chocolate Truffles, 190
jelly roll pan, 234
Jerk Chicken with Cilantro Mango Salsa, 59
Jicama Slaw, 134
julienne, 234

Kathy Casey Food Studios®, 117, 226
Kebabs, Beef, 61
Kimball, Christopher, 10, 44, 151, 198, 226
Kinkead's Restaurant (Bob Kinkead), 56, 134, 226
kombu, about, 153
Kornick, Michael, 77, 226
kosher salt, 234
Kumquat, Spinach Basil, Salad with Raspberry
    Vinaigrette, 124

lactose-free substitutions, 217
Lair, Cynthia, *Feeding the Whole Family,* 24, 89, 227
lamb:
    Chops, Sautéed, with Goat Cheese on a Roasted Bell
      Pepper Sauce with Sun-Dried Tomatoes, 115
    internal temperature, 115
    Leg of, Butterflied, 47
    marinade, 47
lasagna:
    meat variation, 51
    Vegetarian, 51
Leary, Dennis, 72, 226
leek(s):
    Pan-Fried Chicken with, 38
    Potato Puree, 72
    and Saffron Soup with Sautéed Shrimp, 77
lemon:
    Cake, 194
    Glaze, 194
    Spinach Sautéed with Garlic and, 146
lettuce(s):
    Baby, with Beets, Pumpkin Seeds, and Pesto, 123
    Baby, Cumin-Seared Tofu with Corn and, 109
    Butter, with Caramelized Nuts, 122
Lime-Cilantro Cream, 158
Living Without magazine, 186, 228

lobster:
  Mexican Green Soup, 68
Lucques Restaurant, 210, 226
lunch ideas, 219-22

Macaroni and Cheese, 154
Macaroons, 183
Madeira, Pork Tenderloin with Pancetta and Brussels
  Sprouts in, 108
Mahi-Mahi, Grilled, with Tomatillo Sauce, 56
mail order, 12, 229
mango(es):
  about, 35
  Cilantro Salsa, 59
  Salsa, 34
marinades see beef, chicken, tofu, lamb, or specific fish
marinara sauce:
  Cannelloni in, 106
  Spinach Chèvre Pasta with, 37
Margaux, Café, 79, 116, 136, 226
Marsala, Pan-Fried Chicken in, 85
Mashed Potatoes, Garlic, 140
Master Recipe for Long Grain White Rice, 151
measurement conversion chart, 230
Meat Loaf, 101
Mexican:
  Green Soup, 68
  Salsa, 25
  Wedding Cakes, 188
millet, 7, 214, 232
mince, 234
Minestrone Genovese, 110
Mint, Yellow Tomato Soup with Avocado, Red Onion,
  and, 63
mise en place, 13, 234
Miso Soup, 89
mk restaurant, 77, 226

Molasses Cookies, 185
Moroccan Chickpea Stew, 86
muffins:
  Blueberry, 175
  Carrot, 174
  Hazelnut Zucchini, 177
mushroom(s):
  Black Trumpet, Mustard Crusted Black Cod with
    White Asparagus, Leek-Potato Puree, Seville Orange
    Vinaigrette, and, 72
  Chanterelle, Stuffed Quail with Spinach, Pine Nuts,
    and Fresh, 102
  cleaning, 103
  Cremini, Soup, Caramelized, with Fresh Rosemary, 97
  Mélange, 146
  Portobello, Carpaccio, "Groovy" Gnocchi with, 93;
    Grilled Garlic-Studded, with Roasted Tomato-Basil
    Sauce, 136; Red Wine Sauce, Sautéed Salmon with
    Caramelized Onion-Strewn Grits and, 70
  Roasted, 150
  Shiitake, Warm Winter Scallop Salad with Apples
    and, 125
  Wild, Sherry Sauce, 116
mussels:
  Mexican Green Soup, 68
  Northwest Paella, 40
mustard:
  Crusted Black Cod with White Asparagus, Black
    Trumpet Mushrooms, Leek-Potato Puree, and
    Seville Orange Vinaigrette, 72
  Honey Glaze, 64

New Potato Salad, French, with Summer Herb Coulis, 127
Nguyen, Thoa, 92, 227
nonreactive, 234
Northwest Paella, 40

nuts:
  see almonds, cashews, chestnuts, hazelnuts, pecans,
    pine nuts, soy nuts, or walnuts
  Caramelized, with Butter Lettuce, 122
  flour, 214, 231
  nutrition of, 16, 17

oats, gluten status of, 4, 215
oils, healthy selection of, 13
Omelets, 90
onion:
  Strewn Grits, Caramelized, and Portobello Mushroom-
    Red Wine Sauce, Sautéed Salmon with, 70
  Red, Yellow Tomato Soup with Avocado, Mint, and, 63
orange(s):
  Blood, Floating Islands with Caramel, 212
  Cheesecake, 201
  Seville, Vinaigrette, 72
organic shortening, 7, 13, 180, 217, 229
outdoor cooking, 12, 222-23

Pacific Rim Flank Steak, 42
Paella, Northwest, 40
Palmer's, Charlie, Aureole Restaurant, 97, 98, 212
pancakes, 20
  Potato, 144
Pancetta, Pork Tenderloin with Brussels Sprouts and, in
  Madeira, 108
pan-fried:
  Chicken, and Black Bean Salad, 67; with Leeks, 38; in
    Marsala, 85
  Crab Cakes with Tomato Coulis and Cilantro Oil, 46
  Pork Chops with Lime Juice, 91
Panna Cotta with Dried Fruit Compote, 210
Pan-Roasted Pork Tenderloin with Fennel, Radish, and
  Arugula Salad, 98
pantry basics, 11, 223-24

Papaya, Green, Seared Sea Scallop-, Salad with Cranberry
    Essence, 66
pasta:
    Cannelloni in Marinara Sauce, 106
    Hearty Spaghetti Sauce, 114
    Macaroni and Cheese, 154
    with pesto, 42
    Red Sauce with Sweet Butter Clams and, 62
    Salad, 126
    Spicy Tomato Sausage, 78
    Spinach Chèvre, with Marinara Sauce, 37
    Tinkyada brand, 229
Pasta & Co., 28, 37, 62, 84, 110, 227, 229
patient support organizations:
    Canadian Celiac Association (CCA), 7, 9, 216
    Celiac Disease Foundation, (CDF), 7, 9, 216
    Celiac Sprue Association, (CSA/USA), 7, 9, 216
    Gluten Intolerance Group, (GIG), 7, 9, 216
pea(s):
    Snow, Fried Rice with Cashews and, 36
    Split, Soup, 160
    Sugar, 143
Peach Salsa, 31
pear(s):
    Baked, 207
    Cheese Board, 26
    Gorgonzola Salad, 121
pecan:
    Apricot, Chicken, 105
    Paste, with Green Beans, 145
pepitas see pumpkin seeds
pesto:
    Artichoke, 27
    Baby Lettuces with Beets, Pumpkin Seeds, and, 123
    Homemade, 69
Pico de Gallo, 111
Pie Crust Dough, 202

pie(s):
    Apple, 204
    Pumpkin, 203
Pineapple-Banana Sauté, 135
pine nuts:
    Brown Rice with Currants and, 152
    Homemade Pesto, 69
    Stuffed Quail with Spinach, Fresh Chanterelle
        Mushrooms, and, 102
pizza, 69
    Crust, 171
    Sauce, 69
planning, 12-13
poaching, 234
poblano chile, about, 34
Polenta, Creamy, 148
pork:
    Chops, Pan-Fried, with Lime Juice, 91
    Enchiladas Cazuela, 113
    Fried Rice with Cashews and Snow Peas, 36
    Hearty Spaghetti Sauce, 114
    Nine Bean Soup, 157
    Slow Barbecue Baby Back Ribs, 74
    Split Pea Soup, 160
    Supper Nachos, 100
    Tenderloin, Medallions, 45; with Pancetta and
        Brussels Sprouts in Madeira, 108; Pan-Roasted,
        with Fennel, Radish, and Arugula Salad, 98;
        Roasted, with Pinot Noir Sauce, 81
portobello mushroom(s):
    Carpaccio, 93
    Grilled Garlic-Studded, with Roasted Tomato-Basil
        Sauce, 136
    Red Wine Sauce, Sautéed Salmon with Caramelized
        Onion-Strewn Grits and, 70

potato(es):
    Fries, Homemade, 148
    Leek Puree, 72
    Mashed, Garlic, 140
    Pancakes, 144
    Pancakes with Dill Yogurt Cheese and Smoked
        Salmon, 19
    Red, Oven Roasted, 139
    Salad, French New, with Summer Herb Coulis, 127
potato starch flour, 181, 214, 231
Pound Cake, 195
pressure cooking, 234
pretzels, dough for, 169
produce, 11
pumpkin:
    Bread, 173
    Glaze, for Bread, 173
    Pie, 203
    Seeds, Baby Lettuces with Beets, Pesto, and, 123;
        Roasted, 28
puree, 234

Quail, Stuffed, with Spinach, Pine Nuts, and Fresh
    Chanterelle Mushrooms, 102
quesadillas:
    cheese, 35
    Roasted Asparagus, with Cactus Salsa, 48
quick breads see sweet breads
quinoa, 7, 11, 162, 163, 180, 228
    Almond Cookies, 182
    Bread, 164
    flour, 214, 232
    Pizza Crust, 171
    Pumpkin Bread, 173

Radish Salad, Pan-Roasted Pork Tenderloin with Fennel, Arugula and, 98
raspberry:
    Sauce, 191
    Vinaigrette, 124
recipe conversion ideas, 217
recommended flours, 181
red:
    peppers *see* sweet peppers
    Sauce with Sweet Butter Clams and Pasta, 62
    Snapper Fillet with Spaghetti Squash, Saffron, and Tomato Cream, 82
    Wine Jus, 71
reduce, 234
Refried Beans, Homemade, 153
rice:
    Brown, with Pine Nuts and Currants, 152
    Fried, with Cashews and Snow Peas, 36
    Master Recipe for Long Grain White, 151
    Northwest Paella, 40
roast:
    Beef, Sunday Slow-Cooked, with Half a Bottle of Wine and a Cup of Garlic, 117
    Chicken, 49
roasted:
    Asparagus, 137
    Asparagus Quesadillas with Cactus Salsa, 48
    Beets, 142
    Butternut Squash, 140
    Chestnuts, Butternut Squash Soup with, 107
    Chiles, Fresh, 34
    Mushrooms, 150
    Pork Tenderloin, 81
    Pumpkin Seeds, 28
    Red Bell Pepper Sauce, Sautéed Lamb Chops with Goat Cheese, Sun-Dried Tomatoes with, 115
    Red Peppers, Smoky Chipotle Chili with, 158

roasted (*continued*):
    Red Potatoes, 139
    Root Vegetables over Warm Goat Cheese Medallions, 112
    Tomato-Basil Sauce, 136
roasting, 234
Rocky Road, 189
rosemary:
    Caramelized Cremini Mushroom Soup with Fresh, 97
    Gnocchi Sautéed with Sage, Almonds, and, 104
Rosene, Marcella, *Pasta & Co. By Request,* 28, 37, 62, 84, 110, 227
roulade, 234
roux, 234
Royal Icing, 186
Rubicon Restaurant, 72, 226

sablefish *see* black cod
saffron:
    and Leek Soup with Sautéed Shrimp, 77
    Northwest Paella, 40
    Red Snapper Fillet with Spaghetti Squash, Tomato Cream, and, 82
sage:
    Fried, Green Beans, 139
    Gnocchi Sautéed with Rosemary, Almonds, and, 104
salad(s):
    Baby Lettuces with Beets, Pumpkin Seeds, and Pesto, 123
    Basil Spinach, 121
    Black Bean, 130
    Butter Lettuce with Caramelized Nuts, 122
    Chicken, 55
    Classic Spinach, 123
    Cole Slaw, 128
    French New Potato, with Summer Herb Coulis, 127
    Gorgonzola-Pear, 121

salad(s) (*continued*):
    Granny Smith Chicken, 55
    Jicama Slaw, 134
    Pan-Roasted Pork Tenderloin with Radish, Fennel, and Arugula, 98
    Pasta, 126
    Seared Sea Scallop-Green Papaya, with Cranberry Essence, 66
    Seasonal Greens and Garden Cucumbers, 128
    Spicy Winter Tomato, 129
    Spinach Basil Kumquat, with Raspberry Vinaigrette, 124
    Spinach with Dried Cranberries and Roasted Pumpkin Seeds, 132
    Tomato Bread, 131
    Warm Beet, with Walnuts, 133
    Warm Winter Scallop, with Shiitake Mushrooms and Apples, 125
salmon:
    Apple Cider-Dijon, 64
    Mexican Green Soup, 68
    Northwest Paella, 40
    Sautéed, with Caramelized Onion-Strewn Grits and Portobello Mushroom-Red Wine Sauce, 70
    Smoked, Potato Pancakes with Dill Yogurt Cheese, 19
salsa:
    Mango, 34, 59
    Mexican, 25
    Peach, 31
    Tomatillo, 32
Sandtorte, 195
sandwich bread:
    Amaranth, 164
    Brown Rice, 163
    Buckwheat, 164
    Quinoa, 164

sauce:
 Bittersweet Chocolate, 206
 Marinara, 37
 Pinot Noir, 81
 Pizza, 69
 Portobello Mushroom-Red Wine, 70
 Raspberry, 191
 Red Wine Jus, 71
 Spaghetti, Hearty, 114
 Tomatillo, 56
 Tomato-Basil, Roasted, 136
 Wild Mushroom Sherry, 116
sausage(s):
 Assorted, and Mustards, 76
 Hearty Spaghetti Sauce, 114
 lasagna variation, 51
 Northwest Paella, 40
 Spicy Tomato and, Pasta, 78
sauté, 234
sautéed:
 Lamb Chops with Goat Cheese on a Roasted Red Bell
  Pepper Sauce with Sun-Dried Tomatoes, 115
 Salmon with Caramelized Onion-Strewn Grits and
  Portobello Mushroom-Red Wine Sauce, 70
scallop(s):
 Salad, Warm Winter, with Shiitake Mushrooms and
  Apples, 125
 Sea, Seared, -Green Papaya Salad with Cranberry
  Essence, 66
 Mexican Green Soup, 68
scant, 234
sear, 234
seeds:
 nutrition of, 16
 Pumpkin, Roasted, 28
 Sunflower, 16

Semifreddo, Grand Mariner, with Bittersweet Chocolate
 Sauce and Local Blackberries, 206
Seville Orange Vinaigrette, 72
shellfish:
 about wheat slurry, 12
 see specific shellfish
Shiitake Mushrooms, Warm Winter Scallop Salad with
 Apples and, 125
shrimp:
 Mexican Green Soup, 68
 Northwest Paella, 40
 Sautéed, with Leek and Saffron Soup, 77
 Simple Sushi, 88
 Spicy, Skewers, 31
simmer, 234
Smoked Salmon Potato Pancakes with Dill Yogurt
 Cheese, 19
Smoothies, Fruit, 18
snapper:
 Mexican Green Soup, 68
 Red, Fillet with Spaghetti Squash, Saffron, and
  Tomato Cream, 82
Snow Peas, Fried Rice with Cashews and, 36
sole, Mexican Green Soup, 68
sorghum flour, 214, 231
soufflé:
 beet variation, 141
 Cranberry, 208
 Turnip Timbale, 141
soup(s):
 Butternut Squash, with Roasted Chestnuts, 107
 Caramelized Cremini Mushroom, with Fresh
  Rosemary, 97
 Chicken Noodle, 156
 Cream of Yellow Squash, 79
 Leek and Saffron, with Sautéed Shrimp, 77
 Mexican Green, 68

soup(s) (continued):
 Minestrone Genovese, 110
 Miso, 89
 Nine Bean, 157
 Split Pea, 160
 Tomato Basil, 84
 Yellow Tomato, with Avocado, Red Onion, and Mint, 63
sources, 228-29
Sour Cream Coffee Cake, 193
soy:
 beans see Edamame
 Braised Tuna with Ginger and, 44
 as a dairy-free substitution, 217
 flour, 214, 231
 nuts, about, 17
specialty food stores, 11-12
spicy:
 Shrimp Skewers, 31
 Tomato and Sausage Pasta, 78
 Winter Tomato Salad, 129
spinach:
 Chèvre Pasta with Marinara Sauce, 37
 Salad, Basil, 121; Basil Kumquat, with Raspberry
  Vinaigrette, 124; Classic, 123; with Dried
  Cranberries and Roasted Pumpkin Seeds, 132
 Sautéed, with Garlic and Lemon, 146
 Stuffed Quail with Pine Nuts, Fresh Chanterelle
  Mushrooms, and, 102
Split Pea Soup, 160
spread(s):
 Artichoke Pesto, 27
 Channa Dal, 30
 Dill Yogurt Cheese, 27
 Hummus, 24
 Tapenade, 29

squash:
 Butternut, Oven Roasted, 140
 Butternut, Soup, with Roasted Chestnuts, 107
 Spaghetti, Red Snapper Fillet with Saffron, Tomato
  Cream, and, 82
 Yellow, Cream of, Soup, 79
Standard Gluten-Free Flour Blend, 181
steam, 234
stewing, 235
Stew, Moroccan Chickpea, 86
stir-fry:
 defined, 235
 Fried Rice with Cashews and Snow Peas, 36
 Vegetable Tofu, 83
Stock, Chicken, 156
Stone, Larry, 72, 226
Sugar Peas, 143
sugar substitute(s), 180, 229
Sun-Dried Tomatoes, Sautéed Lamb Chops with Goat
 Cheese on a Roasted Red Bell Pepper Sauce with, 115
Supper Nachos with Homemade Corn Tortilla Chips, 100
Sushi, Simple, 88
Svalesen, Christian, 46, 60, 68, 227
sweat, 235
sweet breads:
 Banana, 176
 Carrot, 174
 Chocolate Zucchini, 172
 Hazelnut Zucchini, 177
 Pumpkin, 173
sweet peppers:
 Chicken Fajitas with, 43
 Sautéed Lamb Chops with Goat Cheese on a Roasted
  Red Bell Pepper Sauce with Sun-Dried Tomatoes, 115
 Smoky Chipotle Chili with Roasted Red Peppers, 158
sweet rice flour, 181, 214, 231

Swordfish Steak, Grilled, over Grilled Eggplant Tapenade
 with Basil Oil, 60
Szmania, Ludger, 41, 93, 102
Szmania's Restaurant, 93, 102

36° Restaurant, 46, 60, 68, 227
taco(s):
 beef, 80
 chicken, 80
 seasoning, 80
tahini, 21, 24
tamari, 229
Tapenade, 29
 Grilled Eggplant, with Basil Oil, 60
tapioca starch flour, 181, 214, 231
Taquitos, Lopez, 50
tart(s):
 Apple, 205
 Savory Crustless, with Artichokes and Bacon, 39
Tartar Sauce, 58
teff flour, 7, 214, 232
Thyme-Marinated Flank Steaks, 65
timbale, 235
Tinkyada Pasta, 229
tofu:
 Cumin-Seared, with Corn and Baby Lettuces, 109
 freezing, 83
 Fried Rice with Cashews and Snow Peas, 36
 marinade, 83
 Miso Soup, 89
 Vegetable, Stir-Fry, 83
tomatillo:
 about, 32
 Salsa, 32
 Sauce, 56

tomato(es):
 Basil Sauce, Roasted, 136
 Basil Soup, 84
 Bread Salad, 131
 Coulis, 46
 Cream, Red Snapper Fillet with Spaghetti Squash,
  Saffron, and, 82
 Hearty Spaghetti Sauce, 114
 to remove skin, 84
 Scratch Pizza Sauce, 69
 Spicy, and Sausage Pasta, 78
 Spicy Winter Salad, 129
 Yellow, Soup with Avocado, Red Onion, and Mint, 63
tortilla(s):
 chips, fried, corn, 100
 Flour, Homemade, 167
 shells, fried corn, 80
Trader Joe's, 109, 123, 222, 229
Tri Tip, Barbecued, 57
Trotter's Restaurant, Charlie, 70, 150
Truffle Oil with Capers, 129
Truffles, Java Chocolate, 190
Tugrul, Erol, 79, 116, 136, 226
Tuna, Braised, with Ginger and Soy, 44
turnip:
 about, 141
 Soufflé, Timbale, 141

utensils, cooking, 11, 225

VanRoden, Joanne, (Wellspring), 47, 227
Vea, Lynne, 104, 112, 125, 127, 129, 145, 147, 227

vegetables boiled:
    Artichokes, Fresh, 138
    beets, 133
    Corn on the Cob, 147
    Edamame, 152
    Green Beans, Fried Sage, 139
    Green Beans with Pecan Paste, 145
    New Potato Salad, French, with Summer Herb
        Coulis, 127
    Peas, Sugar, 143
    Potatoes, Garlic Mashed, 140
vegetables grilled:
    Eggplant Tapenade with Basil Oil, 60
    Kebabs, 61
vegetables roasted:
    Asparagus, 137
    Beets, 142
    Fries, Homemade, 148
    Potatoes, Red, 139
    Squash, Butternut, 140
    Squash, Spaghetti, 82
    Vegetables, 149; Curry, 143; Root, 112
vegetables sautéed:
    Spinach, with Garlic and Lemon, 146
    Yams, Sweet, 142
vegetables *see also* specific vegetables
vegetable soup(s):
    Leek and Saffron, with Sautéed Shrimp, 77
    Minestrone Genovese, 110
    Split Pea, 160
    Squash, Butternut, with Roasted Chestnuts, 107
    Squash, Cream of Yellow, 79
    Tomato Basil, 84
    Yellow Tomato, with Avocado, Red Onion, and
        Mint, 63

vegetables steamed:
    Brussels sprouts, 108
    squash, spaghetti, 82
Vegetarian Lasagna, 51
vinaigrette:
    Raspberry, 124
    Seville Orange, 72
vitamin supplement, 221

Waffles, 20
Walnuts, Warm Beet Salad with, 133
water bath, 235
Wendy Wark's:
    Gluten-Free Flour Mix, 181
    Living Healthy with Celiac Disease, 14, 20, 21, 165,
        167, 169, 181, 227
wheat-free diet, 7, 9
whisk, 235
white rice flour, 181, 214, 231
White Rice, Master Recipe for Long Grain, 151
Wild Mushroom Sherry Sauce, 116

xanthan gum, 181, 231

Yamada, Linda, 66, 227
Yams, Sweet Sautéed, 142
Yellow Butter Cake with Chocolate Frosting, 192
yogurt cheese:
    Dill, 27
    Smoked Salmon Potato Pancakes with, 19

Zeller, Debra-Daniels, 30, 227
zest, orange or lemon, 47
zucchini:
    Chocolate, Bread, 172
    Hazelnut Bread, 177

KAREN ROBERTSON BEGAN HER JOURNEY into the gluten-free world when her children were first diagnosed with celiac disease in 1997. As a food lover, she was determined to find gluten-free recipes for baked goods that were moist, delicious, and similar to their wheat-based counterparts. Additionally, it was important to develop high-quality meals the entire family would enjoy. Karen has served on the board for the Gluten Intolerance Group and teaches gluten-free cooking classes in Seattle, Washington.